Bound to Respect

Bound to Respect

Antebellum Narratives of Black Imprisonment, Servitude, and Bondage, 1816–1861

KEITH MICHAEL GREEN

THE UNIVERSITY OF ALABAMA PRESS
Tuscaloosa

The University of Alabama Press
Tuscaloosa, Alabama 35487–0380
uapress.ua.edu

Typeface: Granjon

Manufactured in the United States of America
Cover illustration: Frontispiece from George Thompson's *Prison Life and Reflections*
Cover design: Kyle Anthony Clark

∞

The paper on which this book is printed meets the minimum requirements of American National Standard for Information Sciences—Permanence of Paper for Printed Library Materials, ANSI Z39.48–1984.

Cataloging-in-Publication data is available from the Library of Congress.
ISBN: 978-0-8173-1883-3
E-ISBN: 978-0-8173-8887-4

To My Grandmother,
For Teaching Me How to Love;
To My Mother,
For Loving Me into Life;
To My Wife,
For Being the Love of My Life

Contents

Illustrations

Acknowledgments

Chapter 27 of the book of Acts records the story of Paul's shipwreck off the shore of Malta. On his way to Rome from Jerusalem as a prisoner, Paul finds himself in the midst of a nor'easter. While the crew and passengers despair of their lives, Paul explains to them: "Not one of you will be lost; only the ship will be destroyed." True to his prophecy, the vessel splinters against a sandbar, but all the passengers manage to swim ashore or otherwise reach land. At several points throughout this project, I thought I would have to lose the ship in order to make it to the shore. But thanks to a God who is ever faithful (and who knows my poor swimming abilities), I find myself well equipped to go seafaring again and from my old port even. I thank God for surrounding and steadying me with an army of Pauls, who buoyed me to safety and completion in the midst of the storm.

This book started a long time ago, maybe as far back as when I discovered the meaning of literature and learning at Camden High School. In this regard, two of my first pilots were Ms. Betty Hankins and Coach Thames. At Morehouse College, Dr. Delores Stevens, Dr. Robert Taylor, Dr. Carole Raybourne, and Dr. Melvin Rahming deserve special recognition, but Dr. Steven Baker was more than a professor. I told you my dream, and you believed it. No mention of Morehouse is complete without a reference to all the Big people: Mike, Sam, Shea, and Owen. You hold my songs, stories, and dreams; you hold my life. Let's keep on holding on. The UNCF/Mellon Foundation has been exceedingly good to me. For the summer institute and continued support, I am eternally grateful. One of my fondest memories is of Dr. Byrd telling me, in his inimitably stern-faced but deeply loving way, "Keith, you have a lot of work to do." I am still working, Dr. Byrd. I remember my Spice House peers with great affection but none more so than my sister-friends, Andrea Armstrong and Jaisha Bruce. The SSRC–Mellon Mays Foundation continues to do incredible work. To Cally Waite and Emma

Tatti, you stepped in right on time. At the IRT, Kelly Wise and a host of remarkable administrators, professors, and students continue to do tireless work.

Several local and regional institutions and libraries were invaluable throughout this process, including Camden's Free Public Library, Rowan's Keith and Shirley Campbell Library, Stockton's Undergraduate Library, Temple's Samuel L. Paley Library, the Community College of Philadelphia's Main Library, and the University of Pennsylvania's Van Pelt Library. At Rowan University, I also want to acknowledge the careful attention and good advice of Cathy Parrish, Tanya Clark, and Cindy Vitto.

The University of Michigan deserves special thanks. I cannot say enough good things about Rackham's summer institute, especially Mary Clark. I continue to reap the benefits of the Center for the Education of Women's generosity; thank you, Valerie. Megan Sweeney, Tiya Miles, and Xiomara Santamarina saw my work in ways that I did not and perhaps still do not; I hope this work does their influence some justice. Sidonie Smith, you continue to inspire and surprise me. Nothing in this life has been more humbling than having the privilege to write for you. For the rest of Michigan, with all its power and wonder, I will say three names: Kelleen Milton, Meilee True, and Elizabeth Agunloye.

At Rutgers University in Camden, I have found my way home one more time. This project would have been inconceivable without that institution's guidance and support. My special thanks to Chancellor Wendell Pritchett, Dean Kriste Lindenmeyer, Camie Morrison, and Dee Jonczak. While at Rutgers, generous support from the Christian R. and Mary F. Lindback Foundation made various research trips, learning experiences, and access to archival material possible. Many parts of this work are a direct result of that foundation's funding and assistance. Matching their good faith with their good work, several English Department members read drafts of this manuscript in part or in total. For working through early versions of this book, you deserve much more than my gratitude, but certainly no less. Thank you, Shanyn Fiske, Howard Marchitello, Chris Fitter, and Rich Epstein. Along with reading various versions of this work, the following colleagues also navigated me through some very turbulent waters: Geoffrey Sill, Tyler Hoffman, Carol Singley, Ellen Ledoux, and Holly Virginia Blackford, readers and among readers. For all of you, I am eternally grateful. If I started to list the many students who have touched this project, the trees and their descendants would curse my name, so I will say Tara K. Wood, diligent and uncompensated researcher, reader, and friend.

My heartfelt appreciation goes to the Board of Directors at the University of Alabama Press as well as its incomparable editorial and production staff. It has been a pleasure to work with you on seeing this project through to completion. My deepest gratitude goes to Daniel Waterman for seeing the value in this project and understanding why this story needed to be told. In the winter of 2013, you asked me to pull up a chair and that propitious half-hour conversation has led us to this moment. I also want to acknowledge the anonymous reviewers from the press whose incisive comments made this project's arguments and expression more consistent and lucid by a hundredfold. Of course, any remaining lapses in this book's argument or execution are my own.

So many family members have knowingly and unknowingly shaped and supported this project, so I can only name a few. To Mum, I have no fear of silence or sacrifice (and in some ways, what else is the writing of a book?) because of you; you are a woman warrior. To Auntie, summers and the Brooklyn Public Library—a recipe for success. To Dave, you show me how to get back up. To Makissa, we have never needed words; like creation, it has been from the beginning. To Grandmummy, you and I both know that you were the first doctor in the family. You are my first teacher. To Mr. and Mrs. Allen, the names I call you by can never adequately say how much you mean to me. To my church family at St. Matthews (especially Rev. Dr. John Randall and Rev. Leonard Greene), I know you have been praying for me; and it has made all the difference.

To my kids—Joshua, Rebekah, and Zion—the love you give me is the definition of love. I see and feel God in each of you. To my wife, Kale, what else in this life might we build together? You have borne this project as long as I have, and (even more importantly) carried it in ways that I could not. We often joke that you wish I could have carried our children, even just for a part of the time. Well, this has been my child, but you have helped to bear this one as well. And that is why I dedicate this last word to you: Iwalu.

Bound to Respect

I
Uncommon Sufferings

Rethinking Bondage in *A Narrative of the Uncommon Sufferings, and Surprizing Deliverance of Briton Hammon, A Negro Man,—Servant to General Winslow, of Marshfield, in New-England*

> Although often identified as a slave narrative, Hammon's work is not really part of that genre. . . . Hammon's narrative deals with bondage and freedom in vastly different ways than do slave narratives. Hammon emphasized his bondage only when discussing his experience as an Indian captive, as a bondsman for the Cuban governor, and as a prisoner for resisting the draft. . . . Hammon's narrative obviously does not assume the same definition of slavery or agree with the depiction of slave life. The slave narrative pattern from south to north and from bondage to freedom has not yet developed.
>
> Frances Smith Foster, "Briton Hammon's Narrative" (185)

One way to tell the story of the variety and complexity of black bondage in the New World is to start with the story of Briton Hammon. On Christmas day in 1747, the Massachusetts bondsman was compelled to leave his master's house and join a shipping expedition en route to Jamaica and the Bay of Campeche, a resource-rich expanse located to the west of Mexico's Yucatán Peninsula. The trip was a risky, but routine, one. Known as the Campeche run, it entailed travel down the eastern seaboard, a potential layover in Jamaica to purchase sugar, two-week journey from there to Campeche, followed by negotiations with the ex-sailors and pirates who cut and sold the dye-producing logwood, all the while avoiding capture by the Spaniards patrolling the peninsula (Rediker 60, 139). If things went well, captains could then steer their ships toward the generous Gulf Stream current that flanked the East Coast and complete the entire trip in about six months (Desrcohers 154). The fact of this particular journey and of Hammon's existence, then, would probably have gone unremarked by fellow New Englanders if it had not been for a singular occurrence: Hammon would not make it back to Massachusetts for another twelve years. When he did return in the summer of 1760, accompanied by his former master no less, New Englanders were eager to find out what had happened to him. They wanted to know what had happened to the ship, who remained from the crew, how Hammon had survived, with whom he had stayed, and, of course, how he had miraculously made it back "home." Likely with the permission of his master, if not at his urgent behest, Hammon related a version of his adventures, which was then arranged into a fourteen-page account and published by the Boston publishing firm of Green and Russell, the abbreviated title of which reads *A Narrative of the Uncommon Sufferings, and Surprising Deliverance of Briton Hammon, a Negro Man,—Servant to General Winslow, of Marshfield, in New-England* (1760). This would eventually come to be known as the first slave narrative by a person of African descent in North America.[1]

For reasons that might already be making themselves clear, Hammon's narrative reveals very little, at least on purpose, about his bondage to New England whites and much more about his captivity to people beyond Massachusetts. The account's action, for instance, begins in earnest on the return voyage from the bay, when Hammon's ship strikes a reef off the eastern coast of Florida. Though the crew advises the captain to chuck the heavy logwood, and thus enable the ship to escape into deeper waters, the captain refuses and the vessel continues to idle. Expecting to be engulfed by the crushing surf at any moment, the crew imagines that they are delivered when they see another smaller vessel rapidly approach, apparently bearing an "English Colour" (Hammon 21). But their feelings of deliverance quickly turn to dismay when they realize that their prospective saviors are actually "*Indians* of which there were Sixty" (21). The Natives board the vessel, murder the captain, dispatch several other crew members, and burn the ship, all the while "making a prodigious shouting and hallowing like so many Devils" (21). Eventually, the entire crew is killed, except for a fleeing Hammon, who is captured, flogged with a cutlass, strapped to a boat, and whisked off to the shore (21). The narrative presents Hammon as fearful for his life, but it also confesses that the Indians actually "us'd [him] pretty well" and explains that he remained with them for "about five Weeks" (22).

Although it is possible that Hammon might have been spared so that he could be sold as a slave (Bolster 28), at least one researcher has suggested that Hammon's encounter with these Natives should be interpreted as a rescue and not as an abduction. Identified as the Calusa by historian Jeffrey Gagnon, this tribe of coastal Natives had been the victim of British raids for Indian slaves throughout much of the eighteenth century. Consequently, they may have viewed the "Negro Man" Hammon as a fellow victim of English cruelty (Gagnon 84–7). What is more, Hammon may have known and worked alongside Native American indentured servants in the Winslow household and was "probably networking among New England Natives for most of his life before ever setting foot on

Florida soil" (78). This braided history might explain why, of all the crew members, Hammon was the only one to be kept alive and, even more tellingly, why they "us'd [him] pretty well." Nonetheless, the narrative presents this episode as Hammon's first "captivity," one that would have probably thrilled eighteenth-century colonial readers, raised on such staples of Indian captivity writing like Mary Rowlandson's foundational tale of white female abduction, *The Sovereignty and Goodness of God*.[2]

Hammon's captivity, such as it is, does not last long. After over a month of apparent exile in Florida, a Spanish schooner from Saint Augustine, Florida, piloted by one of Hammon's former acquaintances from Jamaica, kidnaps him and transports him to nearby Cuba, where the Natives pursue him a few days later in the hopes of reclaiming "their Prisoner" (Hammon 22). Subsequently, the Spanish governor of Havana, Francisco Antonio Cagigal de la Vega, agrees to pay the Natives ten dollars for Hammon and, furthermore, instructs them to bring future captives for ransom to Havana. The Natives agree, and thus commences Hammon's detention in Havana. Just as his bondage in Florida is relative, uneven, and ambiguous, so is his captivity in Cuba. Though Cuba would become a thriving slave society and the leading producer of sugar by the mid-nineteenth century, neither slavery nor sugar production had been introduced there on a large scale in the mid-1700s (Fuente, "Slaves" 663). In fact, Cuba's slave population paled in comparison to neighboring islands like Haiti and Jamaica (McNeil 43), and free blacks made up more than a third of the entire black population (Thomas 36). Indeed, through *coartacion*, the system by which Cuban bondspeople could gradually purchase their freedom, blacks often had ways to end or temper their slavery that were not available in other parts of the New World (Thomas 36).[3] Domestic slaves in Havana (as opposed to the countryside) fared particularly well, often having the ability to "work on their own in conditions close to liberty" (Thomas 37). As Hammon almost seems to brag at one point, "I had my Liberty to walk about the City, and do Work for my self" (23).

But though Hammon is apparently free to explore Havana, he is still obliged to "live" with the governor in "the Castle." At least since the late sixteenth century, Havana was fortified by three such structures: El Morro, La Punta, and La Fuerza, massive stone edifices that were crucial to the outpost's defense (Fuente, *Havana* 73–77). By the time of the British seizure of Havana in 1762, the governor's residence was in La Fuerza (Thomas 16), the fortress most internal to the harbor, and it is likely that La Fuerza was the residence of Cagigal de la Vega during Hammon's time in Cuba. The narrative alternatively presents this "Castle" as a potential sanctuary and cell. After he is redeemed from the Natives of Florida, the account explains that he "lived with the Governor in the Castle about a Twelve-month" (Hammon 22), implying that he was some kind of royal servant or even semi–house guest. But later when he tries to escape from the island he is "ordered back to the Castle, and there confined" (23), indicating that he was a de facto prisoner. Indeed, it is unclear what the nature of the "living" is that Hammon does with Cagigal de la Vega. Did Hammon have to labor for the governor? Was he a member of the cadre of bondsmen who helped to fortify the castles and cut timber for the shipyard? And if he was not a slave of the state, then what kind of relationship, if any, did Hammon have to bondage? Indeed, how would he compare his "living" with the governor to his "living" with General Winslow?

Whether one reads Hammon's stay with the governor as a precarious liberty, complicated captivity, or a fusion of both, it is compromised after about a year. While walking down a city street, a Spanish press gang seizes him and throws him into the city's "Gaol" or jail (22). The next day they ask him to help man four newly built ships headed to "Old Spain," but he adamantly refuses (22).[4] Most African Americans, if forced to choose, would probably opt for impressment (or forced military enlistment) over enslavement on the land because the sea offered greater opportunities for independence (Bolster 31; Brunsman 121). However, after experiencing what appears to be the relative autonomy of urban life in Havana, impressment might have meant a genuine interruption of the quasi freedom Hammon had found. Perhaps of even greater importance, strained war-time relations between the British and Spanish would have made a forced tour of duty to Spain even less desirable by decreasing the chances of Hammon's return to New England. Certainly from the perspective of the text's Boston publishers, as John Sekora, Robert Desrochers Jr., and others have suggested, resisting Spanish impressment would have made for a much more patriotic and marketable story (Serkora, "Red, White" 94; Desrochers 165). At any rate, the narrative notes that Hammon refuses Spanish naval conscription, and for this act of defiance, he is thrust into "a close Dungeon" for "*four Years and seven months*" (Hammon 22).

It appears that Hammon may have rotted away in this condition for an even longer period of time if not for the intervention of a sympathetic Englishman waiting for the repair of his vessel. He informs the governor of Hammon's whereabouts, and he subsequently releases him. At this point, Hammon is remanded into the custody of the governor and attempts to get off the island. He makes two unsuccessful attempts, the second of which leads to yet another form of bondage. After he is returned to La Fuerza, he is "set at Liberty, and order'd with a Number of others to carry the Bishop from the Castle, thro' the Country, to confirm the old People, baptize Children, &c" (23). In language that is typical of the ambiguous bondage that structures *Uncommon Sufferings*, Hammon is granted "liberty" in one breath and then "order'd" to serve the bishop in another. While the narrative presents this latest form of subjection as a papist plot to defraud the Cuban people (the bishop apparently "receives large Sums of Money" [23] for his blessings), Bishop Pedro Agustin Morel de Santa Cruz's 1754 tour also constituted the first comprehensive census of Cuba's population in the eighteenth century. He visited nearly every town on the island and took meticulous notes on the arrangement of households, from areas in the northwest section near Havana to his ecclesiastical seat in Santiago de Cuba, the island's most southeasterly region (McNeill 35–39). In language reminiscent of his stay with the Natives in Florida, Hammon notes that he "lived very well" during this seven-month tour of the island (23), suggesting the ambiguity and complexity of his relationship with the Bishop.

At the end of this expedition, Hammon is once again remanded to "the Castle" (23). This return from and to captivity precipitates Hammon's final attempt to get off the island. On his proverbial third try, he stows aboard the ship of another sympathetic Englishman, who refuses to give Hammon up to the Cuban authorities. From there, Hammon flees to Jamaica, and the rest of the narrative details his involvement in the Seven Years' War, naval engagement with the French, subsequent disability as a result of a skirmish (23), convalescence at the British naval hospital in Greenwich, and eventual destitution in the London streets (24). Likely as a means of fending off starvation, Hammon's relationship to black bondage takes on perhaps its strangest turn when he enlists on "a large Ship bound to *Guinea*," that is, a vessel headed to Africa to buy slaves. While African-born blacks did serve as deckhands and interpreters in the Atlantic slave trade (Bolster 51–52), Hammon's choice appears curious in light of his earlier refusal to join a Spanish naval convoy. But here, the necessity of survival seems to override the protocols of race.

Hammon is saved from this fate, however, when he learns of another vessel, which is bound to Boston and in need of a cook. It is while he is "at Work in the Hold" of this vessel that he learns that a gentleman hailing from Massachusetts is also aboard the ship (24). After a few days of confusion about the identity of a "General Winslow"—"For I never knew *my good Master*, by that Title before" (24)—Hammon discovers that the traveler is none other than his former owner from Marshfield: "My good master" (24). He and Hammon return to Massachusetts, and thus, if ironically, concludes this foundational "slave narrative."

As I hope this extended critical summary makes clear, far from being exclusively a record and representation of New England chattel slavery, *Uncommon Sufferings* is a text that implicates multiple genres and geographies of unfreedom, including but not limited to Indian captivity, naval impressment, maritime shipwreck, Native American enslavement, Native American indenture, and Cuban imprisonment, not to mention systems and examples of bondage for which we do not have ready-made names. The fact that this more complicated account of black bondage comes to us at the cost of a more straightforward narrative of captivity to New England whites might give us pause. However, the means by which this story comes to us should not automatically undermine its import. Both because of and despite its white editors' attempts to downplay chattel slavery in Massachusetts, the account illuminates stark differences in the conditions of captivity for blacks in various parts of the New World. Blacks abducted by the Calusa appeared to have far different prospects for freedom and unfreedom than blacks serving as royal slaves in Cuba or as domestics in New England households, highlighting the fluidity and inconsistency of categories like "bondage," "escape," and "freedom." One form of bondage does not patiently wait for another to end before it begins in Hammon's narrative: captivities jostle for supremacy, conceal their power and intentions, make simultaneous claims on the person of the captive, broker asymmetrical contracts with each other, overemphasize their differences, and regularly, if sometimes unintentionally, frustrate the restrictions caused by one form of constriction only to introduce new possibilities and limitations. As typified by Hammon's rescue by his "good master," bondage can paradoxically enable opportunities for escape and reunion even as it reinstates other strictures of enslavement.

I read these apparent contradictions as a productive confusion, what Philip Gould has referred to in another context as an "enabling ambiguity" ("'Remarkable Liberty'" 117). That is, the generic and experiential instability present at the inauguration of the slave narrative presents a singular opportunity to reimagine what narratives of black bondage are and how we might read them. Along with a host of other eighteenth-century black autobiographers, like Venture Smith, John Marrant, and Olaudah Equiano, Hammon could not have understood himself as participating in the pre–Civil War autobiographical accounts that we have become comfortable in identifying as "fugitive slave narratives." This genre might be defined as representations of bondage to whites in the upper South, followed by eventual escape to and relative self-sufficiency in the industrialized North, what Frances Smith Foster calls the "narrative pattern from south to north and from bondage to freedom" (185) in this chapter's epigraph. Instead, Hammon's over-a-decade-long adventures are more reflective of the geographical mobility and linguistic diversity that historian Ira Berlin observes of "Atlantic Creoles" in the fifteenth century and beyond or people of African descent who lived in between, and on the edges of, several Atlantic empires (23). As a result, I do not invoke Hammon here as a historical-literary model that applies to all times and places but rather as a poignant example of what black bondage has been, what it might still be, and what it might look like. Understood as one of many scenes of instruction for black life and writing in the New World, the tale discloses a point that I believe bears on African American cultural production well beyond the time the text was produced: even in the context of chattel slavery—perhaps the most conspicuous, influential, and menacing historical reality of the New World—multiple kinds of captivity, confinement, and bondage structured the lives and stories of people of African descent.

If slave narratives constitute "the ground on which later black writing is based," to use John Sekora's phrasing, much depends on the curious and insistent presence of multiple forms of confinement and compulsion at the "beginning" of this genre ("Black Message/White Envelope" 482). In the language of the epigraph, if "Hammon's narrative deals with bondage and freedom in vastly different ways than do slave narratives," then what are the nature of those differences, and what do they mean for reading more "traditional" accounts of bondage? If the "slave narrative pattern of from south to north and from bondage to freedom has not yet developed," what are the narrative patterns that are present in Hammon's account? What do they look like, and what geographic movements and ideological orientations do they point us toward? More specifically, if Hammon's text is "not really part" of the slave narrative genre, then what genre or genres is it a part of, and, just as importantly, what texts proceed from those genres? In short, if we do not read Hammon's text retroactively—that is, as always having already produced the seemingly discrete genre of the antebellum African American slave narrative—what other historical, rhetorical, and representational possibilities emerge from this account?

Inspired by the richness of Hammon's story and the provocative questions it raises, *Bound to Respect: Antebellum Narratives of Black Imprisonment, Servitude, and Bondage, 1816–1861* is an exploration of the many underappreciated forms of captivity—"uncommon sufferings," if you will—blacks experienced and recounted in the first half of the nineteenth century. It rereads traditional antebellum slave narratives as well as recovers lesser known autobiographical and biographical accounts as they reveal marginalized forms of black suffering and confinement. By shifting attention to mechanisms and metaphors of constriction both beyond and in the shadow of slavery to southern whites, this study hopes to restore to antebellum African American life writing the heterogeneity of captive experience and representation suggested by Hammon's multifaceted narrative. Loosely signifying on just a few of the wide-ranging models of unfreedom implied in Hammon's inaugural text (imprisonment, Indian captivity, servitude, and maritime shipwreck/capture), this project focuses on four often underappreciated, and sometimes wholly neglected, archives of nineteenth-century African American bondage: the representation of enslaved incarceration in southern penal structures, the memory of slavery in Indian Territory to Native Americans, the rehearsal of child indentured servitude in narratives by northern, black women, and the depiction of African Americans in North African captivity. In doing so, it understands African American writing about imprisonment, servitude, and captivity as part of, and integral to, a larger network of images, vocabulary, narratives, and histories related to bondage and submission in the nineteenth-century world, a world of myriad and mutinous captivities reminiscent of the dizzying world of unfreedoms suggested by Hammon.

Bound to Respect argues that antebellum writers, both in the context of slavery and within systems relatively removed from it, tapped into this imaginative matrix in order to facilitate two of the most important goals of almost all pre–Civil War black writing: legitimizing claims to personhood and framing articulations of protest. Seen as the opposite sides of the same coin, calls for personhood and for protest contributed to the recognition and articulation of black humanity. As Samuel Cornish and John B. Russwurm argued in the inaugural issue of *Freedom's Journal* (1827), the first African American newspaper, blacks "form a spoke in the human wheel" (1). *Bound to Respect* maintains that if the spokes of the wheel correspond to various constructions of humanity, then the language of incarceration, bondage, servitude, and captivity provided one axis around which definitions of humanity turned. As the connected narratives of financial self-sufficiency, spiritual conversion, self-possession, and literacy also did, writing about bondage functioned as a humanizing discourse, transforming despised black subjects into more acceptable ones, a kind of Slotkinian regeneration through strategically narrated confinement.

More than just rehabilitating or denigrating specific racial identities, however, narratives of black unfreedom simultaneously participated in as well as produced the fictions of racial, gender, and cultural difference that they assumed. If blackness is the "product of partial synchronization" and "engagement across cultural boundaries," as Stuart Hall has argued (28), then it cannot be disentangled from, or understood as existing discretely before, the constellation of identities that it is defined against. Likewise, the "black" in black prison narratives, for example, is not a stable, self-identical reference point around which more dynamic forms of cruelty and dispossession move; it is made visible and becomes operational through instances and iterations of bondage. Since the condition of possibility for Hammon's narrative is, in large part, the overwhelming suppression of his racial difference, the production and rehabilitation of his blackness is conspicuously muted. Nonetheless, inasmuch as this nominally "Negro Man" invites the interest of a white readership, his narrative reveals the potential for generating sympathy and respectability for despised and dispossessed black subjects in the context of narratives of captivity.

Antebellum slave narrator Henry Bibb provides a couple of noteworthy examples of this. Detained in Kentucky's Covington jail while attempting to rescue his family from slavery, Bibb laments: "This was the first time in my life that I had been put into a jail. It was truly distressing to my feelings to be locked up in a cold dungeon for no crime" (65). After he reunites with his family, they are eventually transferred to the Louisville workhouse while a slave driver collects more bondspeople for sale in the Deep South. The narrative uses their group incarceration as an opportunity to reiterate their innocence and, just as importantly, to underscore the depravity of those around them: "The people of color who were in there were slaves there without crime, but for safe keeping, while the whites were some of the most abandoned characters living" (93). Bibb and his family's imprisonments become a sign not only of their reprehensible treatment but of their psychological fortitude and moral rectitude. Bondage is the stage on which they can declare their desire for freedom and affirm their personhood. In the twentieth century, the prison writings of Martin Luther King Jr., Angela Davis, and Nelson Mandela underscored the ways that incarceration can concretize spiritual integrity and catalyze political dissent.

At the same time, if "all living is not in protest," to invoke Kevin Quashie (8–9), then neither is all writing. Antebellum narratives of black bondage display the self-interest, hubris, and playfulness that characterize literature in general. As my analysis of *The Narrative of Robert Adams* demonstrates, the desire for economic compensation and even minor celebrity were two of the primary motivations for Robert Adams's multiple retellings of his sensational African captivities. Alleging that he had discovered the route to the legendary city of Timbuktu during one of his abductions, the African American sailor probably cared much less (if at all) about protesting racial injustice than he did about being paid for his story and enjoying the temporary renown it granted him. Similarly, Hammon's editors and owner certainly had unabashedly economic motives in mind when they published his story, and Hammon himself may have relished the opportunity to be at the center of a fantastic advent narrative. Therefore, these accounts are not just engaged in what Kenneth Warren calls the "instrumental" and "indexical" purposes of African American literature—writing designed to fight injustice and measure black intelligence (10–11)—but they are also complicated stories of inflated egos, imperial conquest, and chance encounters that may or may not align with the objectives of black racial uplift and respectability politics.

Whether in the service of protest, personal gain, or individual expression, the price of such authority was often the marginalization, if not demonization, of other groups, many of whom occupied similarly denigrated positions in relation to Euro-American norms and values. Adams's representation as a civilized Western subject is predicated on the misrepresentation of Arabs and indigenous Africans as barbaric and childlike, just as Hammon's identity as a God-fearing "Englishman" is achieved through a depiction of "Indians" as devilish and irrational.

Engaged in the dynamics of what Roderick Ferguson and Grace Kyungwon Hong refer to as "comparative racialization," Hammon and Adams emerge as sympathetic characters by virtue of their marked differences from, and denigration of, racial, linguistic, religious, and geographic outsiders. This problematic racial zero-sum game refashions embattled "black" subjects into respectable, sympathetic, and authoritative ones but with the collateral damage of constructing racial, cultural, and sexual minorities in problematic ways.

The title of this book, *Bound to Respect*, compactly expresses the uncomfortable affinities between bondage and respectability, the way that accounts of bondage can engender power and humanity for some people while simultaneously rendering the complexity of other populations invisible. Significantly, the phrase emerged from a document that is often cited as an archetypal statement of American whites' disregard for African American personhood: Supreme Court chief justice Roger B. Taney's majority decision in *Dred Scott v. Sandford*. Originally filed in 1846 in a Missouri trial court, the case began when bondsman Dred Scott asserted that he and his family were free based on their transportation by their former owner, army surgeon John Emerson, to territories where slavery had been prohibited, thereby emancipating them. The case meandered through the lower courts for several years, alternatively denying and granting the Scotts their freedom, eventually making its way to the Supreme Court in 1856. By a decision of 7–2, the court sided against the Scotts, sealing not only Scott and his family's fate but the fate of blacks throughout the United States (Fehrenbacher 239–316). As legal historian Don E. Fehrenbacher explains, the Dred Scott decision meant that "Negroes were not citizens of the United States and therefore had no right to bring suit in a federal court" (323).[5] Taney defended this ruling by contending that people of African descent had always been understood as inassimilable in American society, a precedent that the court was now "bound" to follow. "They had for more than a century before been regarded as beings of an inferior order," he reasoned, "and altogether unfit to associate with the white race, either in social or political relations; and so far inferior, that *they had no rights which the white man was bound to respect*; and that the negro might justly and lawfully be reduced to slavery for his benefit" (emphasis added, Taney 407). Along with providing legal sanction for the myth of black inferiority, Taney's synopsis of American racial history effaced the many subtleties of African Americans' relationship to bondage and freedom. As Fehrenbacher explains, "One of the truly striking aspects of Roger B. Taney's opinion" was that it ignored the legal distinction between free and enslaved blacks: "His discussion of [free blacks'] legal status invariably slipped over into a consideration of their racial ties with slavery" (15). For the purposes of a unified narrative of black inferiority, then, it was easier for Taney to remand all blacks to the condition of slavery and, furthermore, to imagine that bondage as an expression of ineluctable difference and subhumanity.

My use of the phrase "bound to respect" for this book's title purposely confounds the language and logic of Taney's opinion, both thinking of black bondage beyond an exclusive reference to chattel slavery and asserting that bondage could broker and organize relationships to respect and power. More than just admiration or feigned deference, respect should be understood as the condition of possibility as well as the imagined horizon of black social, economic, and political struggle. As Patricia Hill Collins's reading of Aretha Franklin's 1967 soul classic "Respect" explains, the word is a "metaphor for the conditions of African Americans in a racist society," and at the same time it speaks to the specific desire of "'we' Black women" (116).[6] In its deployment as a greeting and affirmation used between Caribbean men (the phrase "nuff respect," for example) the expression addresses and redresses colonial histories of black male vilification and invisibility. The *Oxford English Dictionary*'s gloss of respect as "direct[ing] one's gaze towards" underscores the potential for this kind of interpersonal recognition ("respect" def. I.1.a). Thus, to respect someone or something is to honor that entity with genuine contemplation. As such, the word encapsulates the need for, and the declaration of, a defiant, dialectical humanity in a world that seeks to ignore, injure, and expunge people of African descent.

Motivated by a desire for this kind of acknowledgment, tales of black unfreedom offered literary rites where political rights had been denied. As Henry Louis Gates Jr. and other scholars have noted, writing in the Western world has been largely understood as synonymous with full personhood, and black people's manipulation of the written word has been integral to affirming their development (25). If only because of the mystery and indignity often surrounding experiences of captivity, bondage prompted the production of writing and thus could further the project of materializing black humanity. Whether literally "bound" through the process of book binding or metonymically bound through the more general processes of publication, writing about bondage facilitated African American self-fashioning and self-expression.

Given the limits placed on black attempts at literacy and expression in the context of a dominant white culture, the nature of this "writing" is complicated. As with Hammon's account, it is likely that a white amanuensis is partly responsible for much of the language, and even in the absence of heavy-handed editorial intervention, Hammon would have had to craft his story in a way that it would be acceptable to a British, colonial reading public. Nonetheless, black people's deep immersion in West African and then African American vernacular traditions meant that they were masters of the spoken word and other modes of articulation, Grey Gundaker reminds us, even when they were not masters of themselves. Prompted by the exigencies of bondage, they "bound" their listeners and interlocutors through stories of their confinements, often with an eye toward their own humane self-fashioning or even financial self-interest.

Reflecting the global dimensions of this book's thesis, the phrase "bound to respect" also registers the assorted ways that bondage, incarceration, servitude, and other forms of submission have animated world history. From a contemporary vantage point, New World chattel slavery might appear to be an anomalous phenomenon, but it is hardly the only such instance. As the research of Orlando Patterson, M. L. Bush, Kevin Bales, and others has shown, slavery, detention, and sundry forms of coerced labor have existed in virtually all human societies, whether it took the form of slavery in antiquity, serfdom in Russia, indentured servitude in the Caribbean, indigenous slavery in New France, penal deportation in Australia, kinship slavery in Western Africa, mass incarceration in the United States, human (sex) trafficking, or debt bondage at the present moment.[7] Moreover, these practices have often functioned, as Patterson suggests, not in opposition to the expressed ideals and objectives of those societies but in concert with, and as expressions of, "the most profoundly cherished ideals and beliefs in the Western tradition" (viii). Both as a negative example of freedom as well as a practical method by which freedom is achieved, bondage has been a fundamental way in which human societies articulate independence, power, and progress.

As one moment within this much longer history, the first half of the nineteenth century offers a window into the multifarious ways that the use of bondage and claims to respectability and efficiency were articulated as complementary projects. In a search for more humane ways of punishing apparently deviant people, for example, the American penitentiary supplanted the widespread use of corporal and other physically aggressive forms of punishment from the colonial era (Rothman 45–56). More than just a logistical solution to the management of unruly populations, the invention of the penitentiary contributed to the young republic's image of itself as progressive, humane, and exceptional. Not too differently, southeastern Native Americans, particularly the Cherokee, adopted chattel slavery as a way of cementing their connection to white, southern planter models of "civilization" as well as a way of negotiating the erosion of traditional gender roles brought about by decades of white settler expansion (Perdue, "Cherokee Planters" 110). The creation of the Cherokee Nation, in fact, was simultaneous with their adoption and codification of black slavery and antiblack racism (Miles 108–11). Since the colonial era, child indentured servitude, or binding out, represented an acceptable way in which towns could manage poor, unprotected children and provide a means of cheap labor for middle-class families. Relocating already vulnerable children with host families under the guise of guardianship and stewardship, child indentured servitude represented a system of coercive labor that some scholars speculate may have been "second only in importance to slavery" (Herndon and Murray, "'Proper and Instructive'" 18). Looking beyond the borders of the United States, the North African principalities known as the Barbary States (Tangier, Algiers, Tunis, and Tripoli) used the abduction of European vessels, seamen, and travelers as a tool of political diplomacy and financial gain for centuries (Baepler 3). Their ability to demand tribute from foreign nations was in large measure dependent upon their ability to transform human beings into captives. To be sure, all of these uses of captivity and coercion were frequently contested, both by the members of these groups as well as by the populations they targeted, but the widespread use of such tactics suggests that bondage and efficiency, captivity and democracy, incarceration and respectability were not mutually exclusive categories but interdependent ideas and practices that helped nations and communities to make sense of themselves.

The dates for this study (1816–61) correspond to an approximate forty-five-year period in which America was attempting to make sense of itself after its final intercontinental conflict with the British in the War of 1812, a redefinition that required the relocation and disfranchisement of (among others) people of African descent. The year 1816 marks the inaugural year of the American Colonization Society (ACS), a group composed of well-to-do white men, whose expressed purpose was to "civilize" Africa by sending America's free black population to colonize the continent. While presuming the inherent inferiority of American blacks, it earnestly attempted to reproduce a black nation modeled after the United States (Kazanjian 91). Though it managed to resettle a relatively small number of blacks, about thirteen thousand (Fairhead et al. 10), the formation of the ACS is symbolic of the precarious position of people of African descent, free and unfree, in the American body politic. From the domestic slave trade in the South, which orchestrated the movement and detention of some two million bondspeople throughout the South (W. Johnson 7), to various state laws and unofficial practices that compromised the safety, movement, and opportunities of free blacks throughout the United States (Bracey et al.), to the Fugitive Slave Law of 1850, which significantly buttressed slave owners' abilities to retrieve fugitives in the North (Pease and Pease 11–12), hardly any of the approximately 3.5 million black people in America in 1850 (roughly 3.2 million of them enslaved) could feel their lives were protected, much less respected. Certainly, questions and anxieties about the status of African Americans persisted and even intensified after the beginning of the Civil War in 1861, but the passage of the Emancipation Proclamation in 1863 and the Thirteenth Amendment in 1865 meant that the terms under which those questions could be posed were radically different from before.

Read as rehabilitative and reintegrative rituals, antebellum accounts of black imprisonment, servitude, and captivity encode the possibility of reinserting black subjects into economies of personhood, belonging, and desire. Like Briton Hammon's narrative before them, however, their claims to self-expression and humanity are not made in, or possible by, the safety of an idealized freedom but through and against the mechanisms and metaphors of bondage that attempted to ensnare them. They speak in a voice that is haunted by the prospect of unfreedom. Equally important, these stories are haunted by the white accounts of captivity and bondage that necessarily influenced and echoed their own. From Henry David Thoreau's account of a one-night stay in a Connecticut jail in "Civil Disobedience" to James Riley's best-selling Barbary captivity account, *An Authentic Narrative*, black writers had to negotiate the stories of detention and captivity that had been previously told, or that were even likely to be told, from the perspective of white subjects.

The notion of mimicry, as theorized by postcolonial critic Homi Bhabha, provides one way to think about the ways that black narratives of bondage are shadowed by their white antecedents and contemporaries. According to Bhabha's argument, any act of repetition in a colonial context enacts an imitation that is "the same, but not quite." Bhabha notes that such imitation tends not only towards flattery but mockery, encoding a repetition that "is at once resemblance and menace" (Bhabha 123). Understood as a subtle and even sinister strain of imitation, menace produces unscripted, anomalous, and potentially resistant doubles, such as a British colonial officer with "dark" skin or the recitation of a national anthem with a foreign accent. Even as it maintains the status quo, it "must continually produce its slippage, its excess, its difference" (122). These eruptions of the "the same but not quite" complicate the seemingly submissive act of imitation, introducing diversity where we might only imagine domination or calling attention to alterity where we might only see conformity.

The connected but contrasting impulses of "resemblance" and "menace" illuminate the simultaneously conservative and subversive potential of black stories of bondage. On the one hand, these accounts "resembled" white accounts of captivity inasmuch as they terrorized the lives and representations of other disenfranchised groups. At least since Mary Rowlandson's *The Sovereignty and Goodness of God* in 1682, Anglo-American stories of abduction and confinement have encoded the demonization, objectification, and dehumanization of Native American subjects, among other dispossessed groups. Black accounts of "Indian captivity" transmit many of the same misperceptions. In fact, we might even say that the humanization of African American subjects is often proportionally inverse to the dehumanization of, say, Native Americans, North Africans, poor whites, and illiterate subjects. As made clear from Hammon's narrative's representations of Florida Natives and then the Spanish bishop, achieving respect in the context of such brutality is often a contest between racial and cultural others that requires the defamation of one subject in order to elevate another. From Moors in North Africa to disfranchised whites in southern workhouses, the illustrations of bondage considered here disparage the full spectrum of nineteenth-century pariahs and have-nots, trading on the perceived deficiencies of one group to celebrate the redeeming qualities of another.

But if black accounts of imprisonment obscure the suffering of white prisoners or white child workers, they also successfully fail to reproduce the white power, historical amnesia, cultural dislocation, and psychic violence that have often attended white captivity writing. When read as a function of the operations of "menace," they, in fact, hijack narrative forms that had often been used by Anglo-American whites to displace and dispossess people of color and, in the process, undermine those accounts. Moreover, even as stories of black abduction carry on the racist, ethnographic impulses of Indian captivity and Barbary captivity narrators like John Williams and James Riley, respectively, they also participate in the captive's prerogative to lament her own condition as well as to chastise her captor. As a person of African descent, Hammon's "captivity" in Cuba raises questions about black freedom and relationships to other blacks in the New World. As such, these early narratives have the potential to contribute to the restoration of the full and complex context of black suffering, highlighting black dispossession and deconstructing myths of white privilege. Such reimaginings of who might be at the center of a narrative of bondage or suffering opens up opportunities to consider the discriminations practiced against other groups. As my discussion of bodily "disability" and indentured servitude in Harriet Wilson's *Our Nig* makes clear, that text accommodates communities of physically ill and somatically different people within its vision of an ideal and healthy society. More than just "copies" of white models, they institute their own resistant representations and meanings. Tales of black suffering and bondage thus have the capacity to turn ethnocentric narratives back onto themselves, directing their classist, chauvinistic, and able-bodied perspectives back at the groups and institutions who most benefit from them and granting that power back to the least powerful. While they can never fully disentangle themselves from the ethnocentric and sexist assumptions embedded in these narratives, they can menace them enough to thwart the complete reproduction of their elitist perspectives.

Finally, we should also note that stories of black bondage are menacing because they record and rehearse yet another way in which people of African descent were brutalized. Inasmuch as the writing considered here reconstructs the violent maltreatment of people of African descent, it tells the story of black imprisonment, domestic abuse, illness, abduction, shipwreck, abuse, chaining, and other painful and life-threatening situations. Consequently, this is a body of texts that adds more horrors and suffering to the already too-long catalog of black agony in the New World. In this unfortunate but ever-significant sense, these texts menace black lives and literature.

Critical Interventions

As part of a third wave of African American literary criticism, *Bound to Respect* is in conversation with several studies that seek to challenge the frameworks that have defined African American literary study. No longer attempting to establish the legitimacy of the field (as in the first wave) or to advance the field through (for instance) the application of the insights of contemporary critical theory (the second wave), this phase of African American literary criticism interrogates its constitution, assumptions, and future directions.[8] As one voice within this larger chorus, *Bound to Respect* takes part in the "soul searching" (Carpio 387) that has come to define African American literary study at the present moment, an ethos that is cogently articulated in Roderick Ferguson's powerful essay, " Lateral Moves of African American Studies."

Ferguson, writing against what he calls "the hegemonic mode of plotting African American racial formations" (114), urges critics to resist an origin narrative of African American (literary) history that "starts with the middle passage, moves to slavery, proceeds to Emancipation, stops briefly at Reconstruction, passes through Jim Crow segregation, and arrives at civil rights" (116). In its place, he asserts the primacy of "lateral moves" within black experience and representation, such as migrations that challenge a US nationalist framework or queer of color critiques that contest heterosexual and male privilege. Doing so, he continues, problematizes the seeming "transparency, linearity, and homogeneity" associated with black history and cultural production. *Bound to Respect* likewise moves laterally by situating black bondage within a constellation of confinements, constrictions, and oppressions that were in place at the same time as slavery. It shows how black unfreedom did not only emerge in the void left by slavery but operated laterally—that is, along with and sometimes through the techniques of slavery. I underscore this point in order to trouble the apparent one-to-one and self-evident relationship between black bondage and slavery to southern whites and to highlight African American unfreedom in unexpected places, from Cherokee plantations in Oklahoma Indian Territory to nomadic communities in North Africa. Moving laterally, *Bound to Respect* tells the truth of black bondage and suffering, but it tells it, as Emily Dickinson would have appreicated, slant.

This purposely off-center approach to African American literature finds its corollary in several studies. Moving away from a focus on spaces that would have been owned or ordered by the white planter class, William Tynes Cowan's *The Slave in the Swamp* explores the importance of watery recesses like bogs, marshes, and swamps in actuating and imagining bondspeople's resistance. Rethinking lines of influence in a transatlantic context, Julia Sun-Joo Lee's *The American Slave Narrative and the Victorian Novel* queries the impact of American slave narratives on nineteenth-century authors like Charles Dickens, who have typically been read as shaping minority discourses but not shaped by them. Hoping to dislodge the "bound book" from the center of nineteenth-century African American literary analysis, Eric Gardner's *Unexpected Places* investigates "*the* central publication outlet for many black writers" (10): black periodicals. By way of this approach, he hopes to defy "our near-obsession with specific kinds of narratives" (9) and thereby make available rich and unexplored sites of analysis. In the same spirit, John Ernest's magisterial *Chaotic Justice* uses chaos theory to elucidate the "fractal dimensions" (27) of African American literature in an attempt to wrestle with the "sheer messiness of history" (36) and to come to terms with the "negotiated instabilities" (253) of black writing.

By calling attention to the "chaos" precipitated by slave incarceration, Cherokee slavery, child indentured servitude, and Barbary captivity, *Bound to Respect* similarly desires to expose and wrestle with the irregularity, anomalies, and enigmas of African American experience and literature—black subjects trapped in constrictive systems for which they were never intended, held by groups who had similarly antagonistic relationships with Euro-Americans, and equipped with representational tools that were originally meant for others. As in my discussion of Briton Hammon's "slave narrative," this project does not attempt to bend "problematic" texts to fit the established models of what African American literature is always and already supposed to be; rather, it sits inside the "chaos" of those accounts in order to find the rules that govern their apparent disorder, the improbable method in their disorienting madness.

The book more specifically benefits from and hopes to build on the innovative and inspiring work done by scholars in the particular fields and disciplines at the crossroads of its concerns, such as Caleb Smith's *Prison and the American Imagination* in the area of prison and cultural studies; Tiya Miles's *Ties that Bind* in the area of African–Native American history; Ruth Wallis Herndon and John E. Murray's *Children Bound to Labor* in the area of child labor studies; Jeffrey Bolster's *Black Jacks* in the field of black maritime occupations; and Paul Baepler's *Whites Slaves, African Masters* in the study of Barbary captivity writing. Through synthesizing this scholarship and the traditions they represent, this study hopes to illuminate the multilayered levels of black captive experiences and representations, articulating a story that is only partly, or even implicitly, told in other studies. Michelle Burnham's impressive *Captivity and Sentiment* provides one of the most sustained examinations of captivity and bondage in this broad and comparative way, including Mary Rowlandson, for example, in conversation and in the same discursive milieu as Harriet Jacobs's writing. But Burnham's innovative study only explores black bondage as part of a larger discussion dedicated to mostly white representations and cultural productions. *Bound to Respect* is the first study to think and link multiple narratives of African American confinement, bondage, servitude, and captivity in the first half of the nineteenth century.

By attending to multiple and simultaneous captive formations, this book aims to provide a corrective to the neglect and misreading of alternative forms of African American subjugation, blind spots that emerge in even the most sensitive studies of confinement, captivity, and constriction. In a landmark and field-shaping study of prison discourse in American cultural production, *Prison and the American Imagination*, Caleb Smith notes that a "whole generation of authors," namely, "Dickinson, Hawthorne, Melville, Poe, Douglass, Emerson, Thoreau, not to mention forgotten prisoner-poets such as Harry Hawser" wrestled with the "new subject of the prison" in the first half of the nineteenth century (18). But, significantly, the names of imprisoned African American bondspeople, save for Douglass, are not numbered in this "generation," figures like Lundsford Lane, William Wells Brown, Henry Bibb, and Harriet Jacobs, whom I examine here in the context of southern jails and workhouses. They too had sustained, intimate, and quite literal relationships with changing meanings of the carceral, and their refractions of it deserve and repay critical attention. The recent discovery of black freeman Austin Reed's manuscript detailing his detention in various New York State correctional facilities, which is being edited by Smith, promises to direct serious attention to antebellum African American prisoners (Bosman). Even so, the necessary work of unpacking and historicizing Reed's invaluable story still threatens to conceptualize black imprisonment primarily as a function of emancipated life. Indeed, in the overwhelming majority of studies of nineteenth-century prison literature, African American imprisonment does not begin in literal and practical ways until after the Civil War.[9]

In contrast, *Bound to Respect* contends that several forms of bondage shaped African American life and culture during the antebellum era. Perhaps unintentionally, eminent sociologist of prison culture Loïc Wacquant gets at this more complicated story of black unfreedom when he asserts: "Not one but several 'peculiar institutions' have successfully operated to define, confine, and control African Americans in the history of the United States" (41). By these "peculiar institutions," Wacquant means, and in this chronological order, chattel slavery, Jim Crow, the ghetto, and the hyperghetto, and prison (42). But even this sophisticated periodization of black subjugation imposes too regular an order on the history of African American subjugation, suggesting a steady and even evolutionary sequence of black discrimination and stigmatization, not all too different from the "hegemonic plotline" Ferguson criticizes. Wacquant's schemata, in fact, is indicative of a more general outline of the way that black subjugation has been chronologized and spatialized in much critical work. Painting with an admittedly broad brush, one might observe that in the eighteenth century, Indian captivity dominates maps of the frontier and colonial settlement; the plantation explains the entrenchment of slavery up until the Civil War; convict leasing on various state-run farms accounts for the second half of the nineteenth century, and finally mass incarceration brings us to the supermax prisons of the later twentieth and early twenty-first centuries. Though these paradigms bear some resemblance to reality and still have important explanatory power, they ignore the variety and confluence of discourses about bondage in any given historical moment, the ways that those histories and hermeneutics haunt, anticipate, and inflect other forms of bondage.

Against the relatively continuous and stable models sketched out above, I argue that African American confinement and captivity was a much more unpredictable and incongruous affair, similar to what we see in Hammon's chaotic narrative. My project seeks to menace the kinds of subjugations we might typically associate with slavery as well as to unhinge antebellum literary study from its moorings in the plantation South, thereby complicating and expanding the map of what constitutes nineteenth-century writing about African American bondage. Certainly, a deep appreciation for the politics and poetics of slavery is still at the heart of this project, but it is not bound to slavery as the exclusive context in which to comprehend black life and letters.

Reading African American literary history in this way is not without risks. In the context of the black experience in the New World, the word *slavery*, unlike, say, *servitude* or *captivity*, carries with it a long and sacred history of suffering and black dispossession; the memory, or more properly the lack thereof, of the anonymous millions who died in the Middle Passage; the trauma of those who lived under the regime of chattel slavery; and the legacy of those who had to (and still have to) construct a rudimentary existence out of the meanest economic, political, and social resources. Consciously deciding to challenge the explanatory power of this concept has the potential to produce pernicious long-term consequences. Just a few years ago, in 2010, a politically charged debate raged throughout the United States over the Texas Board of Education's attempt to rename the "Atlantic Slave Trade" the "Atlantic Triangular Trade," thereby erasing that crucial word from the vocabulary of some five million school children ("Politicized Curriculum"). Although the initiative ultimately failed, such a move would have obscured the centrality of slavery and its racial economies as one of the most horrendous acts of genocide in world history. Just as importantly, it would have disgraced the memories of the children, women, and men who understood the inexpressible terror of that experience as one bound to systems of slavery.

However, by centering the significance of imprisonment, servitude, and captivity to rethink African American literary production, I do not mean to minimize, dishonor, or elide the suffering of African American bondspeople. Rather, just the opposite, my purpose is to understand more acutely and concretely the varied shapes that the misery of people of African descent took, to augment the ways in which we understand black pain in the New World, to recognize the rhetorical questions and discursive formations that attended such suffering, and, ultimately, to cultivate a more subtle appreciation of the ways that people of African descent were bound in the antebellum era, ways that may not be adequately expressed by invoking the notion of slavery. Thus, what is at stake in this project is not the mainstreaming or whitening of enslaved experience and black life but rather, the more sophisticated accounting of the lives and cultural production of people of African descent. The vocabularies and interpretive frameworks of unfreedom I use here to remap African American (auto)biographical writing do not disavow black agony and humanity; instead, they honor the pain, inventiveness, complicity, desire, and duress that attend it. In tandem with a continuing recognition of the importance of slavery, alternative paradigms of bondage and captivity help to provide a "fully loaded cost accounting" of African American suffering, to draw on historian Nell Irvin Painter's memorable phrasing (16). Indeed, a dependence on the construction of African American experience as only one kind of narrative ultimately leads to another kind of bondage, a species of subjugation in which we are tethered to the fictions of black difference, inferiority, and suitability for particular forms of suffering that undergird racism and white power. Envisioning an alternative narrative, this book is a gesture toward still honoring the absurd tragicomedy that is black life in the New World while not being bound to slavery's history and hermeneutics.

Organization

Following from this desire to account for the variety and fluidity of black experience and cultural production, each chapter of this study explores a different location and elocution of "binding" that informed antebellum African American (auto)biographical writing. Accordingly, it is organized into two sections, "Bound in Slavery" and "Bound in Freedom." The former analyzes subjugations in the context of slavery, as in my examinations of prisons in antebellum slave narratives or the relationship between Native American's enslavement of blacks and chattel slavery in the American South. The latter explores constriction in the context of relatively free spaces, as in my investigation of North African captivity in the account of the black sailor, Robert Adams. This schema reflects the project's desire to move from the more familiar locations and texts of African American suffering, such as chattel slavery in the South, to increasingly unfamiliar ones, such as indentured servitude in the Northeast. As a consequence, the entire book is organized topically and spatially, rather than chronologically, beginning with arguably the most recognizable (of late) text and site of antebellum black bondage, *Incidents in the Life of a Slave Girl*, in the American South and ending with a relatively unknown account and location of black captivity, *The Narrative of Robert Adams*, in North Africa. Breaking from the American South, the book enlarges the map of black unfreedom to include the American Midwest, Northeast, and eventually North Africa. Though this organization means that the study moves chronologically backward, it is truer to the project's motivating purpose: the deconstruction of slavery as the exclusive site of black bondage and the recovery of marginalized formations, spaces, and narratives of black confinement.

Each chapter of the monograph is organized around a consortium of concepts and identities that were implicated in specific forms of African American bondage, such as the "Genteel Slaveholder" or the "Civilized Native." Chapter 2's "Imprisoned Slaves, Genteel Slaveholders, and Virtuous Prisoners: Slave Incarceration in *Incidents in the Life of a Slave Girl, Written by Herself*" situates *Incidents* and other antebellum slave narratives within the histories of the modern penitentiaries and local jails of the first half of the nineteenth century. Paying particular attention to the incarceration of Jacobs's children, brother, and aunt in North Carolina's Chowan County jail, the chapter explores *Incidents*'s provocative reimagining of imprisonment as a breakdown of the family, a place of resistance, and a site of domestic tranquility. As the narrator mockingly notes when Jacobs's daughter is returned to the town's jail: "She knew she was loved in the jail" (105). At the same time, my discussion demonstrates how the technology and language of incarceration was a vexed inroad into professional masculinity for Jacobs's master, Dr. James Norcom, creating and consolidating an image of himself as genteel but efficient, the "genteel slaveholder." Such readings reframe this seminal "slave narrative" as a multivalent account of the significance of penal structures in the first half of the nineteenth century, linking it in unexpected conversation with texts as diverse as novelist Charles Dickens's prison writing to political prisoner George Jackson's readings of 1960s' penitentiary life.

Chapter 3, "Mild Slavery, Sympathetic Abolitionists, and Courageous Husbands: Cherokee Slavery in *The Life and Adventures of Henry Bibb, an American Slave*," explores the reality and representation of black enslavement to southeastern Native Americans. A number of first-person testimonials from the perspective of bondspeople exists that document the thousands of African Americans who were enslaved to Native Americans, but Henry Bibb's *Life and Adventures* is the only sustained account to be produced in the antebellum era. Depicting a mild and essentially forgivable model of slavery, it has taken on an iconic, if not mythical, status within the study of what black slavery to Native Americans meant. Grounded by a focus on the rhetorical function of "Indian slavery" in Bibb's slave narrative as well as an understanding of the brutalities that characterized such an experience, the chapter shows how Bibb's particular depiction of Cherokee slavery is a function of his desire for a courageous settler masculinity as well as an attempt to critique the hypocritical practices of white slaveholders. The chapter also traces this sympathetic portrayal to white abolitionists' surprising tolerance of Native American slaveholding as a means of critiquing white chattel slavery, illuminating the ways that some stories of black bondage made it hard for other stories to be told or understood. In the process, the chapter reveals how southeastern Native Americans' dependence on black chattel slavery buttressed claims to progress and civilization even as they were attempting to defend themselves against the encroachment by federal and state governments on their land. Fighting their own battle to remain sovereign and achieve respectability, they paradoxically bound and formed relationships with those who were also the victims of white power and privilege.

Moving into my discussion of the ways that black bondage occurs in spaces and times of apparent freedom, chapter 4, "Bound Children, Benevolent Caretakers, and Disabling Service: Indentured Servitude in Harriet Wilson's *Our Nig*," sheds light on the invisible world of black children's indentured servitude in white households in the antebellum North. In a system that may have been second in numbers only to chattel slavery, municipalities and middle-class families earned cheap labor, managed expendable populations, and otherwise benefited from the mental and physical exertions of poor and vulnerable children of all races. Not surprisingly, African American children, particularly girls, fared the worst in this system. Harriet Wilson's *Our Nig* represents the only book-length representation of an African American child's indenture in the first half of the nineteenth century. Using theories of disability to articulate the connections between bodily pain and sympathy, my discussion foregrounds the ways *Our Nig* mobilizes the figure of the sickly child (and eventually adult) servant to challenge the myth of the indestructible black child laborer. The chapter reveals the ways that the language of disability and vulnerability, specifically invalidism, make visible the disavowed suffering of indentured African American children.

Reprising Briton Hammon's abduction at sea as well as some of the authorial and editorial questions his complex narrative raises, chapter 5's "Savage Moors, African Companies, and Mulatto Explorers: North African Captivity in *The Narrative of Robert Adams*" considers the reality and representation of African Americans sailors who were held captive by Moors and Arabs in North Africa, what was then known as Barbary captivity. It is likely that only a handful of American blacks found themselves in this position, but fragmentary reports from white captivity narratives indicate that people of African descent suffered from this form of bondage as well. Due to its highly mediated character, Adams's narrative, however, is perhaps less useful as historical record of American or at least foreign-born blacks in Barbary than what it means when a "mulatto" protagonist is situated within a predominantly white narrative genre. Sponsored by the Company of Merchants Trading to Africa, a London-based commercial company, the expressed purpose of the account was to show that during Adams's captivity, he was taken to and thus inadvertently discovered the route to the legendary city of Timbuktu. Stories of black captivity in Africa thus brokered European claims to geographical mastery, but also troubled the basis of that privilege and knowledge.

Considered together, Jacobs's *Incidents*, Bibb's *Life*, Wilson's *Our Nig*, and Adams's *Narrative* shed light on an array of discriminatory discourses and dynamics that hindered the actualization of African American humanity and expression in the first half of the nineteenth century but also the way that those mechanisms made available alternative routes to claim respectability and authority. At the same time, they point us toward the larger world-historical investment in forms and fictions of bondage as a means to define, appreciate, and articulate formations of freedom and authority. These stories are thus larger than the specific individuals that sit at the center of them and encourage a greater appreciation for how bondage and liberty, captivity and democracy, sovereignty and servitude are intimately and insistently paired and produced. They render the ambiguous and overlapping representations of bondage that structure Hammon's account and speak to the ways in which the nineteenth century, though dominated by the ever-present specter of slavery, might have also represented a veritable sea of captivities, fluid and dangerous and ever-ready to engulf black subjects.

In this way, they bear witness to the truth that the possibility for multiple captivities for people of African descent did not die with a man like Briton Hammon but, if anything, might have taken on an added and even more robust life than it had before. Though not much is known about Hammon's life after the publication of his narrative, Robert Desrochers Jr. contends that his last appearance in the public record might have been as "Briton Nichols" in the census of 1790 (168), the same year in which the first US "Penitentiary House," the forerunner of later fullscale state penitentiaries, was commissioned (Johnston 26). African Americans made up as much as 44 percent of the prison population in late eighteenth-century prisons (Lawrence-McIntyre viii). At the present moment, scholars have labeled the explosion of prisons and detention facilities in the United States as a prison industrial complex, given the 400 percent increase in the prison population from 1977 to 2005 (Pfaff 547). Indeed, the United States holds approximately 20 percent of the world's prison population though it makes up only 5 percent of the world population (A. Davis, *Are Prisons Obsolete?* 11), statistics that underline the ways in which detention and punishment reflect and influence our national ethos, social policy, and even models of selfhood. Inside and beyond the borders of America, the presence of human (sex) trafficking, child slavery, political imprisonment, Somali piracy, FARC abductions, and debt bondage suggests the global dimensions of the captive matrix in which we live. Hence, our own historical milieu is just as replete with instances and images of bondage and detention as in the first half of the nineteenth century. Hammon's captivities may appear remarkable in the context of certain understandings of antebellum slave narratives, but, in the context of these realities, his narrative appears eerily familiar, if not prophetic. If he were alive today, it is conceivable that he may not have been surprised at the shape of the world we live in. Having lived a life marked by so many disparate instances and systems of captivity, he may have found them, in contrast to the titling of his narrative, quite common.

I
BOUND IN SLAVERY

2

Imprisoned Slaves, Genteel Slaveholders, and Virtuous Prisoners

Slave Incarceration in *Incidents in the Life of a Slave Girl, Written by Herself*

> It is not clear from the scattered references in private letters, plantation records, and testimonies of former slaves how common unruliness was among slave women because most of their "crimes" were punished *within the household*.
>
> Victoria Bynum, *Unruly Women* (emphasis added, 39–40).

Of all the images of suffering that have emerged from the antebellum slave narrative, few have probably received more critical attention than the figure of Frederick Douglass's Aunt Hester hanging by her wrists from a kitchen joist while receiving a brutal flogging.[1] Hester, it is alleged, has been offering her affections to a free black man in the neighborhood, and her master, Captain Anthony, wishes to punish her in a way that reflects his unmitigated power over her body. To this end, Anthony applies several stripes to her back after ordering her to disrobe from the waist up, underscoring his ability to undress, inspect, and violate her body. The scene takes places on a plantation, the narrator informs us, "about twelve miles north of Easton, in Talbot County" (Douglass 8), the nearest site of county or state governance, and anticipates what Douglass notes in the subsequent version of his life story, *My Bondage and My Freedom*, of the southern plantation generally: it is "a little nation of its own. . . . The laws and institutions of the state apparently touch it nowhere" (64). According to this paradigm, slave discipline and suffering, particularly for women, was a domestic, unmediated, and private affair.

A less sensational, but nonetheless noteworthy, model of female slave discipline is suggested by Harriet Jacobs's *Incidents in the Life of a Slave Girl*, Jacobs's autobiographical account of her life in slavery as voiced through the character of Linda Brent and a host of other fictitiously labeled characters. In chapter VII, the appropriately named Dr. Flint, her abrasive and sexually aggressive adversary, learns that Brent intends to marry a free black man, thus physically and (with her eventual purchase by her suitor) legally removing her from Flint's sexual advances and circle of influence. Like Captain Anthony, Flint resents the potential usurpation of his power over the slave woman's person, but unlike Captain Anthony, when Brent tells the envious Flint of her proposed marriage, Flint does not resort to direct physical violence. Instead, he threatens her with this punishment: "How would you like to be sent to jail for your insolence?" (40). Interestingly, Flint's solution to the problem of the recalcitrant black female subject is not to strike her but to confine her, not to act independently but to involve local authorities, and not to exclude other institutions but to employ the penal system.

Motivated by the possibilities for redefining the representation of black women's subjugation as expressed through Flint's pointed question, this chapter seeks to chart how imprisonment (and even the threat of imprisonment) might have been a crucial part of what it meant to be a slave and especially an enslaved woman. As suggested by the epigraph from Victoria Bynum's *Unruly Women*, the overwhelming majority of slave women's discipline occurred "within the household," but this is not to say that public institutions and structures were never involved. Local antebellum jails played a crucial role in the control and punishment of bondspeople, both female and male. What is more, the reality of slave incarceration meant that the way that slaves and ex-slaves imagined their bondage cannot exclusively be understood through the settings, histories, and ideological orientations of chattel slavery but also through newer and older technologies of imprisonment.

A handful of critics have begun to unpack the implications of imprisonment in and around the world of *Incidents*, elucidating, as Douglas Taylor provocatively does, how Dr. James Norcom, the lascivious Dr. Flint of the narrative, was a private pupil of the father of American penology, Benjamin Rush.[2] Such important examinations have considerably enhanced our appreciation of how slavery and imprisonment are "mutually constitutive institutions," to invoke Caleb Smith's concise phrasing (18). Many more studies have addressed the various psychic, social, and bodily constrictions represented in the narrative, particularly focusing on Jacobs's miraculous seven-year self-exile in her grandmother's crawl space.[3] In fact, virtually every published discussion of *Incidents* makes some obligatory, if fleeting, reference to this astonishing confinement, what Jacobs herself calls "my long imprisonment" (127). Yet, these provocative examinations have almost unanimously neglected the quite literal jail that sits at the heart of the text and that still sits at the center of Edenton, North Carolina: the Chowan County jail.[4] This is the jail that the fictionalized James Norcom refers to when he threatens Brent with imprisonment, and this is the jail that structures much of the text's involvement with and representation of penal technologies. Jacobs's children, brother, aunt, and uncle (sometimes on multiple occasions) were all detained there, and Jacobs would have almost certainly been imprisoned there as well, save for the vexed hiding space she finds in her grandmother's three-by-seven-foot garret. In this way, the Chowan County jail, and the notion of imprisonment in a penitentiary more generally, deeply influenced what slavery looked like and meant in *Incidents*.

Similar invocations of the carceral, I argue below, appear throughout antebellum slave narratives, but most historiographies of African American prison writing identify the beginning of black American incarceration with the end of the Civil War, when legal emancipation precipitated the passage of various Black Codes that required the imprisonment of former slaves for any number of "crimes," such as vagrancy, loitering, and unruly behavior.[5] These studies show that disproportionately high rates of African American incarceration continued throughout the twentieth century and crested in the social violence and student protests of the 1960s, producing such classics of black prison literature as Malcolm X and Alex Haley's *Autobiography of Malcolm X*, George Jackson's *Soledad Brother*, and Angela Davis's *Angela Davis*. More recently, anthologies like *Interrupted Life* detail the manifold ways the US prison industrial complex ravages the lives of some two million persons, of which the fastest growing demographic is women (Frost, Greene, and Pranis).[6] Written over one hundred years ago, however, Harriet Jacobs's *Incidents in the Life of a Slave Girl*—and the slave narratives that intersect with it—still testifies to the possibility of African American female incarceration and its multifaceted refraction in writing. Properly understood, centering the role of the Chowan County jail and these larger histories of incarceration in *Incidents in the Life of a Slave Girl*, resets the terms and starting point of the entire tradition of African American prison writing.

Read as a product of the era in which the prison as well as the plantation had come to permeate national consciousness, *Incidents* reveals how mechanisms and metaphors of imprisonment animated ex-slave narrators' critiques of the peculiar institution, but also how personal and municipal claims to reformation, respectability, and authority depended on incarceration. If the literature of imprisonment is conceived as a "battleground" over a crime's "punishment" and "memory," as Michel Foucault has suggested (67), then reading the carceral inside of slavery has the potential to show the often contradictory uses of imprisonment for southern towns, slaveholders, and slaves. Within the domain of "punishment," on the one hand, penal structures like the Chowan County jail ensured the effective functioning and buttressed the authority of municipal governments and individual citizens. Working within the domain of "memory," on the other hand, the main currency of the ex-slave narrator, Jacobs's narrative dramatizes punishment and imprisonment in order to declare her and her family's humanity as well as to frame her protest against the gendered abuses of slavery. As such, the text discloses how one system of unfreedom could paradoxically limit and even trouble another, creating unexpected opportunities for bondspeople to renegotiate and even resist their constricted conditions.

The Chowan County Jail: Historically Considered

Though *Incidents* is a text that is ordered by the politics and poetics of slavery, its reference to "the felon's home in the penitentiary" (31) suggests a keen awareness of the ways the penitentiary was reshaping discipline for all Americans and, in the process, impacting what slavery meant for black people. Inspired by theories of penal reformation emerging from thinkers like Cesare Beccaria (in Italy) and John Howard (in England), America's first penitentiaries were born in the first half of the nineteenth century and were designed to remedy the overcrowding, disorder, and corporal punishments that had attended colonial and post-revolutionary jails (Rothman 45–56, 89–94). Placing a premium on silence and penance (hence the name "penitentiary"), this new era of discipline sought to attack the problem of deviancy at the level of the "soul" (Foucault 29). Despite the fact that African Americans were "ideologically barred from the realm of morality"—and thus had no souls to save (A. Davis, "Race, Gender" 39)—they immediately assumed disproportionate numbers within the prison population, particularly in the North where the gradual abolition of slavery required different methods for regulating the black population than in the slave South. Antebellum America's most famous penitentiary, Philadelphia's Eastern State Penitentiary in Cherry Hill, for instance, imprisoned "153 white males, 52 African American males, and 4 African American females" in its first four years (Johnston 48). As Kali Gross observes, "State prisons in New York, Pennsylvania, and elsewhere were not created exclusively for blacks, but they were designed to arrest and counteract slavery's traits without ending slavery itself" (104).

The structure in which Harriet Jacobs's aunt, uncle, brother, and children were held, however, is less emblematic of the huge penitentiaries that were erected in the early nineteenth century and more representative of the army of local jails, poorhouses, and workhouses that had been in use since the colonial era. One- or two-floor structures that contained only a handful of cells, their explicit purpose was to serve as holding stations before corporal or capital punishment was meted out; they made no pretension to moral reformation as the penitentiary would. Conceived as "part of the earliest plan of the town" (Brodsky 15), the Chowan County jail confirms the narrator's remark in Nathaniel Hawthorne's *Scarlet Letter* that one of the "earliest practical necessities" in the founding of a new colony was the erection of a jail (45). Colonial North Carolina was no exception;

its jails were built at or around the same time as other essential public structures such as courthouses, warehouses, and bridges (Watson 427).

The latest version of the Chowan County jail was erected in 1825 after the previous building burned down the year before.[7] Built by Ebenezer Paine, the newer edifice was a two-story brick jail with two rooms on each floor, two windows in the front, a shingled roof, and possibly a plank floor interior (Brodsky 65). Of the four rooms, one was a debtor's room, and the most used room was the large east room on the first floor, which was thought to be the most secure (65). Situated directly in front of the jail but behind the courthouse were stocks and a whipping post, collectively considered the "court yard" reserved for prisoner's corporal punishments and other activities (Brodsky 53; *True Tale of Slavery* 225).

Located at the back of the estimable Chowan County Courthouse, the oldest public building in North Carolina (Watson 443), the jail was intimately tied to the town's pragmatic attempts to maintain order as well as its desire to project municipal power and respectability. Chowan County Courthouse historian Marc Brodsky suggests their close connection in this way: "As the two primary county buildings in Edenton, the courthouse and jail were often paired together when it came time to assess the condition of county buildings and to repair deficiencies" (12). As such, the Chowan County jail constituted a fault line on which the town's aspirations to state respectability were precariously balanced. One notable example from the town's colonial history suggests this purpose. Defending a claim that "anarchy reigns" in the town, one early visitor noted: "If a man is imprisoned, the jail is broken open" (qtd. in Brodsky 20), underscoring the notion that the jail might have held the key, quite literally, to Chowan County efficiency and dignity.

This building, and perhaps even just the threat of its use, was likely crucial to the regulation of Edenton's African American population; one of the most important ways it did so was as a space of "safekeeping." In the context of the domestic slave trade, some two million slaves, Walter Johnson speculates, were transported from the upper South to the lower South (7), and public jails were a crucial part of this infrastructure. Between 1837 and 1857, for instance, nearly 500 slaves were imprisoned in Baltimore jails, many of whom were recaptured runaways (Wade 219; Christianson 153). Similarly, slave traders lodged 452 slaves at the District of Columbia jail between 1824 and 1828 (Bancroft 53; Christianson 153). According to *Incidents*, the Chowan County jail was crucial to similar "safekeeping." In the chapter, "The Slave Who Dared to Feel Like a Man," Jacobs dramatizes her uncle Joseph's (remembered as Benjamin in the narrative) unsuccessful escape from slavery and consequent detention in the jail. "That day seems but as yesterday," Jacobs recalls, "so well do I remember it. I saw him led through the streets in chains, to jail" (20). Dramatizing Dr. Flint's spiteful reaction to Benjamin's escape, Jacobs relates that Dr. Flint felt "he should be kept in jail till he was subdued, or be sold if he got but one dollar for him" (21). After a total of six months, Benjamin is sold to a slave trader who transports him to New Orleans (22). Though Jacobs is never imprisoned in the Chowan County jail, the narrative makes it clear that a similar fate awaited her if she had ever been captured after her escape. While the reward only boasts $150 for Jacobs's recapture in state, it offers a "$300 reward if taken out of the state and delivered to me, or lodged in jail" (97). Reflecting this same truth, Mrs. Flint exclaims after Brent's disappearance from the plantation, "When she is caught, she shall stay in jail, in irons, for one six months, and then be sold to a sugar plantation" (105).

Douglas Taylor maintains that *Incidents* is "one of the few slave narratives that might also be read as a kind of proto-prison narrative" (430); however, *Incidents* refracts the representation of slave incarceration for "safekeeping" that occurs repeatedly throughout antebellum slave narratives. As Frederick Douglass recorded in his 1845 *Narrative*, detention in a public jail awaited him and his compatriots when they were thrust in Maryland's Easton jail after a botched escape. Douglass remembers: "We had been in jail scarcely twenty minutes, when a swarm of slave traders, and agents for slave traders, flocked into jail to look at us, and to ascertain if we were for sale" (60). Though Douglass was eventually sent back to Baltimore, he notes that Captain Auld's original intention was to sell him into Alabama after his approximately month-long detention in the jail (61). Similarly, after being literally run up a tree by patrollers' dogs during a flight from the plantation, William Wells Brown is sent to the Saint Louis jail until his master, the ironically named Mr. Freeland, retrieves him (32). In a later chapter, Brown leaves his sister in this same jail before making another jaunt for freedom (56), only to be recaptured and to find himself back in the Saint Louis jail weeks later (61). Having served as an assistant to a slave trader traveling to and from the New Orleans slave market, Brown's narrative provides one of the most extensive accounts of slave incarceration in the antebellum era. Though much less well known, but no less important, slave narrator William Anderson's 1857 narrative, *Life and Narrative of William J. Anderson, Twenty-Four Years a Slave*, laments that he is thrown in jail an astonishing sixty times after myriad escape attempts.

Kentucky slave Henry Bibb, a self-described master in the "art of running away" (15), was detained in four different Kentucky penal structures during his various attempts to retrieve his family. He was held in the Bedford jail for two days, the Covington jail for one night, the Louisville jail for perhaps a week (with his wife, Malinda, and daughter, Mary Frances), and the Louisville workhouse for three months (91).[8] Though we do not have direct access to Bibb's wife's experience, her incarceration underscores the point that enslaved women (and children) were not exempt from carceral structures, even as they struggled against specifically gendered forms of abuse. Bibb reveals that Malinda is taken from the Louisville workhouse on two separate occasions by the slave trader Madison Garrison and notes that "a most disgraceful assault on her virtue" was attempted (98). While his narrative implies, by way of the sympathy the prisoners express for Malinda, that she is safe from sexual violence in the prison, the despair and anomie that Bibb describes in the workhouse belie this assumption. According to the narrative of African American hairdresser and diarist, Eliza Potter, antebellum bondswomen were routinely held for safekeeping at the Louisville jail, and at least one fugitive bondswoman was taken there and subsequently "stripped . : . of every piece of her clothing, and whipped . . . till the blood ran from her neck to her heels" (172), indicating that the Louisville jail functioned as a site for bondswomen's sexualized abuse, not just containment.[9]

To be clear, structures like the Saint Louis, Bedford, and Louisville jails were not slave depots, and thus sites particular to the experiences of bondspeople, but part of each town's established strategy for managing disobedient subjects, a system into which African American subjects unfortunately and frequently fell. As with Jacobs's family's detention in the Chowan County jail, the reason for their incarceration was specifically related to slavery, but the site of their detention was no different from whites who had committed offenses, both related and unrelated to "the peculiar institution." Their confinements not only blur the lines between slavery and imprisonment but compel us to consider how those categories and experiences shaped one another.

The cases of Alanson Work, James Burr, and George Thompson provide a pointed example of the interconnected histories and meanings of imprisonment and enslavement. As recorded in their collaboratively produced journal, *Prison Life and Reflections*, the three white abolitionists' were detained for four months in Missouri's Palmyra jail and then for almost five years in the Missouri State Penitentiary on a charge of "stealing slaves" (G. Thompson 18). At least two of the men (Thompson and Burr) were students at Illinois's Mission Institute, a school that sought to redeem the world through the spread of Christianity. Partly as an extension of this deep evangelical commitment, the institute was adamantly antislavery, and both faculty and students actively participated in rescuing slaves from the upper South in the late 1830s (Harrold 91). As Silvan Tomkins explains, suffering, particularly in the form of incarceration, was a means by which white abolitionists, like William Lloyd Garrison, intensified their bonds to the antislavery cause and quite literally to enslaved blacks (161, 166–67), allowing them to claim, as Thompson and his companions repeatedly do, "We can now sympathize with the slave as never before. We know how the chain feels" (19).

With this goal in mind, *Prison Life* makes a point to record Burr's, Work's, and Thompson's encounters with enslaved blacks in the context of their imprisonments. It mentions the case of Albert who "sold south—ran away—was taken up and put in Palmyra jail—was there during all our time" (89). From Albert, they glean information about other bondspeople in Missouri, such as a Lewis County slave who has a hole cut through his ear so that his master can grab him by it during whipping (35). Of their time in the Missouri State Penitentiary, they relate the experience of "three runaway slaves" brought there "in chains, for safe-keeping," one of whom is apprehended, much like Henry Bibb, while trying to meet his enslaved wife in Kentucky (345). Soon after Thompson is set to be released, a bondsperson asks him to write him a "free paper" (362), and another approaches him "for directions to liberty" (368). Most dramatically, the text's front piece showcases a woodcut drawing of Burr, Alanson, and Thompson posed (in chains) next to what are presumably enslaved blacks in Palmyra jail (see fig. 1). *Prison Life* does not reveal any particulars about the bondspeople, but it is possible that they are there for "safekeeping" after running away or as punishment for some other infraction. As their textual representations of enslaved prisoners do in the narrative, the image proves their expressed commitment to "*remember them in bonds as bound with them*" (vi), per the instructions of Hebrews 13:3. At the same time, the distance between the white and black prisoners and the differing postures begin to suggest how dissimilar their experiences of incarceration might have been.

Archival evidence suggests that the Chowan County jail, like Palmyra jail, was also employed in the services of daily slave management, particularly with respect to crimes against property. An 1826 arrest warrant, for instance, ordered the capture and assumed the jailing of an enslaved man identified as Bill for "driving a horse and cart through the streets of the town of Edenton and as to injure a horse."[10] Similarly, an 1857 warrant implies that the slaves Edward and Anthony, accused of "battery upon each other," were temporarily housed at the Chowan County jail before they received several lashes at the "common whipping post."[11] Since slaves were considered property, their assault on each other was probably considered an offense on par with the "injury" of the horse. In contrast to these uses of the jail to punish so-called crimes against property, *Incidents* probably means to suggest Norcom's manipulative nature with his essentially psychological uses of detention. In one scene, Dr. Flint sends William to the jail in order to "reflect upon his bad conduct" (61–62). Parodying and exposing the logic of what Michael Meranze identifies as the ideology of reformative incarceration, *Incidents* suggests that Norcom might have employed the jail as a space that he could use to "reform" his slaves' conduct. Extorting information was another function of detention, as when Norcom imprisoned Jacobs's

Figure 1. Inside cover image from George Thompson's *Prison Life and Reflections*.

children, brother, and aunt after her flight from his son's plantation. For approximately three months, Jacobs remembers, they were "thrust into jail, as means of compelling my relatives to give some information about me" (101).

The Chowan County jail was also complicit with more physically aggressive acts of intimidation and punishment, particularly through the use of the stocks and whipping post situated in its front yard. Jacobs's brother John outlines the cruelties of slavery in "A True Tale of Slavery." He explains that "at the back of the court-house and in front of the jail, is a whipping post, where I have seen men and women stripped, and struck from fifteen to one hundred times and more" (225). Reflecting a similar use of the jail, Harriet Jacobs notes in the chapter "The Church and Slavery" that the town constable is willing to whip bondspeople "at the public whipping post, in jail or out of jail" (70). Through whipping, the Chowan County jail was probably a crucial part of how Edenton, and probably many communities and cities throughout the antebellum South, defined and defended the social fictions of African American inferiority and racial difference. One 1826 Chowan County ordinance reveals that for "each and every person who may hereafter be convicted of breaking the courthouse windows" the fine would be five dollars for each pane of glass, but for "every slave committing the same offence [he or she will] be punished by whipping not exceeding 39 lashes" (qtd. in Brodsky 44). This intimate connection between African American subjugation and the structure of the jail is illustrated in Mark Twain's representation of Injun Joe, who reveals at the end of *Tom Sawyer* that his lustful anger toward Widow Douglass emerges from her husband's use of the local jails and punishment in a specifically racialized way: "He had me horsewhipped—horsewhipped in front of the jail, like a nigger!" (174). William Wells Brown's 1848 narrative confirms the frequency of such beatings. In one of the most oft-cited moments in the antebellum slave narrative, William Wells Brown recalls his evasion of a beating at a Vicksburg jail while traveling with a chain gang bound for New Orleans by duping a free black man into receiving his punishment. Though Brown's actions have instructively been read as a tactic of the African American trickster (Andrews, *To Tell* 145–48), they also teach an important lesson about the crucial role of penal structures in slave discipline: "It is true that in most slaveholding cities, when a gentleman wishes his servants whipped, he can send him to the jail and have it done" (Brown 51).[12] Likewise, *Incidents* and "A True Tale of Slavery" implicate the Chowan County jail and its agents in the manifold ways that slaveholders and the state could regulate slave "disobedience" as well as invent and sustain the hierarchical relationships between the races.

In the wake of more exceptional cases of disobedience, such as the revolts of Denmark Vessey and Nat Turner, dozens of blacks were imprisoned in local jails before exculpation, transportation, or execution (Christianson 153–54). The Chowan County jail was no exception. The most extensive use of the Chowan County jail in a concentrated period of time, in fact, occurred in the context of the most important slave insurrection in the antebellum era: Nat Turner's 1831 rebellion. According to the *Edentonian Gazette* of that year, approximately "21 Negroes [had] been committed to jail in Edenton on a charge of having been concerned in concerting a project of rebellion" (qtd. in Brodsky 54). "Every day for a fortnight," Jacobs recalls, "if I looked out, I saw horsemen with some poor panting negro tied to their saddles, and compelled by the lash to keep up with their speed, till they arrived at the jail yard. Those who had been whipped too unmercifully to walk were washed with brine, tossed into a cart, and carried to jail" (67). *Incidents* notes that many of these bondspeople were released after Turner's capture, but their detention nonetheless testifies to the close relationship between the regulation of enslaved subjects and the operations of the jail.

In a number of ways, then, places like the Chowan County jail abetted African American disfranchisement and subjugation. In the context of the domestic slave trade, jails served as spaces of "safekeeping" for recaptured runaways and those who would be sold further south. They were also used in daily slave management to control slave behavior, and the employment of whipping through the jail often maintained asymmetrical relationships between blacks and whites. When the slave regime was under particular duress, such as during a rebellion or outbreak of unusual violence, jails could also be relied upon to manage and restrain bondspeople. And for any number of crimes against property, jails served as temporary holding cells for bondspeople until the proper punishment was decided and executed. Therefore, whether it was for disciplining wayward slaves, holding intransigent ones until sale, or housing them on the journey south, penal structures had an important place in southern slavery and in Edenton, North Carolina, in particular.

Jails and Southern Gentlemen

According to *Incidents*, James Norcom, Jacobs's historical tormentor, took full advantage of the Chowan County jail. Above and beyond sending his slaves there, he used it as a threat to extort information and otherwise influence his bondspeople's behavior. Located probably no less than fifty yards from the jail and on the same busy thoroughfare, King Street, James Norcom's physician's office allowed him the ability to keep an eye on whoever might have been locked in the jail while he attended to business in his office or at the courthouse in front of it. What is more, since the jail was located centrally within the community, there were no significant barriers to seeing, hearing, or otherwise knowing what was happening in or around it. Indeed, if someone was being physically punished, either at the whipping post in front of it or within one of the compartments inside of it, any person within a hundred yards would have probably heard their screams. Sitting in his office, James Norcom would have likely heard those cries and, in a matter of moments, could walk over to the jail, inspect the prisoner, and exchange a word with the jailer.

The presence of the jail might have been convenient for Norcom in other ways. If "the language of honor was the dominant language of the men who ruled the slave South," as Kenneth Greenberg asserts (xi), then the use of jails might have been a crucial part of the way in which Norcom and other southern male slaveholders demonstrated their literacy in this regard. Without having to resort to the physically aggressive and messy tactics demonstrated by Douglass's Captain Anthony, I would submit, structures like the Chowan County jail helped propertied southern men to punish their bondspeople, while maintaining an image of themselves as efficient, compassionate, and sophisticated owners.

William Wells Brown's *Narrative* also suggests the crucial role that jails played in the maintenance of southern models of masculinity and respectability. According to Brown's story, it is during a business meeting between the slave trader, Mr. Walker, and several prospective buyers that Brown, an assistant to Walker, spills a glass of wine on one of these "gentlemen," a faux pas that should instantly merit his punishment. However, his owner did not immediately reprimand him and instead simply "apologized to them for my carelessness, but looked at me as though he would see me again on this subject" (47). The next morning, Walker sends Brown to the local jail with a note instructing the jailor to give him twenty lashes. Brown's interpretive summary of these events bears repeating: "It is true that in most slaveholding cities, when a gentleman wishes his servants whipped he can send him to the jail and have it done" (51).

As suggested by Brown's notable invocation of the tendencies and expectations of "gentlemen," the decision to involve the penal system was likely informed by a desire to appear as a composed and authoritative male; it is such "gentlemen" who are indisposed by the spilling of the wine, and it is such "gentlemen" who send their slaves to be whipped at the local jail. Walker is averse to afflicting bodily pain in the presence of his potential buyers because, among other effects, it might make him appear as uncouth or irrational. Given his occupation and the nature of their business (the trading of human property), this might appear contradictory, but Walker, in fact, might have felt even more strongly about maintaining such propriety as his livelihood was one that constantly would have opened him up to charges of inhumanity and callousness. Walter Johnson notes that based on the language used by fellow southerners to describe slave traders—"Southern Shylock," "Southern Yankee," and "Negro Jockey"—they were regarded as "figurative outcasts from slaveholding society" (24). Understood as a class of people quite below and distinct from slaveholders, slave traders were stigmatized as the embodiment of the horrors and brutalities endemic to the entire system, though their treatment of bondspeople was no crueler than any other agent of the peculiar institution. As a result, for Walker, being able to play the role of the stern yet rational slaveholder was likely the most advantageous pose to strike, as opposed to literally striking Brown. With thousands of dollars at stake if he were to lose their confidence, he did not want to use an aggressive display of physical violence to demonstrate his power, but rather, employed the strong arm of the law, quite literally, to manage his bondsperson.

If we read Walker's motivations as emblematic of those of other southern males, Flint's proposal to enlist the jail as a means of addressing Brent's "insolence" is rooted, I would submit, in a desire to keep up "gentlemanly" appearances. Brent's alleged arrogance at accepting the affections of a free black man is not too unlike Brown's boldness in spilling wine on potential clients and "gentlemen," at least in terms of their effects. Both actions trouble the fiction of white male invincibility; they make Walker and Flint appear fallible in the eyes of others and to themselves. Accordingly, both had to punish their bondspeople in such a way as to maintain this fiction, while also retaining their dignity and self-possession. As Greenberg explains of elite southern men, "They were concerned, to a degree we would consider unusual, with the surface of things—with the world of appearances" (3). Through Jacobs's depiction of Dr. Flint's reluctance to use direct physical violence openly, *Incidents* implies that James Norcom was deeply invested in preserving such gentlemanly fictions. Commenting on Flint's specific aversion to employing the whip, Jacobs explains, "The application of the lash might have led to remarks that would have exposed him in the eyes of his children and grandchildren" (35). As a result, Flint's desire to maintain a refined image in front of his family and others discourages him from resorting to acts of villainy and physical aggression, at least in public. Jacobs, in fact, meticulously dramatizes a brutal beating that Flint gives a cuckolded male slave, a dramatization that is almost an identical reprise of the beating that Captain Anthony gives Aunt Hester in Douglass's narrative. Jacobs remembers:

> When I had been in the family a few weeks, one of the plantation slaves was brought to town, by order of his master. It was near night when he arrived, and Dr. Flint ordered him to be taken to the work house, and tied up to the joist, so that his feet would just escape the ground. In that situation he was to wait till the doctor had taken his tea. I shall never forget that night. Never before, in my life, had I heard hundreds of blows fall, in succession, on a human being. His piteous groans, and his "O, pray don't, massa," rang in my ear for months afterwards. There were many conjectures as to the cause of this terrible punishment. Some said master accused him of stealing corn; others said the slave had quarrelled with his wife, in presence of the overseer, and had accused his master of being the father of her child. They were both black, and the child was very fair. (13)

Jacobs's depiction exactly reproduces the sadistic aesthetic of graphic physical violence that Douglass invokes with his representation of Aunt Hester. Captain Anthony's and Dr. Flint's victims are hung from joists, stripped naked, beaten until the blood drips to the floor, and meted punishment for alleged sexual indiscretions. This scene shows Flint's ability and willingness to use bodily pain as a method of punishment, but in a private setting. Significantly, Captain Anthony's victim is female, and Flint's is male, implying that Flint's personal understanding of gentlemanliness and professionalism might have also included restrictions against fantastic public displays (though not uses) of violence with respect to his enslaved women. His reluctance to put the venerable Aunt Marthy (the historical Molly Horniblow) up for sale at a public auction, which emotionally mimics the logistics of Aunt Hester's physical elevation, stripping, and violation, indicates a similar kind of uneasiness with public displays of callousness against women, albeit a very powerful one. Even so, Flint certainly uses physical violence against Brent, and as has been suggested by several critics, the suggestion of sexual violence is insistent and clear. He is thus perfectly comfortable with grotesque violence against his slaves, just as long as those acts are committed behind closed doors and allow him to maintain the veneer of professionalism and respectability that he desired.

The need for respectability we see in Flint was arguably the driving force of James Norcom's life. North Carolina historian Thomas Parramore explains that Norcom was an ardent subscriber to the hierarchical arrangements that pervaded southern antebellum life. A well-respected physician, Norcom, who studied under the eminent Philadelphia physician, Dr. Benjamin Rush, operated a practice that made him the most prominent physician in northeastern North Carolina. He sent all of his children to expensive American northeastern universities (Parramore 82–83). Thus, his fellow Edentonians thought highly of him, but, even more importantly, he thought highly of himself. In his many letters to his wife-to-be and his children, Norcom is nothing else if not a commander of respect, demanding it from his family and insisting that they demand it from others. Commenting on Norcom's letters to his family, Parramore argues, "They reveal a man of almost fanatically high principles who could scarcely compose a paragraph without consciously seeking to add something to the moral uplift, the wholesome practical guidance, of his offspring. Virtually every letter is a small treatise on character-building, a Chesterfieldian exercise in the obligations of self-respect and good citizenship" (83). James Norcom was thus a man who was obsessed with attaining and maintaining respect, to the point of a kind of madness. As Parramore continues, such an insatiable need for dignified treatment made Norcom perpetually suspicious, filling him with a sense of "almost constant betrayal" (84).

Read in the context of Norcom's considerable investment in, and even obsession with, protecting his precarious social status, Flint's threat to send Brent to "jail for [her] insolence" takes on provocative meanings. Not just a slight affront against Norcom's personal dignity, "insolence" speaks to a fundamental attack on Norcom's absolute and thus ever-vulnerable sense of himself as an upright and impervious southern man. Backed by the legal fictions of white privilege and the formidable infrastructure of slaveholding power, Norcom expected complete obedience from his perceived subordinates, and, inevitably, Jacobs's "calculations" foiled his efforts to manipulate and master her life, presenting continuous instances of disrespect and disloyalty. It is not surprising, then, that when Flint learns that Brent has become pregnant by his neighborhood rival, Mr. Sands, he charges her with "insolence and crime" (59). Raising the stakes of her short-lived relationship with a free black man, Brent's sexual union with the accomplished

Sands, a lawyer and future congressman, is perceived as a direct attack on Flint's authority, a critique of his power as well as a "betrayal" of his affection for her. Such "insolence" also frames the birth of Brent's second child by Sands, as she is reluctant to give the child his father's name because "my master would have regarded it as a new crime, a new piece of insolence" (62). Consistent with Parramore's picture of Norcom as a psychologically unstable man who experienced the independent actions of others (slave or otherwise) as expressions of "constant betrayal," Flint repeatedly accuses Brent of failing to appreciate (what he believes is) the benevolent care he offers. After Brent fails to meet Flint for another private meeting in which he will undoubtedly proposition her, the narrator remembers, "Then he launched out upon his usual themes,—my crimes against him, and my ingratitude for his forbearance" (61). Flint interprets Brent's refusal to accept his sexual advances as yet another act of unfaithfulness because he fantastically imagines himself as sincerely dedicated to her well-being.

If such acts of "ingratitude" and "insolence" are read as attacks on Norcom's fragile sense of self, then the Chowan County jail functioned as one of Norcom's most formidable defense mechanisms. According to *Incidents*, on at least one other occasion, Norcom recruited the jail as a specific device for managing the threat of insolence. Upset by William's sympathetic reaction to Flint's latest tongue lashing of Brent, Flint revels in an opportunity to "vent his spleen" when William does not arrive at the doctor's office "so early as usual" (61). For this minor offence, Flint lodges William in jail. As the narrator recalls, "His master was greatly incensed at what he called his insolence. He said he had put him there to reflect upon his bad conduct" (61). As memorialized through the character of Flint, *Incidents* suggests that Norcom used the jail to defend his honor as a respectable southern man. As psychoanalytic theory makes clear, structures like jails and fortresses often appear in dreams as edifices that contain what the sleeping subject wishes to exile or repress.[13] The jail might have provided a convenient psychological and practical model for what Norcom wanted to do with people and things that contradicted his idealized vision of himself: lock them away. As the Chowan County jail stood behind and backed the authority of the Chowan County Courthouse, so too the county jail figuratively stood behind and backed the authority of Norcom. To return to Flint's proposition of "jail" for Brent's insolence, it is clear that the jail was meant to buttress Norcom's flagging sense of authority at a moment of deep personal crisis: Jacobs's expression of affection for a free black man. Norcom invoked the power and terror of the Chowan County jail to suppress her "insolence." "Fanatically" committed to protecting his ever-eroding ego from assaults of disrespect, he used the jail to help reinforce his authority as well as contain those things that threatened him. As a crucial symbol within his own private imaginary, the Chowan County jail functioned as a powerful psychological and physical support to maintain both his noble and invincible vision of himself.

The jail likely offered Norcom other benefits. As historian William Dusinberre explains of discipline on Charles Manigault's capacious South Carolina plantation, "An advantage of the Savannah jail was that a severe whipping could there be imposed by a stranger: the slave's violent resentment would not be concentrated on the overseer" (125). Similarly, the Chowan County jail and its agents might have provided a material and emotional buffer between Norcom and his slaves. In the particular case of Jacobs, Norcom probably would have been reluctant to perform the kind of graphic whipping on Jacobs that he does inside the workhouse on the plantation slave; in a small town such as Edenton and against Molly Horniblow's favored grandchild, this would have almost certainly compromised his ability to "save appearances." Without the messiness of direct, one-on-one punishment, the jail offered a way for Norcom to control his slaves' behavior while maintaining his emotional distance. To return briefly to the case of William Wells Brown, Walker may have similarly disliked the idea of challenging Brown physically as the two had to work closely while transporting slaves to and from the New Orleans slave market. If he had failed to overpower Brown in a violent physical confrontation, as Edward Covey famously fails to do in Frederick Douglass's *Narrative*, it would diminish his ability to manage him afterward.

Finally, the jail might have also helped Norcom consolidate the appearance of financial stability. Unlike less well-off slaveholders, this logic suggests, he can pay to have his slaves punished at a location dedicated to such acts. Recalling William Wells Brown's language, he is a "gentleman" and does not have to resort to the indignity of beating his own bondspeople. Such options in punishment allow him to delegate various disciplinary functions and thereby show his privileged position as one who is a part of the slave system but who does not have to participate in its brutal acts. Instead of striking fear and eliciting the respect of his bondspeople through direct physical violence, as Captain Anthony appears to do, Norcom can intimidate his slaves, in part, through the confinement offered by the county jail.

"The Key on the Inside": Contesting the Chowan County Jail

But if the proximity of the jail meant that Norcom had easy access to it, it also meant that bondspeople could more easily manipulate it. It was a fixed part of Edenton life. For the same reasons Norcom was so easily able to turn the Chowan County jail toward the purposes of slave regulation and personal control, Jacobs and other slaves were also able to contest those meanings and practices and turn them toward their own devices.

William Wells Brown's slave narrative also discloses this potential when it reveals that Brown ultimately avoids the beating that was meant for him. Finding a free black man who will deliver Walker's note to the jailor for a dollar, Brown escapes his punishment from Walker at the expense of this unsuspecting free, black victim. Returning to Walker after he allegedly receives his "punishment," he feigns injury and remorse. In this instance, the jail works to punish a black subject but not the one Walker intends. Though it is meant to function as an extension, repetition, and intensification of the imperatives of slavery, it punishes imperfectly and (with particular respect to Brown) not at all. This might be read, of course, as a function of Brown's iconoclastic ingenuity, but it is also a fundamental feature of the ordinary reproduction of power. As Bhabha makes clear in the arena of colonial power, no act can be repeated in exactly the same way; each reproduction is "the same" and yet "not quite." Brown's trickster behavior similarly operates within the fundamental and inescapable failures that characterize the functioning of slavery's power. The imperfect fusion of the jail's mechanisms to slavery's protocols creates regular opportunities for misdirection and misunderstanding, breakdowns that are as much a function of Brown's cunning as they are the inevitable inefficiencies of the system.

In a similar way, Norcom's jailing of Jacobs's children and family produce ambiguous results that ultimately liberate them. *Incidents*, for example, presents Brent's children's incarceration as a financial burden that eventually abets the children's legal purchase and release from Norcom's control. Revealing Flint's concerns with the costs of imprisonment, the narrator explains, "My brother and the children had now been in jail two months, and that also was some expense" (107). Fees for jailing a bondsperson could be as much as forty cents a day (see fig. 2), so for the two-month detention of Jacobs's three family members and two-week detention of another, Norcom could have potentially racked up jailor's fees around eighty-three dollars.[14] This sum probably weighed heavily on the financially strapped physician. Believing, in fact, that Brent is confined in a New York jail (J. Jacobs, "A True Tale of Slavery" 211), Flint takes out a loan in the amount of five hundred dollars to make his sojourn to New York in search of Brent, forcing him to "merely lighten his pocket hunting after the bird he ha[d] left behind" (H. Jacobs 104). Hence, the combined economic toll of paying for Jacobs's aunt's, brother's, and children's incarceration as well as undertaking a northern sojourn in search of Jacobs likely made Norcom financially vulnerable, a truth that Jacobs reveals in *Incidents* when she asserts: "My friends thought it was a favorable time to work on his discouraged feelings" (107). It is

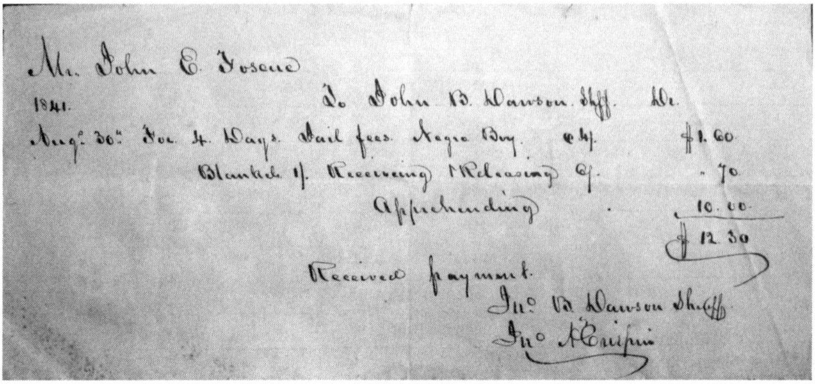

Figure 2. An 1841 jail receipt from a North Carolina jail for an unnamed "Negro Boy," noting $1.60 for four days jail fees at forty cents per day. Picture taken by the author. (Courtesy of UNC, Chapel Hill, Special Collections.)

at this crucial point in the narrative that Flint decides to sell the children to a south-bound slave trader, who, unbeknownst to Flint, is working on behalf of Sands and Aunt Marthy. After the children and Jacobs's brother are sold to the slave trader, he takes them outside the town, where the Chowan County jailor, a man by the name of George Lamb, breaks their chains and turns them over to the ownership of Sands.[15] To be sure, they become the property of another white man, but this transfer of ownerships sets in motion a series of events that will lead to their eventual emancipation. In this way, the children's forced imprisonment constitutes a fortuitous and strategic detention that eventually results in their sale and release to their grandmother. Previously, Jacobs's grandmother had attempted to purchase Jacobs and her children directly, but Norcom had been able to resist. When he is compelled to sell the children, the jail and its agents are thus revealed as mechanisms by which bondspeople can renegotiate if not contest their mastery.

John S. Jacobs's account of his and the children's imprisonment in "A True Tale of Slavery" further illuminates the ways in which the Chowan County jail could trouble, if not subvert, slavery's power. "A True Tale" explains that George Lamb, the Chowan County jailor who breaks his and the children's shackles once they are sold to the trader, "was an old acquaintance of [John Jacobs]" (211). The two had struck up a friendship when John Jacobs began to make frequent calls at the home of a mutual friend, whereby he and Lamb spent "many hours together" (211).[16] Reflecting on his friend's treatment of him in the jail, John Jacobs remembers: "Now that he had me under lock and key, and knowing that it was not for any crime that I was there, he could not be otherwise than kind. He allowed me every indulgence. My friends, such as could come, could call and see me whenever they pleased, and stop as long as they liked; he would never turn the key on them. Sometimes he would give me the key on the inside. While the doctor had me here for safe keeping, I could have made my escape day or night" (211).[17] As suggested by the pregnant statement, "he would give me the key on the inside," though slave subjects often found themselves trapped within constrictive systems and structures, they also had the potential to exercise agency from inside, and through, those structures. John Jacobs's close relationship with Lamb mitigated the Chowan County jail's ability to execute the desires of Norcom and other slaveholders. Knowing he was not there "for any crime," a frequent refrain throughout the literature of slave incarceration, Lamb was not only unwilling to treat John Jacobs harshly, he "allowed [him] every indulgence" and even gave him "the key on the inside." Granted the power to admit his own friends into the jail as well as to let them leave when he pleased, at least occasionally, John Jacobs essentially became his own warden, the master of his own captivity. Hence, even as it contained and restricted the movement of Jacobs's family members, the Chowan County jail also left room for them to renegotiate slavery's imperatives. In a similar way, Norcom's detention and sale of Jacobs's children and brother ironically precipitated their manumission from his control. Just as Lamb gave John Jacobs "the key on the inside," so Jacobs's children's and brother's imprisonment ultimately severed their relationship to Norcom, literalizing the emancipatory potential of jails and their agents in relation to slavery. Working within the field of "punishment," then, incarceration could create provocative possibilities for the critique and attack of slaveholder's powers.

Local jails thus inhabited a nebulous position within the antebellum slave South. As they did for Norcom, they could consolidate relationships to masculinity, refinement, and professional identity, providing a useful disciplinary barrier between the agents of slavery and its victims while also underscoring the elite status of slave owners and overseers. Jail allowed slave owners to execute the uncomfortable and messy work of punishment without being directly involved in its execution. At the same time, jails could expose cracks in the infrastructure of slavery, creating opportunities for the renegotiation and circumvention of slaveholders' powers, giving slave subjects the "key on the inside." Jacobs's children's incarceration, in particular, became a financial burden to Norcom, who was reluctant to sell them but could not afford to keep them detained in the Chowan County jail. The economic realities of incarceration force his hand, ultimately leading to the sale of the children to Sands, their return to their great-grandmother, and their eventual freedom from slavery. As a form of "punishment," then, jail did not necessarily mean the automatic retrenchment of white privilege and could actually precipitate the undoing of slavery's imperatives, even as it consistently abetted the constriction, regulation, and abuse of black subjects.

Maternal Alienation and the Carceral

Within the domain of "memory," penal structures and their invocation offer a range of meanings as diverse as those found under the umbrella of "punishment." As Norcom laid claim to various professional and gentlemanly subject positions through his appropriation of the Chowan County jail, Harriet Jacobs's textual representation of the jail and other carceral structures enabled her to fashion herself in sympathetic and authoritative ways. Fighting fire with fire, she reappropriates the fact of slave incarceration, redeploying it in narrative in order to foreground the suffering and resourcefulness of African American bondspeople. As purposely constructed recollections of past events, these representations are crafted, in the words of Jacobs's preface, to make the "women of the North" comprehend "how deep, and dark, and foul" are the "abominations" of slavery (1, 2). Consequently, *Incidents* not only remembers, as in recalls the details of, imprisonment toward sympathetic or rhetorically useful ends, it reorganizes, reemphasizes, and reuses its elements, in order to claim and declare African American humanity, particularly that of enslaved women. Having a kind of figurative key on the inside, Jacobs's invocations of incarceration disrupt and decode the constrictive structures of slavery.

One of the most important ways in which *Incidents* does so is in its use of incarceration to illuminate slavery's disruption and destruction of enslaved subjects' relationship to the maternal, complementing a reading of *Incidents* as a meditation on what Grace McEntee calls "thwarted motherhood" (202). If we recall, Brent's experience of slavery properly begins when she loses her mother. "When I was six years old," the narrator reflects, "my mother died; and then, for the first time, I learned, by the talk around me, that I was a slave" (6). In this way, slavery for Brent specifically and practically means the absence of the mother. Subsequently, the loss of her mother thrusts her into the services of a white mistress, who was "almost like a mother to [her]" (7) but who also prematurely passes away. Her death sets off a string of events that lead to her ownership by Dr. Flint's five-year-old daughter, Emily. Brent's legal ownership by a female child, of course, underscores her distance from adult, maternal protection, a distance that is further multiplied and ironized when she prematurely becomes a mother, out of wedlock and by a white male, at the age of sixteen. *Incidents* is thus a sustained reflection of the anguish of what I call maternal alienation, an estrangement from the protection, affections, and rights of the mother.[18]

Jails serve as important sites of such ruptures. Commenting on Brent's separation from her children once they are sent to the jail, Mrs. Flint confirms this reading when she notes that if Brent had "so much feeling for her children as a cow for its calf" then "she would have come back long ago, to get them out of jail" (102). According to Mrs. Flint's paradigm, the jail denies the ability of women to mother, and, therefore, demands that even the crudest of mothers (as suggested by the simple cow) end their children's incarceration in order to fulfill those functions. The imperatives of the maternal and the carceral, Mrs. Flint argues, are mutually exclusive and seemingly irreconcilable. *Incidents*, through narrative, reworks this paradigm by rhetorically foregrounding mothers' "feeling[s] for [their] children," emphasizing the pain they feel as women who are unable to care for their imprisoned children, thereby underscoring their earnest desire to be protective and nurturing caretakers. In the process, the invocation of the jail animalizes the agents of slavery who prevent the union between mother and child (they do not have as much feeling as a "cow for its calf," the argument would run) and transforms the imprisoned children and their embattled mother into sympathetic figures. Curiously signifying on the many incarcerated women who are denied the ability to mother in our own historical moment, *Incidents*'s representations of slave imprisonment engender empathy for subjects who cannot mother or be mothered, paradoxically employing the traumatic representation of the carceral to insist on enslaved women's stake in the maternal.

Significantly, the model of sympathetic representation employed by *Incidents* relies on a theory of sympathetic movement outlined in one of the landmarks of penal theory, Benjamin Rush's "An Inquiry into the Effects of Public Punishments upon Criminals and upon Society." This foundational document provided one of the earliest and clearest rationalizations for the modern penitentiary as well as a model for how imprisonment can be understood as a site of sympathy. In " Inquiry," Rush argues that the public display of penal suffering leads to the production of sympathy for inmates since crowds at whippings and hangings frequently cheered for the criminals and jeered at the officers of the court. Understanding this as counterproductive to the hegemonic purposes of punishment, Rush concludes that prisoners' suffering should be removed from public view and contained in a separate structure, a place where their private suffering could lead to inward transformation and social healing. Elaborating on this point, Rush reasons "distress of all kinds, when seen, produces sympathy, and a disposition to relieve it. This sympathy, in generous minds, is not lessened by the distress being the offspring of crimes: on the contrary, even the crimes themselves are often palliated by the reflection that they were unfortunate consequences of extreme poverty—of seducing company—or of the want of a virtuous education, from the loss or negligence of parents in early life" (141). According to this model, the emotional impact of criminals' suffering, like a disease, could spread to and through the crowd, causing them to identify with the lawbreaker and not the law, what Michael Meranze has termed "mimetic corruption," a process by which "the very presence of embodied criminality overwhelmed spectators' virtue and led them to identify with and replicate criminality" (8). Capitalizing on Rush's deepest fears, Jacobs's descriptions of imprisoned bondspeople emphasize their suffering, daring and compelling readers to side with the incarcerated slaves and resist the normative "script of legal punishment" (8). Her reproduction of imprisonment "corrupts" the original intent and function of "punishment," creating sympathy for incarcerated bondspeople where there should only be antipathy. These "deliberate calculations," to recall Jacobs's language, invert Rush's carceral logic of private punishments and inward transformation to relate public punishments that produce outward transformation. Jacobs's "mimetic corruption" of the reformative ethos of "punishment" "whispers foul words" in her readers' ears, thereby indoctrinating them into the "pit of abominations" that is slavery. That is, *Incidents* details the atrocities committed behind jail grates in order to expose the suffering of the incarcerated slave, bringing her pain into public view just as Aunt Marthy's sale at public auction exposes Flint's callousness. In doing so, it urges them to sympathize with its maternally estranged victims, who are locked in the carceral and unable to take succor in the relief of the maternal.

As distinct from Rush's model, it is worth noting that in Jacobs's schema the "crimes themselves are often palliated" not so much by knowledge of the criminals' poverty but by knowledge of the victims' position as casualties of slavery. As a reading of almost any antebellum slave narrative makes clear, slavery compels, in hyperbolic fashion, "extreme poverty," "seducing company," "want of a virtuous education," and, as the current discussion of maternal estrangement makes clear, "the loss and negligence of parents in early life." Deeply invested in both abolitionism and prison reform, Rush accurately, though perhaps unintentionally, lays bare the parallel movements of sympathy in slave and prison narratives.[19] Even more deeply familiar with the intersections of slavery and imprisonment, having lived as a slave and seen the effects of imprisonment on her family, Jacobs too uses the sympathetic operations of prison representation in the services of antislavery.

One of the most provocative examples of how jails engender such sympathy can be seen in Jacobs's rendering of the imprisonment of Aunt Marthy's son, Benjamin, the historical Joseph Horniblow. In the chapter, "The Slave Who Dared to Feel Like a Man," Jacobs dramatizes her uncle's unsuccessful escape from slavery and consequent detention in the Chowan County jail. Here, the exigencies of maternal estrangement are articulated through the sentimentalized representation of the carceral. "At midnight [the jailer] opened the jail door for my grandmother and myself to enter, in disguise. When we entered the cell not a sound broke the stillness. 'Benjamin, Benjamin!' whispered my grandmother. No answer. 'Benjamin!' she again faltered. There was a jingle of chains. The moon had just risen, and cast an uncertain light through the bars of the window. We knelt down and took Benjamin's cold hands in ours. We did not speak. Sobs were heard, and Benjamin's lips were unsealed; for his mother was weeping on his neck. How vividly does memory bring back that sad night!" (22). Recalling the somber mood of Charles Dickens's entrance into the silent "catacombs" of Philadelphia's Eastern State Penitentiary as recorded in his 1842 travelogue, *American Notes*, the scene depends on a poetics of stillness and silence to communicate Benjamin's desperate condition in the Chowan County jail. According to nineteenth-century prison discourse, penitentiaries made prisoners members of the living dead through their program of unending isolation and silence. What Dickens notes of one prisoner in the Eastern State Penitentiary might well be noted of Benjamin: "He is a man buried alive: to be dug out in the slow round of years; and in the mean time dead in everything but torturing anxieties and horrible despair" (113). Though not entombed in a state prison but a local county jail, Benjamin too is encased within an envelope of profound silence. "We did not speak," the narrator remembers, and the gothic moonlight eerily filing through the prison window further communicates the disquieting hush of the scene. Moreover, this outward stillness is the corollary of an internal decomposition. As intimated by Benjamin's condition before his mother and Brent enter the jail—cold hands, sealed lips, and a silently still figure—the incarcerated slave is already dead, a phantom of a soul encased within the shell of a material existence. Accordingly, he is ready for death: "Here I will stay till I die, or till he sells me," Benjamin confesses (22). Clearly exhibiting the effects of "social death" that Orlando Patterson says marks victims of chattel slavery, Benjamin might also be understood as an example of what Caleb Smith refers to as "cadaverous subjectivity," "human lives divested of subjectivity, of humanity itself, persisting as ghosts or monsters in a carceral living death" (28). Combining the poetics of prison representation with the realities of local detention, *Incidents* paints a haunting and despairing picture of a slave's alienation from his mother and figures this estrangement as a kind of death.

Following the model of sympathetic contagion outlined in Rush's "Inquiry," this picture of incarcerated distress inevitably leads to sympathy for the embattled prisoner. Modeling the proper emotional response for the idealized, female reader, Benjamin's mother's tears are the tears of the conscientious reader. As Karen Sánchez-Eppler notes of the operation of sentiment within women's antislavery fiction, "Tears designate a border realm between the story and its reading, since the tears shed by characters initiate an answering moistness in the reader's eye" (*Touching* 27). Dickens's *American Notes* dramatizes a similar scene in which carceral affliction leads to sentimental weeping. Of a German prisoner, who still had to serve three more years on a five-year sentence, Dickens notes, "I never saw such a picture of forlorn affliction and distress of mind. My heart bled for him; and when the tears ran down his cheeks, and he took one of the visitors aside, to ask, with his trembling hands nervously clutching at his coat to detain him, where there was no hope of his dismal sentence being commuted, the spectacle was really too painful to witness" (115). Dickens's "bleeding heart" is the equivalent of Aunt Marthy's tears on her son's neck. Both are eruptions of sympathetic emotion that respond to "spectacles" that are too uncomfortable to witness yet demand the audience's recognition. Just as readers of *American Notes* were meant to disparage the "tampering with the mysteries of the human mind" (111) reflected in Dickens's rendering of the separate system, readers of Jacobs's presentation of the Chowan County jail should recognize the barbarity of tampering with the relationships between enslaved mothers and their children. To be clear, Jacobs is not critical of jails per se (just as Dickens is not critical of the penitentiary system as a whole, only the separate system's techniques), just their particular use to split apart families and deny enslaved subjects the roles and protections of the mother. More focused on the particular use of jails to abet racism and slavery than on attacking jails themselves, the scene calls for an end to the disruption of the bonds between mother and child caused by slavery and its allied systems.

This carefully drawn scene of incarceration foreshadows the most extended representation of imprisonment and fractured maternities in the text, Jacobs's children's, brother's, and aunt's incarceration. As recounted in the chapter "Months of Peril," Brent fears that her children will be sent to the plantation to be "broke in," and thus she escapes from Flint's son's plantation, which immediately precipitates her family's incarceration. Just as the jail compromises Aunt Marthy's ability to care for, protect, and have access to Benjamin, the "old jail" again threatens to sever Brent's relationship with her daughter and son. In *Incidents*'s remembering of this imprisonment, the jail becomes a space where Jacobs can frame her dejected position as a frustrated mother as well as emphasize the suffering of her children. Reproducing the Rushian scheme, where scenes of prison distress lead to sympathy for prisoners, the knowledge of Jacobs's children's detention ultimately leads to tears: "My children remained in jail, where brother William did all he could for their comfort. Betty went to see them sometimes, and brought me tidings. She was not permitted to enter the jail; but William would hold them up to the grated window while she chatted with them. When she repeated their prattle, and told me how they wanted to see their ma, my tears would flow" (101). The children's innocent and natural desire to see their mother motivates the operation of sympathy in the passage. Readers are meant to mourn the children's detention and participate in Brent's ocular effusions, making their tears "flow" for the incarcerated children and for her inability to protect them. The scene thus operates from and makes two connected appeals for sympathy, one for the imprisoned children, who did not commit a crime, but also for their "ma," who cannot rescue them from their deplorable condition. Like the tracing of a finger around the edges of an open wound, the scene invites the reader to reexperience the distress of incarceration, an injury that is distinctly and specifically read as maternal. The inability for the mother to be with her children, despite the easy communication between the light of the distant moon and the interior of the cell, provokes the mocking and free "flow" of her tears. As in Benjamin's confinement, the moonlight might enter in and the children's prattle might escape the confines of the jail, but the imprisoned children are locked behind prison bars and are thus literally barred from their mother. As Michelle Burnham notes of Indian captivity narratives, scenes of bondage are emotionally moving because they dramatize the physical removal of vulnerable (white) female subjects from their loved ones (3). Here, the jail grate represents the immovable border between Jacobs and her children, which is meant to be emotionally moving for *Incidents*'s readers.

This formula of carceral distress followed by sympathetic recognition is well represented throughout antebellum slave narratives. Henry Bibb provides this description of his wife's first sight of him in Kentucky's Covington jail: "When she looked through the dungeon grates and saw my sad situation, which was caused by my repeated adventures to rescue her and my little daughter from the grasp of slavery, it was more than she could bear without bursting into tears" (88). He is in jail on behalf of his wife and daughter, the passage maintains, and the reader should appreciate this fact, as dramatically externalized in Malinda's crying. Bibb himself, in fact, becomes teary eyed when he contemplates his own diminished position inside the jail: "[My master] then had me taken to a blacksmith's shop, and most wickedly had my limbs bound with heavy irons and then had my body locked within the cold dungeon walls of the Bedford jail. . . . My heart was filled with grief—my eyes were filled with tears" (87). He loses self-possession when he must bear witness to his manacled body's distance from the respectable subject positions of husband and father. Likewise, tears are the ultimate result when William Wells Brown plans to escape for freedom but must leave his sister imprisoned in the Saint Louis jail. "I cannot give a just description of the scene at that parting interview. Never, never can be erased from my heart the occurrences of that day! When I entered the room where she was, she was seated in one corner, alone. . . . As soon as she observed me, she sprung up, threw her arms around my neck, leaned her head upon my breast, and, without uttering a word, burst into tears" (56). Public jails and other penal structures thus repeatedly served as a site for the fracturing of relations within the slave family. The representation of these fractures calls on readers to sympathize with the incarcerated slaves, to "burst into tears," make their "tears flow," and "weep on the neck" of these downtrodden subjects.

These scenes of prison jailing and maternal suffering anticipate the splintering of families attendant to imprisonment in later African American prison writing, encoding a recurring trope throughout African American prison literature in which heartbroken mothers must wrestle with the reality of their sons' incarceration. Aunt Marthy and Benjamin's exchange, in particular, anticipates the estrangement of mother and son found in the letters of political prisoner George Jackson. Initially convicted for allegedly stealing seventy dollars from a convenience store, the eighteen-year-old Jackson was sentenced to a term of "one year to life" in 1960 (Mann 21). While still serving this sentence, Jackson and two other inmates (Fleeta Drumgo and John Clutchette) were indicted for the murder of a California prison guard (John V. Mills) in early 1970 (27). The three became known as the Soledad Brothers, named after the California prison in which they were held, and were international symbols of the inequities of American society and jurisprudence. In a failed attempt to force the men's release, George Jackson's seventeen-year-old brother, Jonathan, laid siege on California's Marin County courthouse with a small arsenal of guns on August 7, 1970; however, he was killed in the process (41). Roughly a year later, George Jackson would also be dead when he was shot by a San Quentin prison guard, a killing that many regard as an assassination (28). Before he was slain, Jackson released *Soledad Brother*, the record of his prison correspondence from 1964 to 1970, a text that has been heralded as a classic of American prison writing and revolutionary thought, which he dedicated to his fallen younger brother, Jonathan, Angela Davis, and his mother, Georgia Bea Jackson.

Jackson's letters to his mother, whose repeated salutation, "Dear Mama," echoes like a chant throughout the text, register similar kinds of tension between mother and son that are recorded in *Incidents*. Encoding what H. Bruce Franklin notes as the turn in the mid-nineteenth century from representations by "professional criminals," inmates who blamed themselves for their incarceration, to that of essentially "political prisoners," inmates who located the problem in the larger society (133, 131), Benjamin is a recalcitrant "prisoner," not a penitential "criminal." In *Incidents*, for example, Aunt Marthy instructs her son to accept his master's authority and his fate as a slave: "Put your trust in God," she advises. "Be humble, my child, and your master will forgive you" (22). However, Benjamin angrily retorts: "Forgive me for *what*, mother? For not letting him treat me like a dog? No! I will never humble myself to him. I have worked for him for nothing all my life, and I am repaid with stripes and imprisonment. Here I will stay till I die, or till he sells me" (22). Roughly a hundred years later, in the context of the social unrest and antiestablishment imperatives of the 1960s and 1970s, Jackson's letters reveal a similar frustration with his mother's belief in conventional wisdom and acceptance of traditional hierarchies. Reflecting on his lack of faith in divine authority, Jackson laments: "If there is a god, Mama, he hates me and I'll have to resist what he or it is doing to us. All my life, Mama, I've had to work things out for myself. I've had help from no quarter. I've been alone now for a long time. This is why I've had so much pain and trouble. [My father] gave me nothing. You gave me god and that horrible church. Even god managed to take something away from me. I have nothing left but myself" (88). Like Benjamin, Jackson has no faith in what he calls in an earlier letter "European gods" (88) but rather understands society's evils as a function of the elite's abuse of power. As he states in a March 1966 letter: "I place the blame for the social ills that have caused us discomfort and unhappiness squarely upon the shoulders of those responsible: the people in control!!" (50). As a result, the jail is a site at which the ideological and political differences between mother and son become painfully magnified. Like Benjamin, Jackson disdains the Christian god and instead opts for self-sufficiency. He exposes the increasing distance between him and his mother, as it is routed through the mechanisms of the carceral.

In a contrasting mode, *Incidents* also points to a repeated moment in which imprisoned sons ask their mothers for forgiveness. After Benjamin's outburst against the tyranny of slavery, Jacobs renders this scene: "Mother and son talked together. He asked her pardon for the suffering he caused her" (22). In almost identical language, late twentieth-century rapper Tupac Shakur's maternal anthem, "Dear Mama" (1995), recalls this of a rebellious son, "I reminisce on the stress I caused, it was hell / Huggin on my mama from a jail cell." Rehearsing the oft-used salutation from George Jackson's letters to his own mother, Shakur's "Dear Mama" memorializes the reconciliation between mother and son as mediated through the mechanism of the carceral. His speaker pathetically embraces his mother from the confines of the cell, imitating Benjamin's sentimentalized embrace of his mother in the Chowan County jail. Crucially, Shakur's speaker's ire is not directed toward the state, but at himself, the prodigal son, for not relinquishing his criminal activities and thereby sparing his mother emotional pain. Even so, as the child of Black Panther Party activists Afeni Shakur and Billy Garland, Shakur is also sure to intimate that structural inequities predestine African American (male) life for incarceration from childhood. As his slow and throaty voice queries in the next line of the song, "Who'd think in elementary / I'd see the penitentiary / one day?" For Shakur, imprisonment was more than just a metaphor. While pregnant with Shakur, Afeni Shakur was incarcerated with other Black Panther Party members for allegedly attempting to bomb New York City buildings, prompting the rapper to note in a 1995 jailhouse interview: "My embryo was in prison" (qtd. in Dyson 24–25). Read in tandem with Jackson's provocative prison epistles as well as Shakur's pain-laced homage to motherhood, *Incidents* underscores how long and powerfully African American experience and cultural production have been marked by intertwined narratives of maternal deprivation and carceral subjugation.[20]

Incidents is both an early and prophetic episode in this history, illustrating how penal structures participated in the division and destruction of families during slavery. This deployment of the carceral is in perfect keeping with Jacobs's desire, as voiced in the title page, to expose the "depth of the *degradation*" of slavery. Such scenes of imprisonment underscore the brutality of slavery and the suffering humanity of bondspeople, scenes that are just as important as Douglass's representation of Aunt Hester's flogging by Captain Anthony. As Hester is tied, disrobed, and whipped to prompt the recognition and sympathy of Douglass's readers, so is Jacobs's family bound, chained, and imprisoned to gain the empathy of her audience. The invocation of the carceral "binds" readers to identify and commiserate with the suffering of the imprisoned slave who has been figuratively and literally barred from the roles and protections of the maternal.

Virtuous Prisoners and Criminal Slaveholders

Along with buttressing bondspeople's claim to the maternal, Jacobs's representation of the carceral also actively contests the identification of slaves' behavior as criminal, both calling attention to the misreading of African American identity as inherently deviant and exposing the illicit behavior of the agents of slavery. Writing within and against the "racialization of theft and unethical behavior" that Lovalerie King identifies as characteristic of "American legal and social practice" (56), *Incidents* appropriates imprisonment as a means of deconstructing the assumed self-identity between blackness and criminality. It exposes the perverse moral order propagated by slavery, detailing the ways in which the virtue of the slave is read as "criminal" and the criminality of the slaveholder is interpreted as "virtuous." Against this paradigm, Jacobs's invocations and depictions of slave imprisonment tell of carceral virtues, models of respectability and moral probity emerging from the vocabularies and histories of imprisonment. Anticipating the counterintuitive logic of the vet's claim in *Invisible Man* that "there's always an element of crime in freedom" (Ellison 155), *Incidents* reframes the slave's allegedly unethical behavior as authentically moral and the slaveholder's seeming moral concerns as decidedly corrupt. Denying the conflation of African

American identity with criminality while simultaneously representing and invoking African American imprisonment—a complex move to be sure—Jacobs's narrative sits inside the imputation of inherent African American deviance and, quite literally, makes a virtue out of criminality.

Incidents dramatizes several moments where African American identity is conflated with criminality. On the day of the slave auction, the narrator laments: "At the appointed hour the grounds are thronged with men, women, and children, waiting, like criminals, to hear their doom pronounced" (15). This pathetic scene frames slaves as unlawful, even as they follow the expected protocols for the division of their families. Of a slave who attempts to feed his family by "stealing" a pig from his master, the text notes: "When his own labor was stolen from him, he had stolen food to appease his hunger. This was his crime" (48). As made clear in the ironized use of the word "crime," *Incidents* aims to expose the deviance of slaveholders, which is all too often projected onto bondspeople. Likewise, Flint reads Brent's attempts at self-preservation as "crimes" against him. Upon first hearing that Jacobs is pregnant by her white paramour, Mr. Sands, Flint condescendingly says to Brent, "Though you have been criminal towards me, I feel for you, and I can pardon you if you obey my wishes" (58). Extending the metaphor, Flint maintains that Brent could receive his "pardon" if she would align her will with his, effectively defining her entire existence as a kind of prison, for which only Flint has the key. Later, when Brent reveals that she is pregnant with yet another child from Sands, she explains, "Dr. Flint had sworn that he would make me suffer, to my last day, for this new crime against *him*, as he called it" (77). The thematic of criminality thus organizes Flint's interactions with Brent as well as predicts his later desire, per his runaway slave advertisement, to "lodge her in jail."[21]

Of these several offenses, the greatest "crime" is her voluntary sexual relationship with Mr. Sands in order to deflect Dr. Flint's sexual attentions, her infamous "plunge into the abyss" (53). This is, according to Gloria Randle, "the story that she must tell while at the same time—as the authorial tone reflects—she dreads disclosing" (47). Coming in the appropriately numbered chapter X, the mark of the ineffable and inexpressible, Jacobs's revelation of sexual impropriety is a tale that exceeds the provincial language of domesticity, sentimentality, and piety that governed white female respectability. Having lived a life that was pocked with deviations from the conventional prerogatives of what Barbara Welter defines as "the cult of true womanhood"—chastity, piety, domesticity, and submission—Jacobs was rightfully apprehensive about revealing her sexual history. "The remembrance fills me with sorrow and shame," she confesses to the reader. "It pains me to tell you of it" (53–54).

Jacobs employs the language of the carceral to articulate this vexed decision.

Doubling the screen that is already created by her use of the alias Linda Brent, she positions the language of the carceral between herself and likely judgmental readers, using it as a prophylactic barrier against the messy and uncomfortable details of her criminalized sexual life. Just four sentences before the revelation of Brent's infamous "plunge," Jacobs calls on the rhetoric of imprisonment to make clear the wretchedness of Brent's life with Flint, which, in fact, compelled her to step outside the bounds of normative, white female morality. She explains that Flint had begun to build a cottage for Brent in a "secluded place, four miles away from the town" (53), a move by which Flint intends to "make a lady of [her]" (53). Of course, Brent realizes that this cottage will only be a parody of domesticity, allowing the guarded Flint the privacy to assault Brent, sexually and otherwise, with virtual impunity. The narrator enunciates her refusal to accept this ignoble position as Flint's "lady" by drawing on the rhetoric of imprisonment: "I vowed before my Maker that I would never enter it. I had rather toil on the plantation from dawn till dark; I had rather live and die in jail, than drag on, from day to day, through such a living death" (53). Like the counterintuitive desire for the exhausting labor of the plantation, the preference for an ignominious existence in the jail rhetorically foregrounds the hellish conditions of the cottage. As emphasized by the anaphoristic repetition of the phrase, "I had rather," the choice of the jail is one that foregrounds the paradoxical desirability of the jail in the context of the complete vileness of Flint's "secluded home." In an ironic response to the question Flint proposes that frames this chapter—"would you like to be sent to jail for your insolence?"—Jacobs answers that she would rather indeed be sent to the jail than live under Flint's power. Such a "life" and "death" in a jail would be a paradoxical respite from Flint's perverted model of black womanhood. Jacobs confirms this favorable reading of the carceral in her dramatization of Brent's response to Flint's threat of imprisonment that begins this chapter. "As for the jail," she tells Flint, "there would be more peace for me there than there is here" (40). Jacobs valorizes the carceral in order to express her abhorrence for the criminal, rhetorically binding herself to a despicable jail in order to make clear her vehement disapproval of Flint's program of sexual aggression and violation.

The notion of "life and death in jail" also allegorizes the way that the invocation of the carceral screens her from, or at least deflects, public scrutiny. Jacobs's precise problem in her confession is that it forces her to expose her body; as a "calculating" sexual agent, her body is read as inherently deviant and oversexualized. As Hortense Spillers has compellingly argued, black women's identities in the New World have been overdetermined by white male expectations of African American women's licentiousness and hyperreproductivity.[22] The disappearance of this body is precisely what Jacobs desires at the moment of her confession. What the narrator notes of her memory of sexual impropriety with Sands equally applies to this overdetermined body: she "would gladly forget it" if she could (53). In this light, the Roman numeral "X" that identifies and opens the chapter signals Jacobs's unconscious desire to cross out this section of her life and narrative, to negate and banish the uncomfortable relation of her "criminal" sexual acts.[23] Toward this end, the narrator's expressed desire to "live and die in jail" "forgets" Jacobs's body, crosses it out, and exiles it behind figurative prison walls, where it cannot be seen by the public. Just as early nineteenth-century penitentiaries removed prisoners from the embarrassment of public spectacles like the scaffold, Jacobs's conjuring of the jail screens her from the hostile gaze of her readers. These hidden prisoners represent a historical model of the rhetorical disappearing act that Jacobs's passage hopes to replicate. Preferring the "civil death" that Caleb Smith argues defined antebellum imprisonment (36) for the "living death" Flint proposes with his cottage, Jacobs buries herself alive inside the trope of the dreadful but comparatively desirable prison, concealing herself within its rhetorical structures in order to evade public scrutiny. As I detail below, prisoners had their own bodily baggage that impinged on their ability to elicit sympathy; nonetheless, here, Jacobs deflects the hyperembodiment of the criminalized black female slave with the figure of the righteous prisoner. She is the virtuous prisoner who would rather "live and die in jail" than consent to sexual immorality.

Moreover, the constrictive image of life and death in jail accurately reflects the vexed terms and conditions of Brent's relationship with Sands as well as its consequences. By "plunging into the abyss," Brent does, in fact, choose and create various kinds of "life and death" in jail. Her union with Sands produces two "lives in jail," her children, Ellen and Benny. Following the condition of the mother, they are both legally slaves, indefinitely locked in the "prison house of slavery." Later, when they are imprisoned in the Chowan County jail, these children's lives are literally trapped inside a carceral structure. Brent's vaguely defined and precarious relationship with Sands also constitutes a kind of "life and death in jail," for it foils Flint's plans to remove her to the secluded cottage, but it also imprisons her in a nebulous sexual affair with Sands. Finally, Jacobs's seven-year self-exile in her grandmother's attic almost literalizes this "life and death in jail," as her confined condition allows her to remain within the direct vicinity of her children, enabling her to function as a "hidden guardian," as Stephanie Li has suggested (31). At the same time, her concealment almost makes an invalid of her and even threatens her life. "My friends feared I should become a cripple for life;" the narrator remembers of the garret, "and I was so weary of my long imprisonment that, had it not been for the hope of serving my children, I should have been thankful to die; but, for their sakes, I was willing to bear on" (127).

Dead to the outside world from her "long imprisonment," the crawl space also provides the only opportunity for life near her children.

So, despite the fact that carceral structures are always haunted by the possibility of "death" and disability, they are imagined as paradoxical spaces to maintain relationships to respectable and desirable femininity. This idea that the jail is the paradoxical space for an alternative and desirable model of womanhood is memorably articulated in chapter VI. Dilating on the domestic terrorism that is life inside the house of a "jealous mistress," which is the title of the chapter, Jacobs more explicitly frames the penitentiary as a space where female respectability can prevail. Railing against Mrs. Flint's suspicions of her husband's attraction to Brent and her consequent cruelty to Brent, the narrator proclaims, "I would ten thousand times rather that my children should be the half-starved paupers of Ireland than to be the most pampered among the slaves of America. I would rather drudge out my life on a cotton plantation, till the grave opened to give me rest, than to live with an unprincipled master and a jealous mistress. *The felon's home in a penitentiary is preferable*. He may repent, and turn from the error of his ways, and so find peace; but it is not so with a favorite slave. She is not allowed to have pride of character. It is deemed a crime in her to wish to be virtuous" (31, emphasis added). Located within a larger complex of images related to affliction, the reference to the "felon's home" defends Brent's decision to enter into an illicit sexual relationship with Sands. As Brent's preference for life and death in jail communicates her detestation of Flint's sexual attentions, her choice of the "felon's home in a penitentiary" communicates her abhorrence and ultimate refusal of slavery's perverse moral code. As Flint's "lady," she has no hope for redemption or respectability. Attempts at virtue will, in fact, render her a criminal. As a result, authentic virtue is more likely to abound in the "penitentiary" because slave law despises legitimate virtue. The language of the carceral articulates Brent's refusal of Flint's attentions but also defends her decision to accept Sands's. There is no hope for "pride of character" with Flint's cottage, but Brent's union with Sands preserves such possibilities. The narrator calls on the image of the "felon's home in the penitentiary" to express the truth that female virtue and chattel slavery are mutually exclusive. In order to be virtuous, the slave subject must be "criminal"; she must break free from the moral code of slavery and devise her own complex, tentative, and "abysmal" moral order. Imprisonment's signification as perilous and undesirable communicates the difficulty of such a project.

Significantly, chapters VI and X, which both contain especially provocative revelations, begin with these invocations of inmates in jail and felons in the penitentiary, suggesting Jacobs's profound understanding of the carceral as a way to enunciate the difficult (sexual) choices she is compelled to make. Jacobs begins several of her twenty chapters with philosophical reflections or hypothetical questions before detailing the narration of actual incidents. For instance, in the chapter, "The Lover," Jacobs's first line asks: "Why does the slave ever love? Why allow the tendrils of the heart to twine around objects which may at any moment be wrenched away by the hand of violence?" (37). These musings lead into more or less abstract reflections on the possibilities of love for the enslaved subject before finally and specifically noting, "There was in the neighborhood a young colored carpenter; a free born man" (37), the particular subject of the chapter. Likewise, Jacobs's pronouncements that she would "rather die in jail" and that the "felon's home . . . is preferable" are part of the hypothetical abstractions that frame the narrative details in these chapters. They underscore the centrality of carceral motifs to thinking through and expressing African American female respectability in *Incidents*. Illustrating how her "criminal" acts are actually the deeds of a virtuous and respectable person, Jacobs deploys the language of the carceral to debunk the myth of the deviant and sexually promiscuous slave woman. Pitted against Flint's perverse "lady," life and death in jail and the felon's home in the penitentiary offer paradoxically desirable alternatives that foreground Jacobs's "pride of character." Read together, these scenes suggest that, in the sexually oppressive and morally corrupt system of slavery, to be "criminal" is to be virtuous and to be incarcerated is to be a true woman. As opposed to purity, submissiveness, and domesticity, *Incidents* proposes the cult of true womanhood should be defined by defiance, imprisonment, and criminality. Through the strategic invocation of the jail, then, Jacobs is able to express the particular "abominations" of slavery as well as to defend her own complex, improvised, and tortured responses to personal degradation and sexual violence.

"She Knew She Was Loved in the Jail"

Finally literalizing the idea presented in chapters VI and X that the jail is "preferable" to slavery's abuses, *Incidents*'s depiction of Brent's children's and brother's detention in chapter XVIII depicts the jail as a refuge from injury, surveillance, and punishment. In a section entitled, "Months of Peril," the Chowan County jail becomes a refuge from the menacing schemes of Flint. Envisioning the jail as the setting for domestic tranquility and opportunities for clandestine behavior, *Incidents* rejects the narrative of benign paternalism that proslavery apologists invoked to defend slavery. With its idealized representation of the jail, *Incidents* signifies both on the trope of what Victor Brombert calls "the romantic prison" as well as New Testament models of felicitous incarceration (specifically Pauline), thereby exposing the world outside the jail as necessarily corrupted and even fatal.[24]

Afflicted with a case of measles, for instance, Ellen is removed from the Chowan County jail to receive medical care at Dr. Flint's office, but this unexpected furlough is remembered as an intensification of her suffering: "Poor little Ellen cried all day to be carried back to prison. The instincts of childhood are true. She knew she was loved in the jail" (102). In a reverse of the previous model of prison representation in which detention within jails produces tears, removal from the jail is the source of sorrow. As demonstrated by the fact that Ellen "cried all day," the sympathy that had been previously generated for incarcerated slaves' release from the jail is now generated for their "safe" enclosure inside of it. What is more, the passage suggests that a greater and more insidious malady, besides measles, runs rampant outside the jail; that slaveholding is a kind of moral sickness that pales in comparison to bodily illness. In Mary Titus's reading, "As a slavemaster and thus the source of the systematic illness of slavery, Doctor Flint dispenses disease, and not health" (207). Relying on a Romantic belief in the inherent wisdom of children—"the instincts of childhood are true," the narrator insists—*Incidents* declares that Ellen naturally perceives this contradiction between slavery's rhetoric and its reality. The paradoxes manifested in this scene suggest an understated parallel between the curious sanctuaries created by Ellen's sickness and the "felon's home in the penitentiary" of chapter VI. As it is the felon who ironically displays the capacity for virtue, so here it is the "sick" child who is actually healthy. The text repeatedly relies on these counterintuitive associations in order to articulate the depraved moral order of slavery. As I demonstrate in chapter 4 with my discussion of disabling service in Harriet Wilson's *Our Nig*, strategic representations of illness constituted another way in which African American dehumanization was made legible. Conversely, *Incidents* here suggests that the jail provides the conditions for authentic health, while the slaveholding world outside of it is inherently "sick."

What makes the jail safe is the paradoxical presence of love and other family members inside of it, and their conspicuous absence from the world outside of it, confirming Stephanie Li's thesis that "intra-dependence," or access to social networks, defines fulfillment in enslaved women's writing (11). Of Brent's childhood mistress, who assumes a mother-like affection for her, Brent explains, "I loved her, for she had been almost like a mother to me" (5). In turn, her treatment of her compels her to declare that she felt as free as "any freeborn white child" (5). Conversely, the absence of love is the definition of bondage. While staying at Flint's son's plantation with her mother, for instance, Ellen is left to fall asleep from the exhaustion of her own crying and almost bitten by a "large snake" because the younger Flint compels Jacobs to attend to domestic duties (87). Brent, in fact, leaves the plantation precisely because she suspects that Ellen and Benjamin will be permanently sent there to be "broke in" (94). In the jail, on the other hand, the children are cared for by their uncle William and their aunt, who is described as their closest relative next to their mother and grandmother. The text implies that they experience a measure of safety that is only elsewhere present at Aunt Marthy's. Hence, when Flint appears to act benevolently by removing Ellen from the jail, it is quite consistent with the narrative's logic that Ellen would cry to return to the jail. The jail is a space that makes available the emotional security and familial connections that she had been denied elsewhere in the world of the narrative. As such, the jail serves as a powerful indictment of the invisibility and terror that characterizes black life outside prison walls but inside slavery.

Fellow North Carolina bondsperson Lunsford Lane's narrative of slave life, *The Narrative of Lunsford Lane*, codifies a similarly counterintuitive reading of penal structures. After securing his own freedom by paying his mistress one thousand dollars, Lane attempts to work for and purchase the freedom of the rest of his family. Unfortunately, state laws mandate that he leave North Carolina within twenty days of his manumission, not giving him enough time to raise the required sum to redeem them. When he returns to North Carolina, he encounters, in his own language, a mob "waiting to drink [his] life" (121). However, Lane finds refuge from this multitude, of all places, in the local jail: "The guard then conducted me through the mob to the prison," he remembers, "and I felt joyful that even a prison could protect me" (121). Lane's admission that "even a prison could protect me" speaks less to the actual safety of prisons and more to the domestic terrorism that lies outside its doors. The mob, which is meant to allegorize the bloodthirsty sensibilities of slaveholders and racists, stands in sharp contrast to the paradoxical tranquility and safety of the county jail. As in *Incidents*, the refuge provided by the jail is actually a condemnation of the barbarity of slave society. It is an asylum only inasmuch as the world outside of it is a living hell.

Both Jacobs's and Lane's idealized depictions of imprisonment signify on a romantic and Pauline model of the carceral found in Henry David Thoreau's "Resistance to Civil Government," more commonly known as "Civil Disobedience." Anticipating Jacobs's idealization of jail spaces in chapters VI, X, and XVIII, "Civil Disobedience" imagines detention as a mark of the prisoner's moral decency and even social distinction. To be sure, "Civil Disobedience" has been soundly criticized for the fundamental limitations and even contradictions of its critique of prison systems. Even as it rejects the reformative impulses and homogenizing techniques of prisons and society in general, its valorization of universal ideals, disembodied subjectivity, hierarchical order, and male resistance appear to reestablish those same conditions. Commenting more specifically on the differences between the models of disobedience in Thoreau's and Jacobs's writings, Anita Goldman flatly states, "As a site for disobedience, the state prison into which members of Jacobs's family are thrown is deemed insufficient" (239). For the purposes of my project, such biases would also appear to clash with the women-centered, family-oriented, and material critique of prisons advanced throughout *Incidents*. However, when understood as one particular strain of *Incidents*'s deployment of the carceral (compare the illustration of William's imprisonment with Benjamin's, for instance), it becomes clear that this idealized representation of the carceral is not so much a transcendental reconstruction of incarceration (either in terms of the nineteenth-century philosophical movement or in the sense of escaping material history) but more a calculated recognition and application of a specific narrative about imprisonment in order to deconstruct slavery's imperatives. Like Jason Haslam, therefore, I understand "Civil Disobedience" as "constructing a fictional persona" that can be "used strategically as a means of instigating political action" (47). Put toward counterhegemonic representational purposes, it fashions subjects that do not only replicate the prison's imperatives but contest them.

This refractory "persona" is most evident when Thoreau meditates on the oppositional relation to the state in which his imprisonment places him:

> Under a government which imprisons any unjustly, the true place for a just man is also a prison. The proper place to-day, the only place which Massachusetts has provided for her freer and less desponding spirits, is in her prisons, to be put out and locked out of the State by her own act, as they have already put themselves out by their principles. It is here that the fugitive slave, and the Mexican prisoner on parole, and the Indian come to plead the wrongs of his race should find them; on that separate, but more free and honorable ground, where the State places those who are not *with* her, but *against* her,—the only house in a slave State in which a free man can abide with honor." (76)

Gelling with a carceral model in which criminality equals respectability, Thoreau's incarceration consolidates his "justness" and "honor." Similarly, Jacobs's and Lane's invocation of incarceration prove that they are honorable subjects living in the midst of a "slave State." Literalizing Thoreau's claim that the "prison" is the place where the "fugitive slave" can "come to plead the wrongs of his race," these slave narrators declare their resistance to the state and slavery from their locations behind prison walls. When Jacobs writes that she would rather go to jail because "at least there I should find some peace," she strikes a similar pose as Thoreau, arguing that the Chowan County jail constitutes a place simultaneously set apart from and emblematic of the state's tyranny. Both despite and because of the fact that it is reserved as the location for the state's enemies, it is a place where she can be bound with "honor."

In "A True Tale of Slavery," John Jacobs similarly remembers his imprisonment in the Chowan County jail as a moment where he can stand "against" the prerogatives of slavery and the state. When Norcom offers John an opportunity to be released from jail if his uncle will furnish a bond, he notes: "I was in no particular hurry to get out of jail. I wanted a little time for serious reflection, and this was the only place where I could get an opportunity for it" (213). As opposed to understanding his detention as a form of punishment or reformation, John Jacobs envisions his incarceration as an opportunity for resistant reflection. This defiant characterization of his imprisonment recalls the poetics of his sister's reading of his imprisonment in *Incidents*. When Flint places William (John Jacobs) in jail to "reflect upon his bad conduct" (61), William instead uses that time to encourage a slave trader to purchase him from Flint. There is no "evidence of repentance" (61) on William's part, as Flint explicitly desires, only an attempt to confound Flint's ownership and mastery. In both Harriet's and John's representations of imprisonment, the jail becomes a provisional think tank that can be used to interrogate and challenge the pernicious fictions that mark "free" society. They demonstrate what Dylan Rodriguez calls "radical prison praxis," or writing that elucidates the inequities of the social world by way of its location within them (411). As such, their texts do not rehearse the production of politically reformed subjects but critically reflective ones.

"Civil Disobedience" too incarnates this image of the jail as a space of "serious reflection": "I saw to what extent the people among whom I live could be trusted as good neighbors and friends." Thoreau remembers "that their friendship was for summer weather only; that they were a distinct race from me by their prejudices and superstitions, as the Chinamen and Malays are" (83). With his references to the "distinct race" and superstitions of the "Chinamen" and "Malays," Thoreau demonstrates the significant limits of his "prison praxis," articulating his transformed perspective by way of a disparaging invocation of essentialized foreigners. At the same time, his model of prison representation does not reconcile him back to society as an appropriately reformed subject. Instead, it distinguishes him as a boldly resistant one. Harriet Jacobs's and John Jacobs's invocations of detention similarly set them at odds against Flint/Norcom and the slave system. To once more call on Franklin's useful terminology, their depictions of incarceration dramatize rebellious "prisoners" not remorseful "criminals." Complementing Ellen's desire to return to the jail for its ability to cultivate love and remain close to her family, John Jacobs desires to remain in the jail to "seriously reflect" on ways to foil Norcom. Looking forward to the kind of iconoclastic portrayal of jails in works like Martin Luther King Jr.'s "Letter from

Birmingham Jail" and George Jackson's *Soledad Brother*, the depictions of incarceration here do not consolidate state power; they rethink and contest it.

"At the Beginning and Ending of Everything"

This chapter began with *Incidents*'s dramatization of Flint's curious question to Brent, one which perhaps appears to be wholly rhetorical: "Do you want to be sent to jail for your insolence?" My discussion here has tried to show that this statement was deeply grounded in both historical possibility as well as in rhetorical complexity. The invocation of jails meant quite a few different things for different subjects, involving concessions and unexpected possibilities for captors and captives. For Norcom and other agents of southern slavery, local prisons abetted the regulation and dehumanization of African American subjects, slave and free. Members of the slavocracy could call on jails and their services to detain, whip, or otherwise intimidate bondspeople. In turn, penal structures helped to consolidate southern men's sense of themselves as powerful and yet genteel. For Norcom, in particular, the Chowan County jail was a part of the way he psychologically and literally locked things away that threatened his sense of himself as respectable and professional. However, this form of punishment also came with significant limitations and disadvantages. Along with removing bondspeople from the master's labor economy, imprisonment involved financial costs that could drain owners' resources. Furthermore, once African American subjects found themselves inside jails, they were put into a position to enact plans that might disrupt their master's initial intentions. As John Jacobs's narrative makes clear, they sometimes literally had the "key on the inside." Working within the domain of "memory," Jacobs's and other slave narrators' writings reflect a similar kind of revision of the imperatives of punishment, presenting slave incarceration in rhetorically useful and provocative ways. Jacobs, in particular, dramatizes the persecutions of imprisonment as opportunities to foreground the maternal estrangement characteristic of slavery, emphasizing the tremendous physical and psychic toll of imprisonment. Contrastingly, Jacobs also imagines incarceration as a rhetorical foil for the exigencies and perversions of slavery, particularly the sexualized abuse offered by Flint. The jail is a heaven, the text suggests, when compared to the hell of living under the rule of a lecherous slave master. She takes this favorable view of jails quite literally when she argues that her daughter was better loved and cared for in the jail, in contrast to the "sick" and venomous world offered by slavery. Finally, as John Jacobs's "A True Tale of Slavery" intimates, jails could also provide a space to decode the connected systems of slavery and imprisonment, to hatch plots against white power and privilege, and to imagine politically resistant meanings of captivity, anticipating the revolutionary prison treatises of the 1960s and 1970s.

Expanding and resituating the questions we might ask of "slave narratives," *Incidents* and the other texts that speak through it are monumental contributions to understanding the place of prisons and other penal structures in African American life and cultural production. With Flint's proposition to jail Jacobs, *Incidents* sheds particular light on the current condition of African American imprisoned women. Since the late 1970s, women have constituted the fastest growing demographic in prisons, and African American females make up a significant portion of that population (Frost, Greene, and Pranis). Though Jacobs was never incarcerated, such a fate was almost inevitable had she been captured after her escape, and this reality was certainly the fate of other slave women, including her aunt Nancy. In light of the current status and disproportionate numbers of African American women in the prison system, the narrator's comment that Aunt Nancy was "at the beginning and ending of everything" (12) takes on an added meaning. As a surrogate for the many women of color who now populate American prisons, Aunt Nancy stands at a kind of "beginning" for the trend in African American female incarceration. While we do not get her story of confinement as clearly and as meticulously as we do Jacobs's, her brother's, or the children's, we can only imagine what that experience must have been like. Read in this way, *Incidents* shows us that African American female incarceration finds early and complex expression in the antebellum slave narrative. Not just about slavery, slave narratives reveal the complex story of African American (female) incarceration contained in, and existing alongside, accounts of antiblack racism and discrimination.

My next chapter, addressing the representation of African American slavery to southeastern Native Americans, further deconstructs the homogeneity of the seemingly stable notion of "slavery." Moving away from the South into the midwestern state of Oklahoma, it reveals the role of narratives of Indian captivity and Native American slavery in producing "civilized" and "masculine" subject positions for the African American slave narrator Henry Bibb. In the process, it exposes the curiously productive functions of captivity for both African American slave narrators as well as southeastern Native Americans.

3
Mild Masters, Sympathetic Abolitionists, and Courageous Husbands

Cherokee Slavery in *The Life and Adventures of Henry Bibb, an American Slave*

> $20 REWARD
> Ranaway on the 21st September last, from the subscriber, living on Grand river, near the mouth of Honey creek, Cherokee Nation, a negro man named ALLEN, who is about 25-years old; about 5 feet 2 or 3 inches high; very black; has very white eyes; rather a stoppage in his speech when speaking, and a wen under his thigh. When he left he had on a plaid shirt and copperas colored pantaloons; and also, marks of the whip, inflicted before he came into my possession.
> Any person arresting and returning the said negro to me or lodging him in jail so that I can get him, will receive a reward of twenty dollars.
> PETER HILDEBRAND
> Cherokee Nation, Oct. 22–2w
>
> *Cherokee Advocate*, October 23, 1845

While we don't know much about the man called "Allen" in the runaway advertisement reproduced above, the document created in the aftermath of his escape leaves us some clues about what his life might have been like. Given the year of the advertisement, 1845, we know that Allen was one of thousands of slaves held by the Cherokee, Choctaw, Chickasaw, Creek, and Seminole Nations in Indian Territory, the areas in present-day Oklahoma where southeastern Native Americans were forcibly sent via the Indian Removal Act of 1830. By 1839, the year in which this mass exodus ended, somewhere between 4,500 to 5,000 slaves lived in Indian Territory (Doran, "Negro Slaves" 340). By 1860, the first year in which these nations were tabulated in the US census, that number had increased to 8,376. Slaves constituted roughly 15 percent of the population in Indian Territory, but the vast majority of these bondspeople were owned by wealthy and typically biracial elites descended from Native and Anglo-American intermarriage and relations. Within the class of Indian slaveholders, the Cherokees were the largest group, owning over 2,500 bondspeople (347). Given his age (twenty-five) and the year that he escaped (1845), it is possible that Allen may have helped his owner to travel to and establish his residence in Indian Territory, as many other Native American–owned bondspeople did during removal and resettlement (Halliburton 165).

Because of Allens' residence "near the mouth of Honey creek," we also know that he was a bondsperson in one of the wealthiest neighborhoods of the Cherokee Nation West. Located in the Delaware District, Honey Creek was home to prominent proremoval Cherokees such as statesman Stand Waite, Treaty Party leader John Ridge, and newspaperman Elias Boudinot, the former editor of the newspaper that came to be known as the *Cherokee Advocate* (Miles 180). Peter Hildebrand, Allen's owner, was a member of this community. His father and mother, John Hildebrand and Barbara Eaker, were German nationals. After Eaker died his father married a Cherokee woman in Tennessee, Susannah Womancatcher, thereby making John a member of the tribe. Peter followed suit by marrying a Cherokee woman named Elizabeth Harlan, suggesting the deep personal, generational, and economic ties the Hildebrands developed with the Cherokees. Accordingly, when Harlan died in 1826, Hildebrand migrated with other Cherokees to Indian Territory during removal and even led one of the companies of émigrés (Naylor, *African Cherokees* 251–52). Given the wealth and status of his owner, Allen was probably one of several slaves owned by Hildebrand and may have assisted in the raising of corn, grain, and cattle that was typical of Indian Territory agriculture (*African Cherokees* 19).

Perhaps most importantly, Allen's enslavement during the early years of resettlement (1839–46) lets us know that he might have been subject to especially violent treatment. While slavery in the East had often been characterized by a certain degree of "flexibility" (Miles 157), the increased value of slave labor as well as the moral anomie and cultural dislocation caused by removal meant that slavery in Indian Territory was much more restrictive (Naylor, *African Cherokees* 27–30). One symptom of this is that fugitive slave ads were relatively rare in the pre–Cherokee removal *Cherokee Phoenix*, but in the postremoval *Cherokee Advocate* such notices became much more frequent (Perdue, *Slavery* 79). Despite Hildebrand's contention that Allen received his scars before he "came into my possession," his admission that Allen bore "marks of the whip" suggests the potential for this abuse and maybe even the motivation for this particular flight. This last observation underscores the most important thing that we know about the man identified as "Allen": like so many other blacks enslaved in Indian Territory, he desperately wanted to get away.

The Life and Adventures of Henry Bibb, the only book-length antebellum slave narrative to treat slavery in Indian Territory, suggests a drastically different picture of enslaved life in the Cherokee Nation West. Picking up the story from the second half of *Life and Adventures*, we learn that Bibb has already made his way to the North but repeatedly returns to the South in the hopes of freeing his wife, Malinda, and daughter, Mary Frances. When Bibb fails yet again to lead his family to freedom, his most recent owner, a Louisiana cotton planter named Deacon Whitfield, sells him to a group of traveling gamblers, who buy him for the purposes of speculation. Smitten with Bibb's intelligence and gumption, however, they promise to sell him at their earliest convenience and even to give him a portion of the money from his future sale. True to their word, while gambling on a horse race in Arkansas Territory, they sell him to a "very wealthy half-Indian" and split a portion of the profits with him (150). Bibb represents his sale to this Cherokee slaveholder as a decided improvement in his condition. He is never beaten, starved, or overworked, and when his owner fortuitously dies, Bibb is able to make a quick and relatively uncomplicated escape. "All things considered," he writes, "if I must be a slave, I had by far, rather be a slave to an Indian, than to a white man, from the experience I have had with both" (153). In stark contrast to the narrative of abuse and escape suggested by "Allen's" mini–slave narrative, Bibb's extended account suggests that Cherokee slavery is essentially mild and, in relation to slavery to whites, a comparative refuge.

The purpose of this chapter is to think through some of the reasons why Bibb's depiction of slavery in Indian Territory is so drastically different from the one suggested by Allen's runaway notice, inasmuch as they illuminate the multifaceted realities and representations governing black enslavement to Native Americans. Doing so provides an entrée into larger questions about the ways that so-called Indian slavery has been conceptualized, the purposes to which those conceptualizations have been put, and the various meanings of that enslavement for different groups, from white abolitionists to Native Americans. With its idyllic representation of bondage in Indian Territory, Henry Bibb's account represents a singular moment in the history of thinking about Indian slavery. As the only sustained record of Indian slavery by a black bondsperson from the antebellum era, it has often featured repeatedly and prominently in explorations of black slavery to southeastern Native Americans, often in the services of confirming what Celia Naylor has referred to as a "mythology presenting benign slavery in Indian Nations" (*African Cherokees* 21).[1] But if Bibb's narrative contributes to this narrative, I would argue, it does so for largely underappreciated reasons. Just as Hildebrand had specific reasons for crafting his account of black enslavement in the Cherokee Nation the way he did (in order to present himself as a benevolent slaveholder, for instance), so did Bibb. For while Hildebrand was seeking to recapture his human property through his rehearsal of Allen's personal characteristics, Bibb was seeking to recapture an image of himself as a faithful father and courageous husband, while at the same time critiquing the abuses he and his family had suffered from slavery to southern whites. His lived experience and narrativized memory of the Cherokee Nation West was processed through his desire for what he had been denied in slavery to southern whites. If to remember is often to re-member, or to reconstruct events according to personally useful and culturally acceptable patterns (Bruner 38), then no memory can ever be an objective record of an event. Rather, it is a thread that is pulled from, but still tied to, the fabric of personal, historical, and cultural associations from which it was made. Understood in this way, Bibb's narrative reveals how stories of black enslavement to Native Americans are inextricably bound up with attempts at Cherokee self-determination, abolitionists' arguments for Native rights, and African American men's desire for respectable masculinity and familial reconnection.

Historicizing Cherokee Slavery

For antebellum southeastern Native Americans, holding slaves was a practical way in which they signified and realized their achievement of civilization and their progress toward economic self-sufficiency and assimilation. Indeed, the codification of African American disfranchisement and enslavement was coextensive with the creation of the Cherokee Constitution in 1827. When they were forcibly resettled in Indian Territory, new restrictions on black freedom built into the constitution of 1839 became yet another way in which they created order and defined their national identity at a time of extraordinary transition and crisis. Their path to the adoption of chattel slavery and antiblack racism elucidates the importance of black bondage in projects of Native dispossession, cultural self-determination, and economic viability.

The precarious position of Native Americans in the early national era made the acceptance of chattel slavery a practical possibility. By 1790, the Cherokees had been in contact with whites for roughly a century and had consequently become dependent on European markets, tools, and culture, even as they clung to the long-standing beliefs and activities that had defined their worldview (McLoughlin 3–4). American independence, in particular, brought increased pressure to "civilize" southeastern Native Americans, whose way of life was interpreted as an affront to white ways of organizing the world (34). Native women's farming, for example, positioned them in a role that had been traditionally occupied by white men. Likewise, Indian men's hunting removed them from husbandry and, furthermore, required large tracts of undomesticated land, land which Europeans viewed as essentially wasted and vacant. Desiring to align the Cherokees' gendered division of labor with Western standards, the new government understood their role as "helping the Cherokee [men] to become farmers with one hand and arranging for them to give up their old hunting ground with the other" (58). Indian's civilization, they reasoned, would not only bring sophistication to Native Americans, it would provide cheap, fertile land for American expansion. As in the "Georgia Compact" made between Thomas Jefferson and Georgia in 1802, the state promised to relinquish its claim to lands in the western part of the state (eventually the states of Alabama and Mississippi), if the federal government would extinguish all Indian claims to land inside the state (22), thereby freeing up huge tracts of land for white settlement. Though Jefferson was not able to make good on his promise, white settlers took such agreements as an invitation to overrun Cherokee lands, compelling some Cherokees in the 1820s to move to western states like Arkansas, not without acrimony, to avoid the forcible confiscation of their land (162).

One concerted response to such encroachment was, paradoxically, the adoption of Anglo-American culture and institutions. Facilitated by government "gifts" of farm tools and domestic paraphernalia, Cherokee men began to farm and Cherokee women began to weave (McClinton, "Introduction" 35–36). They also participated in more explicit acts of self-definition and white emulation. They established their own syllabary in 1821, the first American Indian newspaper, the *Cherokee Phoenix* in 1825 (later *Cherokee Advocate* in Indian Territory), and a Cherokee Constitution in 1827 (Conley 105–6), effectively consolidating their identity as a separate and self-ruling nation. Nationhood and its trappings, they imagined, would shield them from white aggression. Based on these significant strides, the Cherokees became known as the elite group of the "Five Civilized Tribes," the other four being the Creek, Choctaw, Chickasaw, and Seminole. And though this was true for a minority of the Cherokee population, they participated in that most American of antebellum enterprises: black slaveholding. Operating both as a practical means of meeting the new demands of agrarian life and as a symbol of racial superiority over blacks, slave owning helped to solidify the Cherokee elites' status as "civilized" (Perdue, "Cherokee Planters" 110; Conley 103).

The use of bondage in Cherokee society was not unprecedented. Well before colonial contact with Europeans, Cherokees held captives (*atsi nahsa'I* or "one who is owned"), whose outsider status was defined by their lack of affiliation with one of the seven clans (Perdue, *Slavery* 4). This class of captives was typically made up of prisoners of war from conflicts with other Native American tribes, but, with the advent of Euro-American contact and settlement, whites and Africans also began to occupy these roles. Since the clan was the basic unit of Cherokee identity, to exist outside that system, as Celia Naylor has argued, was a condition that was uncomfortably close to the condition of blacks in antebellum slavery and may have paved the conceptual way for the Cherokees' adoption of it (*African Cherokees* 11–12). At the same time, as Theda Perdue explains, "the term 'slave' can perhaps only be used inaccurately" because the makeup of slaves was not racially determined nor did it arise out of a capitalistic market economy (*Slavery* 4). Captives' positions in Cherokee society was a function of their being clanless, not of their blackness, and their role was not to expedite the acquisition of wealth, as a profit motive was not a part of traditional Cherokee society (*Slavery* 13).

However, as white ways of seeing the world began to infuse Cherokee society, Native conceptualizations of slavery began to resonate with Euro-American models. The estrangement of Cherokee women from the land and the presence of a class of people who could perform their labor meant that a large class of agrarian slaves, who could have served no practical purpose in Cherokee society before, now had a purpose (Perdue, *Slavery* 50). Perdue elaborates on the interrelated articulations of slavery and blackness in this way: "By the third decade of the nineteenth century . . . the Cherokees had come to view themselves as radically different from Africans. Originally the 'slaves' in Cherokee society had been war captives who were considered to be less than human because they were bereft of kinship ties, but as kinship receded in importance and as Indians began to identify with whites, Cherokees began to consider Africans more suitable for slavery than other Indians or Europeans" (*Slavery* 49). Emboldened by this new sense of what race meant, the Cherokees constructed blackness in many of the same ways as their counterparts in the antebellum South. Under the Cherokee Constitution passed in 1827, for example, people of African descent, whether free or enslaved, were not eligible for citizenship or for suffrage (Miles 108–11). According to Article III of Section 4, "No person who is of negro or mulatto parentage, either by the father or the mother side, shall be eligible to hold any office of profit, honor or trust under this government" (qtd. in Miles 109). The creation of the Cherokee state was thus simultaneous with the legal codification of African American disfranchisement. Moreover, laws were put into place that specifically restricted the activities of bondspeople. Slaves were prohibited from owning property, patrols were created to regulate bondspeople's mobility, and laws were instituted that protected an owner's right to kill slaves with impunity (Miles 112). Even before the codification of such laws, it is evident that some Cherokee slaveholders felt that black life was worthless. In 1805, James Vann, the richest slaveholder (and probably the most violent) in the Cherokee Nation, burned one bondsperson alive and executed another after discovering that they had escaped from his Georgia plantation and stolen $3,500 of his money to boot (McClinton, *Moravian* 64). However, the two whites who were also implicated in the plot were merely remanded to Georgia authorities because the thought of an Indian killing a white person might provoke retaliation (67). Just as we might say of antebellum blacks in relation to white America, blacks had no rights that Indians were bound to respect.

At the same time, the stringency of these laws and the ruthlessness of such practices threaten to ignore the complexity and elasticity of Cherokee slavery. The overwhelming majority of Cherokees, for instance, did not hold slaves, and most Cherokees were, in fact, opposed to slavery (Naylor, *African Cherokees* 18; Miles 75). The preponderance of Cherokee bondspeople was owned by a tiny, biracial elite, and it was this propertied upper crust that constituted the framers of the constitution. Of the twelve signers of the Cherokee Constitution, eleven were slaveholders (Perdue, *Slavery* 57). Consequently, the divisions between slaveholding and nonslaveholding Cherokees created "two distinct classes within Cherokee society," one of progressive slaveholders and one of conservative nonslaveholders (68–69). While "conservatives associated slavery with the white southerners who had forced them from their homes" (68), progressives saw slavery as a practical means of accruing wealth, a demonstration of their ability to run their own affairs, and a tool in negotiations with whites.

Complicating matters further, traditional Cherokee society's focus on kinship and clan, as Tiya Miles has suggested, meant that Cherokee slavery might have presented singular opportunities for unlegislated resistance. In a situation that Miles call "flexibility" (157), preremoval Cherokee owners sometimes treated their bondspeople as part of the family, not just as expendable property (94–95). In the context of mission schools, for instance, Cherokees' slaves were taught to read English (93) and thereby translated sermons and other communications from missionaries and whites (94). Even beyond missionary influence, they served as translators and negotiators for their "full-blooded" Cherokee owners (94), and enslaved women, in particular, helped Cherokee women to learn and practice domestic duties (95). Though undoubtedly harsh and oppressive, Cherokee slavery seems to have also offered opportunities that were unavailable in southern slavery and this likely contributed to its reputation as a kind of sanctuary for fugitive blacks.

Government-sanctioned removal, however, significantly circumscribed the freedoms available in Indian slavery. Framing removal as a benign relocation project that would save Native Americans from white "influence" and facilitate settlement of the southeastern United States, President Andrew Jackson engineered the passage of the Indian Removal Act in 1830, which granted him the authority to negotiate the removal of American Indians from the east of the Mississippi to the west of it. Though many Native Americans continued to resist removal through active protests and simply refusing to move, governmental pressure, white settlers' land greed, and divisions within the Cherokee Nation outlasted their resolve. In 1835, a small group of progressive and proslavery Cherokees met in the Cherokee Nation's capital and agreed to removal terms, what has come to be known as the Treaty of New Echota. Though they had no authority to represent the vast majority of Cherokees, who were antiremoval, they exchanged the rights to the Cherokee homelands for $5 million and land in the West (Miles 152). The treaty gave the Cherokees two years to evacuate, and, accordingly, in the summer of 1838, federal and state troops began physically removing Cherokees and other southeastern Natives from their eastern homelands (153). Approximately sixteen thousand Cherokees were compelled on steamboat, wagon, horse, and foot over hundreds of miles from northern Georgia to northeastern Oklahoma in the Trail of Tears. Conservative figures suggest that some four thousand Cherokees died on this journey (155). While some Cherokees managed to stay behind, marooning themselves in the Georgia and North Carolina mountains, by 1839, most of the Cherokees that were formerly living in the states of Georgia, North Carolina, and Tennessee had been forcibly relocated to the northeastern tip of Oklahoma.

To understand the Trail of Tears as only a physical migration or as a statistical function is to miss the profound ways in which removal transformed and destroyed the Cherokees' worldview. In traditional Cherokee cosmology, the world was conceived as a flat plane that was suspended at four corners. The Cherokees understood themselves as "the principal people" (McLoughlin 4), who existed from time immemorial at the center of this land mass. Since the west was where the sun set, it was conceived as the edge of the known world, a place of death populated by nefarious spirits (McLoughlin 13; Boudinot 73). According to this thinking, Indian removal did not just take the Cherokees from their homes; it sent them (literally and symbolically) to their graves. Just as the Middle Passage of Africans overturned the spiritual ground on which Africans stood, Indian removal turned the world of the Cherokees and other deposed tribes upside down; it shook their sense of what the world was. Miles writes: "Indian Removal disrupted the relationship between Cherokees, their homeland, and the stories that lived there. As a result, the cultural values embedded in those stories could no longer be reinforced through the visible markers of place" (159). Hence, the Cherokees had not just been removed from their homes but their ability even to make sense of themselves. Arriving in Indian Territory in 1839, the Cherokees were a fallen people.

When Bibb becomes the property of a "very wealthy half-Indian" in Oklahoma Indian Territory in 1841, it is just two years after this radical and literally world-changing upheaval. Arriving in the midst of what historians called the resettlement period, Indian Territory was a place of desperation, uncertainty, and increasing socioeconomic divides. Not surprisingly, slavery in Indian Territory inspired blacks to flee from their masters in record numbers, as the runaway slave advertisement that opens this chapter from the *Cherokee Advocate* suggests. The greatest of these escapes occurred in November 1842, just a year after Bibb's arrival in Indian Territory, when twenty slaves absconded from Joseph Van's plantation (son of James Vann) and rendezvoused with bondspeople from other farms and tribes, attempting to make their way to Mexico (Miles 169–73). In 1846, just a year after "Allen" left Peter Hildebrand, Lewis Ross might have discovered the seeds of a similar plot, when he found a cache of guns and ammunition in his slaves' possession (170). Indian Territory was thus a place where blacks regularly plotted and attempted escape.

Mythologizing Indian Slavery

Due to what Naylor calls the "mythology" of "benign slavery in Indian nations" (*African Cherokees* 21), however, such realities have often gone unappreciated. This mythology holds that Native American slavery was generally more lenient and humane than slavery to southern whites. While I think that the word "mythology" perhaps obscures the case, implying that there were no important differences between the treatment of slaves by Native Americans and Anglo-Americans, I do believe, like Naylor, that it is essential to underscore the mistreatment and discontent of African American slaves in Indian Territory.[2] Failing to do so diminishes and distorts the quite real suffering that is at the heart of the runaway advertisement that began this chapter. In order to honor the man called Allen's experience of Indian slavery, and the thousands of bondspeople that were in similar situations, it is necessary to trace the ways that the narrative of lenient Native American slavery came to be, some of which appear to be grounded in purposeful misrepresentation and others in historical reality.

One likely source of the benign picture of Indian slavery comes from the Cherokee elite's conscious propagation of a more humane narrative of Indian slaveholding in order to retain white abolitionist support for antiremoval. As the research of Natalie Joy suggests, several notable abolitionists, including William Lloyd Garrison, Lydia Maria Child, and Thomas Weld, received their first experience in organized reform through the Cherokee antiremoval movement. But in order for the Cherokees to retain this important locus of support, they needed to create a palatable narrative of Indian slavery that would not alienate them from their most influential allies. Joy explains that they consequently crafted a narrative of Native American slavery that depended on three fictions: Native American slavery was 1) harmless and nonviolent, 2) a temporary phase, and 3) an unfortunate, though natural, step in their path toward civilization. An encounter between Elias Boudinot, editor of the *Cherokee Phoenix*, and William Lloyd Garrison, editor of the most prominent antislavery periodical, the *Liberator*, illustrates the softened picture of black enslavement the Cherokees represented. Boudinot and Garrison's meeting was precipitated by the advertisement for a runaway slave, one "Lucy," reprinted in a 4 February 1832 edition of the *Cherokee Phoenix*, an advertisement that made it painfully clear that the Cherokees not only practiced slaveholding but were complicit with bondspeople's capture and return to their white masters. After seeing the advertisement, Garrison was eager to get a response from the Cherokee leadership as well as (presumably) calm the fears of his antislavery readership. The opportunity presented itself while Boudinot was on a tour drumming up resistance to Indian removal in the Northeast. Reprinted in an 1832 edition of the *Liberator*, Garrison's report of his meeting with Boudinot makes Indian slavery look like an unfortunate, but hardly protest-worthy, evil: "We were not aware until [Boudinot] informed us of the fact, that although some of the Cherokees are owners of slaves, slavery is unknown to the constitution of laws of the Cherokee nation, and is sanctioned only by custom." Furthermore, Garrison explains, "[Boudinot] deprecated its existence, and joined with us in hoping that there might soon be moral power enough to overthrow it" (qtd. in Joy 11).

As my above discussion of the Cherokee adoption of slavery makes clear, black disfranchisement and slavery was crucial to the formation of the Cherokee republic. Moreover, Garrison's invocation of "custom," as Joy suggests, implies that black enslavement by Indians is merely a cultural curiosity and an informal relation and not a legally protected institution that radically transformed the meaning and organization of Cherokee life. Furthermore, since Garrison was an avid reader of the *Phoenix*, he would likely have read Boudinot's reprinting of the Cherokee Constitution in the *Phoenix* and thus been well aware that black enslavement was a long-standing institution in Cherokee society. But it seems that both men ignored these inconvenient truths: Boudinot because he wanted to keep abolitionist support and Garrison because he still wanted to give it. Seeing white southern slavery as the common enemy, Garrison was apparently willing to make concessions for *this* kind of slavery in order to better fight other kinds of slavery, specifically that practiced by southern whites. In the process, black slavery in the context of Cherokee slavery went largely uncriticized.

Another important source for the depiction of idyllic Indian slavery was the host of missionary groups, including Moravians, Presbyterians, and Baptists, who had close relationships with Native American slaveholders.[3] Their sympathy toward Indian slaveholders, and their commitment to converting them, likely limited their ability to perceive and render thoroughly the violence, inhumanity, and even ungodliness of slaveholding. As Rudi Halliburton Jr. explains: "Since missionaries knew that to exclude slaveowners from the church and speak out against slavery would bring on expulsion from the Nation, they frequently extolled the benevolence of Cherokee masters in their reports to superiors and governing boards. They contended that slaves were treated more kindly and performed less labor than was required of domestic and industrial workers in the East" (94). Just as problematically, they preached essentially proslavery sermons that sometimes encouraged slaves to submit to authority (Halliburton 28). Care has to be taken, of course, to balance Halliburton's statements against particular representations of Native American slavery made by specific missionary groups and agents to see if this was actually the case. The above relation of James Vann's brutal murder of his escaped slaves is found, for example, in the diaries of Moravian missionaries. So while missionaries' sympathies may have leaned toward "saving" slaveholders rather than documenting or protesting black enslavement, they nonetheless provide an important record of bondspeople's abuses.[4]

Finally, the testimony of former slaves of Native Americans, interestingly enough, has greatly contributed to the idea that Indian slavery was categorically lenient. In the words of former Cherokee Nation bondswoman Nellie Johnson, "Old Chief just treat all the Negroes like they was just hired hands, and I was a big girl before I knowed very much about belonging to him" (Baker and Baker 226). Such testimonies were recorded in the mid-1930s as part of the efforts of the Works Project Administration (WPA), a Depression-era government-funded enterprise that collected the testimony of ex-slaves. Historian Laura Lovett explains that roughly 12 percent of all WPA slave narratives come from African Americans who identified themselves as Indians or were descendants of Indians, and many of these accounts relate tales of slavery to members of the Five Nations (195). Even as scholars have recognized WPA testimonials as an "indispensable source" (Escott 40), they have also acknowledged their limitations. Besides the trite objections that we might raise about the unreliability of memory from the distance of several decades, it is perhaps more important to note that WPA slave narrators often shaped their responses according to what they imagined their (white) middle-class interlocutors wanted to hear (Blassingame 86–87). Moreover, since WPA respondents did not write down their own testimony, the language we do have from their testimonies is mediated by several levels of transcription and redaction by their interviewers and their superiors (86). Just as important, ex-slaves might have been using their recollections of Indian slavery as a kind of "rhetorical refuge," to use Tiya Miles's phrasing (43), to deal with the anxieties of their present circumstances. As seen from the vantage point of the Depression-era South, childhood slavery in the Cherokee Nation might have indeed appeared idyllic. Even so, the significant amount of WPA accounts that acknowledge the benevolence, or at least relative humanity, of Native American masters suggests that we should not dismiss these testimonies as just social posturing or simply more proof of the inevitable limitations of the archive. These ex-slaves perceived a clear difference between the kind of slavery practiced in the Cherokee Nation and that practiced by whites. They understood Indian slavery as appreciably better and easier than bondage to white southerners, and these distinctions certainly contextualize our understanding of the brutalities that were evident in Cherokee slavery, both before and after removal. If we define "myth" as total fabrication, the word cannot apply to their conceptualizations of Indian slavery, but if we understand "myth" as a story that makes sense of the world, then their stories represent legitimate readings of some of the potential differences between slavery practiced by white southerners and southeastern Native Americans.

Narrating Indian Slavery

Bibb's account provides an indispensable companion as well as counterpoint to these depictions of black enslavement in the Cherokee Nation. We do well, though, not to hold it up as a story that finally gives us the unadulterated truth of Indian slavery but rather to see it as one that is as equally motivated as the ones mentioned above. For if no record of "experience" exists separate from the language and context in which it is delivered (Scott 66), then why it is produced is just as important and, necessarily informs, what is produced. Understanding Bibb's particular employments and relationships within Cherokee slavery as well as the motivations for his narrative helps us to understand his idealized illustrations of Cherokee slavery.

Of primary importance here is the fact that Bibb calls his Cherokee owner "the most reasonable, and humane slaveholder that I have ever belonged to" (152). Indeed, he refrains from revealing his name, the only slaveholder throughout the entire narrative who is given this pardon, suggesting the almost family-like affection Bibb might have had for his Cherokee owner, though at other times he is more critical of him.[5] However, such sentiments also appear to be a function of Bibb's advantageous position as his owner's personal attendant. As Bibb readily admits, Indian slavery seemed "favorable" because his prospective owner "wanted [him] only for a kind of body servant to wait on him—and in this case I knew that I should fare better than I should in the field" (150). Serving as his owner's personal assistant, Bibb's experience of slavery would have been markedly different from that of field hands. While Bibb acknowledges that his owner possesses "a large plantation and quite a number of slaves" (152), he never reveals anything specific about how these other, and less advantageously situated, slaves are treated. Rather, of his own labors, he notes that they are easy and, in fact, endear him to his master's affection. On the way from his purchase, for example, Bibb's first job is to transport and guard his owner's money, an amount totaling five hundred dollars (151). As the carrier and protector of his owner's money, Bibb becomes the guardian of the resources that made him a slave. Just moments before he explains that he was purchased for nine hundred dollars and "saw the money counted out" (150), a detail that is clearly meant to excite revulsion for the callous economics of slavery. But on the next page, Bibb reveals that his owner has such "confidence" in him that he allows him to carry and protect the money from which he was purchased (151), information that troubles our sense of Bibb's involvement in and identification with his owner's transactions.

The fact that this "wealthy half Indian" "became much attached" to Bibb suggests one aspect of Bibb's simultaneous antagonism and allegiance toward his Cherokee owner. Bibb's owner is described as a "wealthy half Indian," and Bibb is represented, at various points throughout the text, as a "yellow man," "near white," and "too white" (4, 60, 107). As Halliburton, Perdue, and others have noted, most Cherokee slaveholders not only aspired to the standards and accoutrements of whiteness but they were also racially mixed, often times the products of Cherokee mothers and slaveholding white settlers, as was the case with the prosperous Indian slaveholder, James Vann. Though we can only speculate on this particular Cherokee's motives, it seems plausible that Bibb's pseudowhiteness might have attracted his Cherokee owner to him. Perhaps he prized Bibb as a curiosity or identified with his racial hybridity. Or, maybe like many Americans of the time, he believed that "white blood" had the potential to refine or elevate black people, as in an advertisement for Bibb's account that notes he is "not more African than European in his lineage" and has "some of the finest Kentucky blood in his veins" (Davis and Gates 29). Regardless of his owner's disposition toward "near white" blacks, we know that Bibb was clearly skilled in showing people what they wanted to see from his many acts of (racial) passing to get safely in and out of the North, and it seems quite reasonable that Bibb assessed his future owner's sense of what racial difference or ambiguity might have meant to him and used it to get into his good graces, what the text signifies as an "attachment" and "confidence."

Such an "attachment" between these two racially and culturally hybrid figures meant that Bibb might have appeared, to other Cherokees' slaves, as more white or even Cherokee; and this might have meant that Bibb's experience of Cherokee slavery could have been radically different from other slaves' experiences. As a slave born in the slaveholding South, or a "crossland negro" (Naylor, "'Born and Raised'" 162), Bibb would have been probably viewed as an outsider by other bondspeople who were born or had spent the majority of their lives in the Cherokee Nation. WPA narratives confirm the suspicion, or at the very least difference, between slaves who were born or grew up in the Cherokee Nation and those imported to it later (Naylor, "'Born and Raised'" 166). Having such an intimate relationship with his master even before he arrived at the plantation (with its great "quantity" of black slaves) would have probably only further cemented the impression that Bibb was an untrustworthy outsider. Especially since he was in charge of protecting his owner's money, he might have been seen as sympathetic to, or at least complicit with, the master's interests.

Indeed, much has been made of the fact that Bibb never gives the name of his Cherokee master, but it is an equally telling omission that Bibb never gives the name of any other Cherokee slaves. In his descriptions of his slavery to southern whites, we learn the names of Jack, Malinda, and other bondspeople he has personal relationships with; in the Louisville workhouse, he befriends other white prisoners and even notes how they sympathize with his and his wife's suffering; but in Indian Territory, all the slaves melt into an undifferentiated mass: "quite a number of slaves." Naylor suggests that one reason for Bibb's romanticized vision of Indian slavery is the shortness of his stay, which may have only been a couple of months (Naylor, *African Cherokees* 244). This could have certainly limited his contact with other bondspeople. But what might also have contributed to his apparent alienation from the vast majority of Cherokee bondspeople is the exceptionally kind treatment Bibb received from his Cherokee master and the incredible ambivalence, if not rift, this created between him and the other slaves. If so, Bibb's refusal to give the name of his Cherokee owner thus not only speaks to the leniency of his treatment but also to the fact that he might have been estranged from large numbers of "fellow" blacks and the kinds of labor and treatment they experienced. The statement included in Hildebrand's advertisement that Allen is "very black" invokes the kind of inflexible difference that Bibb did not have to contend with in his own body. Described as "near white" and "yellow," Bibb might have had access to racial and cultural identities that limited and even skewed his perception of bondage elsewhere on his owner's property or the Cherokee Nation West.

"Neither Do They Separate Husbands and Wives"

Other favorable representations of Cherokee slavery appear to be less about Bibb's unique position in Indian Territory than about the unique position Indian Territory has in Bibb's narrative. Put another way, Bibb's representation of Cherokee slavery seems more invested in pointing out the sties in the eyes of white slaveholders, as suggested by the examples of Boudinot and Garrison above, than in relating a historically specific or accurate depiction of Indian slaveholding. An extended analysis of one particularly pregnant passage shows Bibb's commitment to indicting the horrors of white slavery through a curious celebration of the compassion of Native American slavery. Of his anonymous Cherokee slave owner, Bibb notes:

> He raised corn and wheat for his own consumption only. There was no cotton, tobacco, or anything of the kind produced for market. And I found this difference between negro slavery and among the Indians, and the same thing among the slaveholders of the South. The Indians allow their slaves enough to eat and wear. They have no overseers to whip or drive them. If a slave offends his master, he sometimes in a heat of passion, undertakes to chastise him; but it is as often the case as otherwise, that the slave gets the better of the fight, and even flogs his master; for which there is no law to punish him; but when the fight is over that is the last of it. So far as religious instruction is concerned, they have it in terms of equality, the bond and the free; they have no respect of persons, they have neither slave laws or negro pews. *Neither do they separate husbands and wives, nor parents and children*. All things considered, if I must be a slave, I had by far, rather be a slave to an Indian, than to a white man, from the experience I have had with both. (emphasis added, 153)

Bibb presents himself here as an authority on comparative slaveries: having had an experience "with both," he is qualified to judge the relative merits, or demerits, of each. Systematically moving through the main tenets of abolitionist critiques of chattel slavery—squalid food, inferior clothing, brutal physical violence, compromised religious instruction, and fractured families—the above passage is a microcosm of the various offenses remonstrated against white masters, overseers, and slave traders in the antebellum slave narratives but as reflected in the fantastic "tricky mirror" created by Bibb's depiction of Indian slavery.[6] As Dan Pierson has demonstrated, the most frequent and damning charge leveled against antebellum slaveholders was that they were inadequate patriarchs or poor male protectors and providers. Bibb's rendition of Cherokee slavery is an extended critique of white slavery through a celebration of Cherokee owners' patriarchal benevolence.

Bibb starts off by noting that Indian slavery is not related to the vicissitudes and disturbances of the market, a familiar critique of white slavery. "There was no cotton, tobacco, or anything of the kind produced for market," Bibb declares. Harriet Beecher Stowe's *Uncle Tom's Cabin* famously opens with a conversation between Mr. Shelby, the benevolent slave owner, and Haley, the despicable slave trader, to show how slavery's economies of debt and profit crush human beings, both slave and free. Haley presses Shelby to sell some of his slaves in order to satisfy an outstanding debt, and thus the novel shows how the concerns of the indifferent "market" menace African American lives and families. But Cherokee slaveholders in Indian Territory were just as invested in the economic value of slaves and their services as any place in the antebellum South. Salt mining was a lucrative business and the labor of slaves was crucial to this enterprise (Perdue, *Slavery* 99–102). As Perdue summarizes, "The slaveholder accumulated more than he could use himself and the profit made by the sale of the surplus gave him capital to invest in various enterprises" (60). Bibb disavows these truths, however, in order to make Cherokee slavery appear more palatable, and thus the kind of slavery practiced by white southerners as more brutal.

The fact that his Cherokee master does not grow cotton is a crucial part of this claim, as cotton had come to be understood as an iconic symbol of white slavery's brutality during the cotton boom of the early nineteenth century (Plasa; Berlin 130). As Bibb notes of his own experience on Deacon Whitfield's plantation, "The cotton planters generally never allow a slave mother time to go to the house, or quarter during the day to nurse her child" (116). "This is the reason," he continues, "why so very few slave children are raised on these cotton plantations, the mothers have no time to take care of them—and they are often found dead in the field and in the quarter for want of the care of their mothers" (116). According to this paradigm, cotton production destroys the bonds between mother and child and even kills children. In truth, the Cherokees did not cultivate cotton on a large scale, but not because they feared it would kill enslaved children but simply because the land would not sustain it (Naylor, *African Cherokees* 19). Indeed, Bibb's assertion that Cherokee slavery is only for "subsistence" would appear to contradict his own admission that his Cherokee owner possessed a "large plantation and quite a number of slaves" (152). "Large" and "quite a number" are, of course, imprecise quantifiers, but they strongly suggest that Bibb's Cherokee owner's involvement in the "market" was more than academic or experimental. Indeed, the Cherokees' adoption of American-style slavery only became possible because they had moved from an economic system based on subsistence hunting and farming to a society based on the acquisition of surplus money and material goods. As the one-time holder and protector of his owner's money, Bibb would have certainly had some clue about the acquisitive nature of his owner, but an emphasis on such truths in his discussion of Cherokee slavery would have compromised his indictment of white slavery's financial and human costs.

Also crucial to the claim that white slaveholders were inadequate patriarchs was the assertion that bondspeople went hungry and without proper clothing, a point we will later see put to effective use in Harriet Wilson's narrative of indentured servitude, *Our Nig*. Bibb explains in his catalog of differences that "the Indians allow their slaves enough to eat and wear." Proving his own point, Bibb relates in an earlier chapter that he had often gone "without clothes enough to hide my nakedness" (14–15) and " often worked without half enough to eat, both late and early, by day and by night" (15). Frederick Douglass's *Narrative* makes this point even more graphically, when he laments: "My feet have been so cracked with the frost, that the pen with which I am writing might be laid in the gashes" (27). Contrasting these statements, Bibb insists that in Indian slavery bondspeople are adequately fed and clothed. Again, Bibb's sense of Cherokee slaves' food culture might have been disproportionately informed by his own relatively comfortable condition as a body servant, but Perdue also concludes that most slaves had "sufficient food," either by way of their owners or from their own industry (*Slavery* 115). Former bondswoman Chaney Richardson states the case succinctly: "We all had plenty to eat" (Baker and Baker 351). Bibb draws on this idea to highlight Native American humanity and foreground southern, white barbarity.

Toward similar ends, Bibb praises Native American slaveholders for the absence of coercive violence. "They have no overseers to whip or drive them," he claims. As we saw in the discussion of the emergence of the penitentiary in the last chapter, the first half of the nineteenth century ushered in revolutionary measures to move away from corporal punishments and public spectacles to more "humane" forms of discipline such as imprisonment and isolation. Within such a context, acts of whipping came to signify outmoded and barbaric expressions of power, particularly in antislavery literature. Dilating on the ubiquity of such representations, Richard Brodhead writes that antebellum slave narratives "make whipping not just a memorably experienced scene but specifically the scene of initiation into slavery itself" (67). Accordingly, Bibb's account presents this form of brutality more than any other form of punishment, even including several inset pictures portraying the various positions and situations in which slaves are flogged. Just three sentences into the narrative, Bibb intones, "I was brought up in the Counties of Shelby, Henry, Oldham, and Trimble. Or, more correctly speaking, in the above counties, I may safely say, I was *flogged up*; for where I should have received moral, mental, and religious instruction, I received stripes without number" (13). This scene of sadistic "instruction" sets in motion a pattern in which whippings structure Bibb's entire narrated life. As a child he is flogged for attending his duties and flogged for running away (16). Then, as an adult he is "marked from his neck to his heels" with fifty lashes for another escape attempt and then paddled with another dozen or so blows (132). Upon his final parting with his wife, the "gory lash" is used with "hellish vengeance to separate husband and wife" (146). Significantly, Indian slavery is the place where this pattern of violent whipping finally comes to an end. Since Bibb never dramatizes (though he hypothesizes) the beating of a slave in Indian Territory, it would appear that the form of bondage that takes place in the Cherokee Nation West (according to Brodhead's paradigm) is not even "slavery." It does not rule through violent coercion but through love and affection.

The natural consequence of this laxity and leniency is that there is no need for oppressive supervision and regulation. As Bibb contends, "They have no overseers to whip or drive them." But Cherokee slaveholders, particularly the large and prosperous ones like Joe Vann, used overseers like their white counterparts in the American South (Perdue, *Slavery* 97). Their large plantations necessitated the organization and supervision of their slave labor force. Even if there were no "overseers" on Bibb's owner's plantation, they were certainly in use throughout Indian Territory. Bibb ignores or deemphasizes the presence of such figures, however, because they suggest a level of regularity and strictness about Indian slavery that he wants to avoid in order to lambaste white slavery. Indian slavery is meek and mild so that white slavery can be mean and unforgiving.

Bibb takes this narrative of the benignness of Indian slavery to impressive heights. Asserting that if an owner and a slave somehow get into an altercation, "it is as often the case as otherwise, that the slave gets the better of the fight." Bibb suggests that Indian slavery is almost completely maintained by the willful consent of bondspeople, since there are no repercussions for self-defense, resistance, or violence. Indeed, the absence of a "law to punish" further invites the notion that Indian slavery operates without coercion, either physical or juridical. But as my earlier discussion of the proliferation of laws against slaves in the postremoval Cherokee Nation make clear, the legal regulation of bondspeople was an indispensable component of Cherokee slavery. Beyond practical considerations of law, Bibb's depiction of Indian slavery is all the more spectacular because it even lacks spitefulness and resentment. Even after the slave "flogs" his master, that will be "the last of it." Clearly, such representations do not speak to historically specific representations of the nature of Cherokee slavery but to the fictions that accompany a carefully crafted and rhetorically powerful wish. In order for the singular callousness of southern slavery practiced by whites to be underscored, Indian slavery must be free from physical violence and emotional resentment.

Per Frederick Douglass's indictment of slaveholding Christianity in his *Narrative*, the lack of "religious instruction" is a classic indicator of white masters' baseness in the slave narrative. Likewise, Bibb notes that in Cherokee slavery bondspeople have it "on terms of equality." In truth, the missionary presence in the Cherokee Nation East, as mentioned above, did allow for more religious freedom, or "flexibility," for slaves than was possible in the white South. But such freedom did not persist into the Cherokee Nation West. Prohibited from learning to read soon after removal (Naylor, *African Cherokees* 30), slaves would no longer have the means, or the permission, to translate sermons or other documents. And with the slave insurrection of 1842, it seems unlikely that their assembly, religious or otherwise, would have been permitted. According to the testimony of ex-Cherokee bondsman Morris Sheppard, born around 1852, "We never had no church in slavery, and no schooling, and you had better not be caught wid a book in your hand even, so I never did go to church hardly any" (Baker and Baker 381). Of course, Bibb arrived in 1841 and perhaps things were laxer on his plantation, but this certainly would have been the exception moving forward in Cherokee slavery. What seems a more likely reading of the "terms of equality" Bibb notices in the Cherokee Nation West is that they are meant to castigate religious inequality in the South. The editor of Bibb's text, Lucius Matlack, was a Philadelphia minister with staunch antislavery commitments ("Lucius C. Matlack"). One can see the likely influence of Matlack's perspective in the many unflattering scenes of slaveholding Christians. Bibb notes, for example, that the slaves of whites have "no Sabbath schools; no one to read the Bible to them; no one to preach the gospel who is competent to expound the Scripture, except slaveholders" (23–24). But this seems little different from the close and mutually beneficial relationship, as Halliburton and others have pointed out, between white missionaries and Indian slaveholders.

But the point of Bibb's narrative of Indian slavery is not to reveal the entanglements of white missionaries and Cherokee slaveholders but to expose the coldhearted nature of so-called Christian slaveholders. Toward this end, Bibb notes of his previous white owner, Deacon Whitfield: "He looked like a saint—talked like the best of slave holding Christians, and acted at home like the devil" (110). Whitfield, whose name is perhaps an ironic play on the esteemed Methodist evangelist George Whitefield, forces female slaves to "breed" with male slaves, male slaves to whip their own wives, and even asks Bibb to whip other slaves, a task for which Bibb notes he was not "savage enough" (114). With not a little touch of irony, Bibb's depiction of slavery in Indian Territory shows that it is the Cherokees who are "humane" and that it is the deacon who is "savage" enough. The group that had been traditionally disparaged for their ruthlessness, Native Americans, emphasizes the callousness and barbarity of white slaveholders.

In his long list of differences, Bibb saves what appears to be the most important one for last: "Neither do [Native American slaveholders] separate husbands and wives, nor parents and children" (153). That is to say, good slaveholders, being good patriarchs, care for and protect the familial bonds between slaves. Bibb's entire narrative is one that is wholly organized around the will to reunite his family, a "recursive pattern" that sends him back to the perilous slave South three separate times even after he achieves his own individual freedom

(Heglar xxxii). Freedom in the text then is not imagined as individual safety in the North but by familial connection. Accordingly, Bibb recognizes he is a slave by his separation from his mother, just as Harriet Jacobs perceives her position as a slave with the death of her mother. Two pages into Bibb's account he notes that after he was "taken away from [his] mother" that it was "then I first commenced seeing and feeling that I was a wretched slave" (14). This initial rupture of the family unit inevitably extends to Bibb's inability to establish binding relationships with other women under slavery to whites. In chapters 2 and 3, where Bibb outlines his courtship and union with Malinda, he explains the legal impossibility that marriage is in the eyes of southern slavery: "There is no legal marriage among the slaves of the South. . . . A slave marrying according to law, is a thing unknown in the history of American Slavery" (38). Accordingly, soon after he and Malinda marry, Bibb confronts the painful reality that he has no power to protect his wife. When they are confined in the Louisville workhouse, Malinda is taken out of the jail for several days while the slave driver attempts to sexually violate her. Later, Deacon Whitfield sells Bibb to a band of traveling gamblers, effectively terminating his relationship with his wife and daughter. Though Bibb attempts to find information about them when he reaches the North, they are never reunited.

In stark contrast to this grim picture of black family relationships in slavery to whites, Bibb's summary of the practice of Indian slaveholders implies that Bibb's family would have remained intact under them since they neither "separate husbands and wives, nor parents and children." But the historical record suggests quite the opposite. As Theda Perdue writes of enslaved life in the Cherokee Nation: "Rarely did a family remain completely intact" (*Slavery* 111). "Cherokee planters," she in fact maintains, "seem to have made little effort to keep families together" (*Slavery* 110). WPA Indian slave narratives flesh out this truth. In former Cherokee slave Morris Sheppard's description of the activities of an allegedly "good natured and kind" owner, he reveals, "When de [Civil] War come, Old Master seen he was going into trouble, and he sold off most of de slaves. In de second year of de War, he sold my mammy, and my aunt dat was Uncle Joe's wife, and my two brothers, and my little sister" (Baker and Baker 68). Sheppard goes on to note, "Mammy went to a mean old man named Pepper Goodman, and he took her off down de river, and pretty soon Mistress tell me she died 'cause she can't stand de rough treatment" (68). To be clear, the Civil War precipitated even harsher treatment of bondspeople, but even this context does not mitigate the fact that slaves were wrenched from their families. As white slaveholders did, slaveholders from the Five Nations dismantled African American families when it suited their needs, regardless of how it affected bondspeople. Bibb's representation of Cherokee slavery, however, is not concerned with such inconvenient truths; rather, his focus is reproaching the cruelties of white slaveholders. Getting to the heart of Bibb's narrative project, Bibb's curious depiction of Indian slavery elides the harsh realities of Cherokee slavery in order to expose the degradations of white slavery.

The neat and almost perfect opposition of the two forms of slavery here suggests that Bibb's re-membering is influenced by what Michael Awkward calls "strategic nostalgia" or the romanticized remembering of past events in a way that highlights the ills of the present. Bibb indicts the evils of white bondage through an almost perverse celebration of Cherokee slavery. *Life and Adventures* paradoxically critiques (white) slavery by defending (Native American) slavery; it engenders sympathy for African American bondspeople to whites by ignoring the plight of African American bondspeople to Native Americans. The text thus achieves the humanizing and protesting aims of antislavery by rationalizing and idealizing the bondage of human beings.

An examination of African American political activist Martin Delany's antebellum novel *Blake; or, the Huts of America* reveals a similar dilution of black suffering in the context of Indian slavery in order to highlight black enslavement to whites. Published serially, but sporadically, from 1859 to 1862, *Blake* dramatizes the peregrinations of Henricus Blacus (Blake), a free-born Cuban, throughout the Western hemisphere as he rallies support for a transnational conspiracy against slavery. The text has often been recognized for its challenge to US-based models of black identity and revolution,[7] but its descriptions of and allusions to Indian Territory further destabilize the locations of and fault lines in black nationhood. In the chapter "Advent among the Indians" Blake travels to the "Indian Nation" in Arkansas and visits the Choctaw chief, Mr. Culver, to request his support for the impending rebellion but is dismayed when he discovers that Culver is a slaveholder. As a result, Culver must give account for Native Americans' participation in chattel slavery, recalling William Lloyd Garrison's exchange with Elias Boudinot in 1832. As in that encounter, the novel imagines southeastern Native American slavery as an essentially harmless, if not utopic, form of bondage, again displacing the abusiveness and dehumanization of Indian slavery onto slavery as practiced by whites. These differences are made clear when Blake chastises the chief for holding slaves, and a white male slaveholder, Dr. Donald, perceives Blake's critique as a form of impudence, calling him a "nigger." The Choctaw chief calmly observes: "'Now you see,' said Mr. Culver as the Doctor left the room, 'the difference between a white man and Indian holding slaves. Indian work side by side with black man, eat with him, drink with him, rest with him and both lay down in shade together; white man even won't let you talk! In our Nation Indian and black all marry together'" (87).

Like Bibb's depictions of Indian slavery, Delany's invocation of Choctaw bondage ignores the separations in labor, lodging, and daily social intercourse in Native American slavery in order to castigate the hierarchical divisions between the ruling and enslaved class in white, chattel slavery. Anticipating Dr. Flint's disdain of Linda Brent's "insolence" in *Incidents*, Dr. Donald is the epitome of the southern male slaveholder who derives his authority from the subjection and silencing of African American bondspeople. Refusing to countenance Blake's reproof, Dr. Donald briskly retorts: "'We have had enough of that!' with a tone of threatening authority" (85). But while white American slaveholders demand the racial subordination of African Americans, Native American slaveholders simply desire their cooperative labor. Thus, as opposed to theorizing the problem of slavery as a structural issue that emerges from the labor exploitation of one class of people by another, the passage suggests that white male egomania is actually the real root of slavery. Absent of these features, black bondage is actually quite mild and manageable. Wanting to suggest a coalition between enslaved blacks in the American South and Cuba with removed Native Americans in Arkansas, Delany sacrifices not only historical specificity but the real legacy of African American exclusion and pain in Indian Territory. Likely influenced by the narrative of benign Indian slavery of the early 1830s and perhaps even Bibb's narrative, *Blake* fashions Native American slavery as an informal labor agreement between African Americans and Native Americans, devoid of aggression, hierarchy, or exploitation. As Culver maintains, "Indian and black all marry together." To be sure, this is a narrative that is reflected in WPA accounts, as remembered by former Creek slave John Harrison, "Mother has told me that before the [Civil] War, that the people as a whole were living comfortably and satisfied. The Indians, Creek Indians, has intermarried with the white and colored, and [the white and colored] became citizens of the tribe, and that they too, were satisfied with the full-blood in this new land of theirs" (Minges 86). Across the Five Nations, however, intermarriage was discouraged and often illegal, particularly in the postremoval era (Perdue, *Slavery* 49; Joy 6). Tiya Miles's indispensable *Ties That Bind* actually chronicles the experience of an enslaved black woman, Doll, and Cherokee partner, Shoe Boots, who were not legally allowed to marry, thereby sentencing some of their children to a life of slavery and fugitivity. Delany's representation of Choctaw slavery must ignore the complications arising from such illicit unions because his objective is to indict white slavery and racism, not Indian slavery.

The ultimate proof of this elision is that Blake and Culver's exchange (like Garrison and Boudinot's) conspicuously omits the voices of African American slaves. The last sentence of the chapter confesses: "[Blake] left the settlement with the regrets of the people, being the only instance in which his seclusions were held with the master instead of the slave" (87), a statement that reads as an eerie gloss of Bibb's depiction (or lack thereof) of slavery in Indian Territory. Like Blake, Bibb appears to hold his "seclusions" with the master instead of the slave in Indian Territory, and this should give us reason to pause, not only because of the motivations it reveals for his intimate identification with his master but the motivations it reveals for his potential disidentification with other bondspeople. The underlying implication is as clear as it is disturbing: Indian slavery is so mild that even if the slaves were allowed to speak, they would not have much to say in the way of critique or objection. Blake can thus achieve the seemingly impossible feat of orchestrating a rebellion against slaveholders with the help of slaveholders because, quite impossibly, Native American slavery is not really slavery at all. When the time comes to overthrow black domination in the Western hemisphere, Chief Culver and other Choctaw slaveholders will join with their black bondspeople to attack the "common foe": white slaveholders. Such a fantasy is possible because Indian slavery is only so in name, not in reality.

This omission is all the more striking for elsewhere when Bibb is thrust among the "quantity," he is sure to document the conditions of his fellow slaves and even provides fairly extensive descriptions of white and black inmates' squalid food, excessive labor, and otherwise deplorable conditions in the Louisville workhouse. He even mentions the strong bond he develops with white prisoners because they sympathize with his condition, and they help him learn to read and write, skills that undoubtedly assist his future flights north (95). But since they are white prisoners who feel sympathy toward the downtrodden slave, Bibb can more easily assimilate their voices into his slave narrative. Black slaves of Native Americans, on the other hand, threaten to detract attention from chattel slavery in the South and expose Native American brutality; they would show how the problem of slavery is not just a racial (white) and geographic one (South) but a problem that could exist in other places and in other contexts, thereby troubling the binary of wicked southern whites and dispossessed black slaves. If slavery is in multiple places with different captors, the narrative pattern of "southern bondage" and "northern freedom" does not have complete explanatory and political power.

Put differently, the story of Cherokee slavery was too messy and inconvenient for the abolitionist-sponsored slave narrative to handle. As a result, slavery in Indian Territory had to be romanticized and diluted, rendering the voices of actual Native American slaves mute. Produced in the context of exposing black suffering to whites, illustrations of Indian slavery could not also accurately render African American affliction to the Cherokee.

Disparaging Cherokee Slaveholders; Praising Indian Captives

But the abolitionist and polemical historical context of Bibb's narrative did allow for other, less flattering representations of Native American slaveholders that still buttressed Bibb's critiques of slavery and claims to individual respectability. For even if Native American slaveholders were "mild," this is not to say they were not "wild." Though regarded by mainstream culture as morally superior to African Americans, Native Americans were understood as culturally inferior to whites. This chain of cultural and racial being is cogently expressed by an 1854 passage from the proslavery *Southern Quarterly Review*: "How well is the vigilant, active, white man, contrasted with the drowsy, slothful black man, while the copper-coloured race holds the intermediate ground between them" (D. J. M. 74). This image of the "drowsy, slothful black man" is an image that Bibb must deny if he is to convince readers that he is, in fact, industrious and smart. He contests this disparaging representation by relying on what might have been considered an equally damming one: a picture of "savage" Natives.

Midway through his remembering of his time in Indian Territory, Bibb explicitly mocks southeastern Native American's achievement of civilization, calling them the "various half civilized tribes" (158). He avers: "Their hands were almost invariably filled with bows and arrows, tomahawks, guns, butcher knives, and all the various implements of death which are used by them" (158). In doing so, he places his heel on the necks of the precariously positioned Native Americans in order to gain a higher perch near the "vigilant, active, white man." Bibb's critique of the "half civilized" Cherokees allows him to negotiate relationships with southern and northern American models of civilization. As Crispin Sartwell explains of the creation of the "civilized" white subject under slavery, "The master was civilized, Christian, and so forth precisely in relation to the slave" (38). In an ironic inversion of this paradigm, Bibb is civilized, Christian, and literate in comparison to the supposed barbarity of his Native American master. He presents the Cherokees as "slothful and lazy" in order to better his own representation as active and vigorous.

Toward the end of advancing this self-representation, Bibb uses pejorative and racist representations of Native Americans to bolster his self-representation, painting them as illiterate, drunk, and uncultivated. Literally in the next paragraph after his high praise for the mildness of Cherokee slavery, Bibb tears into a stereotypical rant against how undomesticated the southeastern Native Americans were. He observes: "A majority of the Indians were uneducated, and still followed up their old heathen traditional notions" (153). Bibb capitalizes on the presumed uncouthness of American Indians in order to construct an image of himself as learned and rational. As the benevolence of Indian slavery highlighted the barbarity of white slavery, so the riotous behavior of the Cherokee could underscore Bibb's sensible disposition. Perhaps no better example of this studied contrast can be found than his rendition of an "Indian frolic." He remembers: "Their dress for the dance was most generally a great bunch of bird feathers, coon tails, or something of the kind stuck in their heads, and a great many shells tied about their legs to rattle while dancing. Their manner of dancing is taking hold of each others [*sic*] hands and forming a ring around the large fire in the centre, and go stomping around it until they would get drunk or their heads would get to swimming, and they would go off and drink, and another set come on. Such were some of the practices indulged in by these Indian slaveholders" (154). Eschewing the actual complexity of Native American and Cherokee dance that researchers like William G. Speck and Leonard Broom have identified,[8] Bibb's description of Cherokee dance reduces it to stereotypical emblems of Indian difference: bird feathers, coon tails, and intoxication. On the one hand, Bibb's denigration of the ruling caste is unremarkable within the tradition of the slave narrative. Like so many other slave narrators, he upbraids his master's class for vulgar and excessive behavior. On the other hand, this lambaste also intersects with the well-known tradition of "Indian hating" found in Indian captivity narratives and other nineteenth-century cultural productions.[9] Bibb uses such Indian hating to advance his positive self-presentation, turning Indian hating into respectable self-making. His invocation of the word "practices" calls to mind the ethnographic and often culturally chauvinistic reports that marked Native Americans as degenerate, irrational, and violent. Like Francis Parkman's descriptions of Native American behavior and lifestyle in his classic antebellum travelogue, *The Oregon Trail*, Bibb's depictions of alleged Native American life and habits consolidate a picture of himself as objective and sophisticated. To say that his language is ethnographic here is more than metaphorical, since as a geopolitically distinct space from the United States, Bibb was indeed mapping foreign territory. In his identification and labeling of various Native American "manners" and "practices," he is essentially a competent white writing subject, taking on the voice of the seasoned and erudite observer. Bibb assumes the language not just of white observer but of colonial settler. Bibb's remarks on the condition of one group of Native Americans he encounters in Indian Territory makes this explicitly clear: "Not one could talk or understand a word of the English language" (156). In contradistinction to the illiterate and incomprehensible Natives, Bibb is a competent user of the English language, both as evinced in his grammatically correct descriptions of Native American dance as well as in his condescending remarks about their crude behavior. While Bibb uses language to form pointed descriptions of his experience, these untutored Indians cannot even formulate or comprehend a "word" of English. Their ignorance of the "word" and Bibb's careful manipulation of it confirms his intelligence and authority. As we will see later in the case of Robert Adams's narrative, the ability to speak English fluently was a standard way in which "civilization" and "barbarism" were identified in the Barbary captivity narrative as well. Here, the illiterate Native Americans, like the "barbaric" Moors in North Africa, clarify Bibb's position as a rational, Western subject in the midst of stomping and screaming "savages."

Interestingly, Bibb's attribution of these "practices" to "Indian slaveholders" is doubtful since Native American slaveholders were a highly Anglicized group. As ethnologists of Cherokee dance and rituals Frank G. Speck and Leonoard Broom have noted, "From the beginning of missionary contact early in the nineteenth until the present, both native and white religious workers among the Cherokee have regarded the dances as competitive systems and treated them as curious *practices of ignorant savages* to be derided, as symptoms of idolatrous behavior to be challenged, or a as a system of decadent revelry and a focus of infection for the forces of sin equated with the forces of intemperance" (emphasis added, 6). Bibb's account ignores such complexities, however, and instead freezes Cherokee people in time and arrests them in this tableau; he erases all difference, even though his own ethnographic perspective actually mimics those of many of the converted Cherokee elite. Less interested in historical specificity or nuance, Bibb is more concerned with presenting stock portrayals of Indians that buttress his favorable self-presentation. In the words of Kathryn Shanley, these are "The Indians America Loves to Love and Read." Unlike the more sensitive portrayals of Native American dance that appear in African American narratives of slavery to Natives, complete with the indigenous names and corresponding meaning of each dance,[10] Bibb's rendition of the "frolic" is merely a repackaging of what white, American audiences always and already knew about Indians: they are enigmatic, atavistic, and infantile people. Such a narrative does not require the voice or authentic description of Native Americans. In this way, Bibb's sensational picture of the Cherokee participates in the displacement and reappropriation of Native American identities consistent with the literary removals of the first half of the nineteenth century. Published in 1849, over a decade after the tragic Trail of Tears, *Life and Adventures* speaks in the absence of southeastern Native American voices and populations, placing Bibb in the position of the privileged white observer of obscure, "heathen" behavior.

As suggested by their "frolic," a word coded to suggest primitive debauchery, Bibb furthers this critique, and thus his own favorable self-presentation, by emphasizing the fact that these Native American slaveholders drink intemperately. The temperance movement was one of the largest and most influential movements in the antebellum era, a concerted campaign against what W. J. Rorabaugh has called the "veritable national binge" of the late eighteenth and early nineteenth centuries (ix). Bibb, relying on his Christian, northern audience's aversion to excessive drink, is sure to include the "drunk" dancing of his Native American captors as a way of underscoring their immorality and depravity. Giving this discussion its own paragraph, he notes that it is a "practice" that is more reprehensible than any another Native American habit. "But the most degrading practice of all," Bibb informs his readers, "was the use of intoxicating drinks, which were used to a great excess by all that attended these stump dances" (153–54). He continues, "At almost all of these fires there was some one [*sic*] with rum to sell" (154). Native Americans have long been unfairly associated with the abuse of alcohol and struggled with the infusion of alcohol into their communities, as the work of Peter C. Mancall has shown, but Bibb takes advantage of these unfortunate historical narratives to frame his own decency and temperance. In the midst of drunken "heathens," he is an exemplar of sobriety and integrity.

Relying on the fiction of the supposed childlike innocence of American Natives, on the other hand, Methodist itinerant preacher John Marrant uses his captivity among the Cherokees to demonstrate his spiritual maturity and readiness for the ministry. As recorded in his 1785 account, *The Lord's Wonderful Dealings with John Marrant*, the precocious Marrant wanders from his childhood home during a period of prolonged fasting and spiritual devotion. In the process, he encounters, and is eventually abducted by, a group of Cherokees living in the South Carolina "wilderness" (81). As opposed to dying at the hands of his abductors, Marrant actually learns their language and converts his captors, even the incredulous "king" of the tribe. He notes: "A great change took place among the people; the king's house became God's house. . . . The king would take off his golden ornaments; his chain and bracelets like a child, if I objected to them, and lay them aside. Here I learnt to speak their tongue in the highest stile" (87). Marrant's comments rehearse the narrative of Native American naïveté that structures Bibb's disparaging representations of the Cherokees. He is the composed, adult spiritual adviser of the disrobing and presumably vulnerable Cherokee leader. What is more, his depiction of the Cherokees' willingness to accept Christianity underscores his aptness for evangelism. Marrant's account was originally delivered as the ordination sermon that would authorize his induction into the countess of Huntingdon's evangelical sect and thus help him to become "a major missionary voice between England, Nova Scotia, and Boston" (May 557). Speaking in and possessing the Indian "tongue," a graphic image of the implicit violence suggested by Native American conversion, Marrant is authorized to witness to foreign peoples through his representation of his Cherokee captivity. While Bibb uses his mastery of the English "word" to mark his cultural authority, Marrant uses his appropriation of the Native "tongue" to articulate his spiritual power, speaking in a narrative voice "marked not by race, but by piety" (Weyler 43). Yet, if Marrant constructs his spiritual identity by way of his closeness to and eventual conversion of his Cherokee captors, Bibb establishes his cultural authority by way of his strict differentiation from his captors. The Cherokees in Indian Territory are "heathens" with superstitious "practices," and Bibb is an aloof and rational observer. While Marrant earns admiration from religious authorities (and becomes a religious leader) for his intimacy with the Cherokees, Bibb earns respectability for his studied difference from them.

Leaving the Territory

The resonance of these representations is suggested by the fact that even when Bibb leaves Indian Territory,[11] abduction by "savage" Native Americans is still symbolically useful in the narrative. As noted earlier, Bibb achieves individual freedom relatively early in the narrative, making the rescue of his family the central drama of the narrative (Heglar xxxii). The narrative, therefore, not only depends on the logic of the abolitionist refrain, "Am I Not a Man and a Brother?" but also its connected query, "Am I Not a Husband and a Father?" Relying on the poetics of the Indian captivity narrative, the account frames Bibb as a praiseworthy father and devoted husband bent on reuniting his fractured family.

Interestingly, Bibb's last invocation of Cherokee slavery occurs well after his narration of his time in Indian Territory. Never one to suffer slaveholders for long, Native American or otherwise, Bibb sets out on his way north early the next day after his Cherokee owner, who he described as "sickly" from the start, conveniently dies (155).[12] Before leaving the territory, however, he notices three white men on horseback who follow closely behind. Once he passes into the slave state of Missouri, he again notes the men's approach and begins to suspect that they are slave catchers. Within Indian Territory, such patrols for Cherokee slaves were common in the early 1840s as the Cherokee Nation's leadership attempted to avert the possibility of slave escape and resistance amid the chaos of the resettlement period (Perdue, *Slavery* 87). Apparently suspecting that these men were sent to carry him back to the Cherokee Nation or to the slaveholding South, he steals a horse in order to create some distance between himself and the strangers. In the following passage, Bibb justifies his theft of the horse by a curious appeal to the importance of family in the context of Indian captivity. "But I ask," he wonders, "if a white man had been captured by the Cherokee Indians and carried away from his family for life into slavery, and could see a chance to get back to his family; should the Indians pursue him with a determination to take him back or take his life, would it be a crime for a poor fugitive, whose life, liberty and future happiness were all at stake, to mount any man's horse by the way side, and ride him without asking any questions, to effect his escape? . . . Such an act committed by a white man under the same circumstances would not only be pronounced proper, but praiseworthy" (163).[13] Like Harriet Jacobs's confession of her illicit relationship with Mr. Sands, Bibb is here faced with explaining questionable, even criminal, behavior that might warp his image in the eyes of his white, middle-class audience. However, as a white captive of Indians—whose status as "civilized" is already suspect—his theft is "proper" and even "praiseworthy." In comparing his act to that of a "praiseworthy" white Indian captive, Bibb effectively resists the derogatory readings that attend his own picaresque characterization. It is a way of resolving what Raymond Hedin calls the "dilemma" of the picaro, "to keep himself clearly on the side of morality while depicting actions often hardly moral at all" (636). In this way, his theft proves his manliness; he is doing what any "white man" separated from his family would do. Equally important, coming immediately after his section on Indian slavery, Bibb actually extends the reading of himself as Indian captive into the "slave narrative" portion of his account. Inasmuch as Missouri is a slave state, it is bound by the same rules of narration governing most antebellum slave narratives. But as a kind of textual and cultural capital, his literal Indian slavery allows him to shape himself literarily and authoritatively according to the rules governing Indian captivity, even in Missouri.

In invoking the threat of slavery to Cherokee Indians, Bibb leans on a model of respectable and aggressive (male) identity found throughout the Indian captivity narrative tradition. Indian captives like John Williams, Daniel Boone, and even the murderous female captive Hannah Dustan had access to a decidedly violent model of behavior under the duress of Indian captivity. Bibb's question to his audience—"if a white man had been captured . . .?"—is an implicit recognition of this narrative and its consequent privileges. Finding the proper and even "praiseworthy" way to be bound, Bibb can justify his theft of the horse and contradict the slanderous representations that compose him as a thief and criminal.

In his justification of horse stealing, Bibb does more than rationalize his questionable means of escape. If we recall, what defined slaves was not only their ownership by another but their inability to own anything else, even and especially themselves. But inasmuch as the crime of theft presumes that the offender can own their transgression, theft problematizes the bondsperson's status as a nonowner and inert being. Elsewhere, the narrative confirms how stealing and possession threaten to unmake slaves. When Bibb half-jokingly tells his readers that he could not have "stolen" a jackass because both he and the donkey were property, he makes this idea clear. There should be, Bibb surmises, "no more sin committed in this than if one jackass rode off another" (122). Similarly, when he and his compatriots are caught and interrogated during an attempted escape, he tells his fellow rebels to "own nothing," implying that the renunciation of all property (even thoughts) is fundamental to being a proper slave.[14] And in the scene directly following his theft of the horse, Bibb feigns legal freedom through his talk of purchasing property, specifically "buying land, stock and village property, and contrasting it with the same kind of property in Ohio" (164). According to Bibb's narrative, for a slave to possess anything besides the vice and stupidity that were associated with him is to disrupt his definition as a slave and forge a tentative freedom.[15] If only momentarily and covertly, to steal is to resist the rules and logic of bondage and to assume a disobedient subject position. In a rough play on Richard III's famous lament, we might say that Bibb gains his kingdom for a horse, for horse stealing threatens to unmake Bibb as a slave and into a free man.

Hence, as an Indian captive, Bibb is authorized to protect his family in ways that slavery insistently denied. Hortense Spillers asserts in her foundational "Mama's Baby, Papa's Maybe" that "legal enslavement removed the African-American male not so much from sight as from *mimetic* view as a partner in the prevailing social fiction of the Father's name, the Father's law" (84–85). In other words, male slaves could not participate in the social fiction of white masculinity, due to both their symbolic removals from the (often white) father's genealogy and their literal prohibitions from protecting and providing for their families. As Bibb notes generally, "It is almost impossible for slaves to give account of their male parentage," and as he explains of his own white father in particular, "I have no personal knowledge of him at all, for he died before my recollection" (14). However, under the same duress as a white man "captured by the Cherokee Indians," Bibb is authorized to behave like the "white father" he never knew. He recollects the adult masculinity that he cannot literally remember, thus giving an "account of his male parentage" by behaving like the father he never had. The restoration of family is precisely what Bibb's invocation of Indian slavery attempts to achieve. What would otherwise have been considered a "crime," the retrieval of "property" from southern slaveholders, is now seen as praiseworthy. Bibb restores the humanity to his family and the need to "get back" to them through the figure of the relentless, resourceful, and aggressive male Indian captive.

Even so, Bibb's self-presentation as powerful masculine savior is dependent on a depiction, for the most part, of othered Native Americans. As Michelle Burnham notes, sympathy for white captives' suffering often worked to elide the larger historical displacements of Native captors perpetrated by the captive group's ruling authorities (4). If we recall, Bibb is sold into Indian Territory in

1841, just two years after the cataclysmic removal of the Cherokees from their eastern homelands from 1838 to 1839. African Americans, of course, did not (nor could they) legislate or execute the removal of southeastern Indians from the East, but Bibb's representation of them in his text certainly reinforces the notion of unmotivated Indian aggression. Similar to how his descriptions of poor and uneducated white prisoners worked as negative examples of the upright and learned man he wished to be seen as, the conventions of Indian captivity narratives work here to displace Indian subjects and resituate Bibb as a member of civilized society, placing him within the "prevailing social fiction" of the father's name and law. In the process, Bibb passes yet again, but this time as a "white man captured by the Indians" on his way to a masculinity and respectability that is largely dependent on, but exclusive of, the Cherokees.

"Hierarchies of Servitude"

If only negatively, Bibb's rendition of black slavery in Indian Territory recalls Hammon's highly mediated narrative of Caribbean and Atlantic captivity in the eighteenth century. Compelled to tell a story of Indian captivity and Cuban imprisonment, Hammon could not reveal a story of white New England slavery. In a reverse of this situation, Bibb is committed to a narrative of white southern slavery, so he cannot express many of the hardships of Cherokee bondage (or slave incarceration, for that matter). The historically specific competition between what Robert Desrochers Jr. calls "hierarchies of servitude" (159) demands that some captivities fall to the wayside while others move to center stage. The context of radical and polemical abolitionism made it difficult for any other narrative of compulsion to be heard, unless it was in the services of aggressively critiquing white southern slavery. Bibb's Cherokee slavery was thus a "mild" slavery so that the barbarity of slavery as practiced by whites could be magnified. In doing so, his representations of Indian slavery helped to critique white slavery and engender sympathy for African American slaves to whites, even as it necessarily obscured the suffering of black slaves to Native Americans.

If "Allen" could have told his own story of Cherokee bondage, perhaps he would tell one closer to the buried story of brutality and mistreatment under Indian slavery I attempt to reconstruct here. Or perhaps not. We know almost nothing about what specifically motivated Allen to flee Indian Territory and what slavery in the Cherokee Nation West meant to him. What we know for sure is that the telling of his story of black bondage and Cherokee slavery in particular would have been mediated by the histories that governed that form of bondage but also by the narratives that surrounded and infused black's slavery to whites as well, which was the dominant discourse on slavery at the time.

Read in this light, Bibb's narratives of slavery reveal the difficulties of deciphering and identifying intersecting accounts of bondage. It suggests that we have to be mindful of the ways that seemingly parallel or complementary accounts of oppression can cancel each other out. Bound inside of the institutional power of antislavery, more specifically, alternative formations and fictions of bondage produce ambiguous and unexpected meanings.

II
BOUND IN FREEDOM

4
Bound Children, Benevolent Caretakers, and Disabling Service
Indentured Servitude in Harriet Wilson's *Our Nig*

> Hard labor and unkindness was too much for me; in three months, my health and strength were gone. I often looked at my employers, and thought to myself, is this your religion? I did not wonder that the girl who had lived there previous to myself, went home to die. . . . I was a poor stranger, but fourteen years of age, imposed upon by these good people; but I must leave them. In the year 1814, they sent me to Gloucester in their chaise. I found my poor mother in bad health, and I was sick also; but, by the mercy of God, and the attention and skill of Dr. Dale, and the kindness of friends, I was restored, so that in a few months, I was able again to go to work, although my side afflicted me, which I attributed to overworking myself.
>
> Nancy Prince, *A Narrative of the Life and Travels of Mrs. Nancy Prince*, 11–12

Railing with as much invective as any ex-slave narrator ever used to denounce slavery, African American political activist Maria Stewart proclaimed in an 1832 speech: "Tell us no more of southern slavery; for with few exceptions, although I may be very erroneous in my opinion, yet I consider [living as a servant] but little better than that" (45). Delivered in Boston's Franklin Hall, the usual meeting place for the New England Anti-Slavery Society, Stewart's statement represents a predictable, but nonetheless provocative, departure from the concerns that we might typically think animated black cultural production in the antebellum era. Most northern states, having implemented several laws for the gradual emancipation of bondspeople in the 1800s, no longer countenanced legal enslavement by the late 1820s (Berlin 104). In its place, various forms of domestic and menial labor came to dominate allegedly free black life, making up as much as 87 percent of black occupations, for instance, in New York City, 68 percent in Boston, and similarly high numbers in other northeastern cities (Litwack 155; Horton and Horton xiv, 10). This is why in 1832—just one year after Nat Turner's bloody slave insurrection, the founding of William Lloyd Garrison's radical abolitionist periodical the *Liberator*, and the creation of the American Anti-Slavery Society—Stewart could challenge the explanatory power and historical relevance of slavery, even as it was poised to dominate national consciousness for the next three decades. In the vitriolic style of her mentor and fellow Bostonian, David Walker, Stewart eschewed the complacency that she imagined characterized newly freed blacks for whom such labor had paradoxically become the definition of freedom. In 1852, African American emigrationist and newspaperman Martin Delany would similarly decry that free northern blacks were too eager to "seek positions, such as servants, waiting maids, coachmen, nurses, cooks in gentlemens' kitchen, or such like occupations, when they can gain a livelihood at something more respectable" (sec. XXIII). As Xiomara Santamarina has pointed out, such caustic reproofs obscure the fact that these humble employments were typically the only kind of work that blacks were allowed to do. Be that as it may, for Stewart, Delany, and many other black leaders, it is clear that the proper framework for understanding African American struggle throughout much of the antebellum North was not just antislavery but antiservitude.

One particular form of service that structured African American lives, and especially the lives of African American children, was pauper apprenticeship. A holdover from Elizabethan poor laws, the system also known as "binding out" emerged from the practice of relocating orphaned, mistreated, and even wayward children to more financially sound and socially stable families, thereby absolving the town of the responsibility for their food, clothing, shelter, and occupational training (Hindle and Herndon 19–20). In turn, charges were required to perform whatever labor their caretakers desired, usually until the age of eighteen for girls and twenty-one for boys (Hernodon and Murray 17). For African American children, whose second-class child status was further compounded by their blackness and poverty, this system could be especially harsh. While white boys were most likely to succeed in pauper apprenticeship, "girls of color benefited the least from the system, exiting indenture with the least literacy training and few work skills" (Herndon and Murray 16). Not only were African American children more likely to leave their host families ill-prepared for free life, they were also more likely to leave it later. Black boys and girls in colonial Maryland and Virginia, for instance, were sometimes indentured until the age of thirty-one, an unprecedented age for white children of either sex (Herndon and Murray 17). Furthermore, once whites evacuated the system of pauper apprenticeship and slavery ended, disproportionate numbers of free black children were thrust into the system as a way of controlling them and exploiting their labor, as was the case in Baltimore (Whitman 57). Though pauper apprenticeship undoubtedly offered some level of protection against hunger and neglect, it could simultaneously function as "a continuation of the exploitation of slavery" (Youcha 20).

The poster child for this truth might well be found in what is often regarded as the first novel published by a black person in the United States, Harriet Wilson's *Our Nig*. Drawing heavily from the details of Wilson's own life, the story dramatizes the abandonment of a biracial child named Frado by her destitute mother and the girl's subsequent "binding out" to a northern, white, middle-class family, the Bellmonts. Arriving as a healthy and even rambunctious girl, Frado's health is compromised through a relentless regimen of menial labor and physical abuse. After her indenture, moreover, marriage to and desertion by a counterfeit fugitive slave compel Frado to relinquish their child to a neighboring white family, an uncomfortable reprisal of her own abandonment by her mother in the novel's opening chapters. Suggesting Wilson's own physical state at the time of the text's production, the work's preface explains that Frado is "disabled by failing health" and has authored *Our Nig* as a means of providing for herself and child "without extinguishing this feeble life" (3).

Since its recovery by Henry Louis Gates Jr. in 1983, after more than one hundred years of neglect, *Our Nig* has been read in any number of thought-provoking ways, illuminating its indebtedness to, and rethinking of, sentimental novels, slave narratives, Indian captivity narratives, children's writing, adoption literature, and white indentured servant narratives.[1] But as my summary of the text suggests, the narrative that undergirds many, if not all, of these interpretations is the account of Frado's development of an immobilizing and chronic illness, a story of "failing health" in the voice of the preface. As potentially "the first example of black autopathography" (James and Wu 7), *Our Nig* uses sickness to underscore the effects of Frado's exploitative labor and caustic treatment as a child servant. As in the excerpt from Nancy Prince's narrative that begins this chapter, illness is the dye that makes visible racism's unremarked presence in the North, what Prince calls "hard labor" and "unkindness." Combining an emphasis on infirmity with emerging ideas about children's fragility and divinity, Wilson shows how the kind of bondage experienced by Frado transformed a spirited black child into a vulnerable adult "invalid."

These entangled discourses of dependency work together to voice what I perceive to be *Our Nig*'s largely self-conscious disability claim. Exposing and supplementing a social world that unevenly and ineffectively provided for the care of several and overlapping vulnerable populations—people with disabilities, African Americans, children, females, and the poor—*Our Nig* recruits the vocabulary of illness and specifically invalidism to make a case for Wilson's entitlement to financial support and emotional sympathy. Reflecting what Rosemarie

Garland Thomson calls a compensatory model of disability (23), illness is constructed here as a catastrophe that can only be alleviated by benevolent intervention. At the same time, *Our Nig* also claims disability in its iconoclastic and redemptive representation of infirm figures, recasting seemingly "defective citizens" (Davidson, Siebers, and Feal 498) as central to a sensitive and healthy society. Rejecting "the ideology of ability" in which infirmity and disability are imagined as kinds of death (Siebers 10–11), Wilson reclaims the vitality and integrity of people with stigmatized bodily differences, what Thomson calls an accommodation model (106–7). As such, *Our Nig* is a memorial to how fictions of disability expose African American children's suffering and servitude in the antebellum North but also to how suffering in African American fictions matters to understanding the meanings of disability.

But if the miseries of servitude inspired blacks to claim disability, albeit in varied and even contradictory ways, it also allowed middle-class families to claim respectability. Wilson's depiction of Frado's arrival on the Bellmont doorsteps suggests that the service this black child will perform will enable them to perform middle-class, New England compassion while also benefiting from the uncompensated labor of an abandoned minor. Indeed, when understood as "early America's first version of foster care," as Geraldine Youcha has suggested (20), child indentured servitude provides a window into how municipalities and town officials shored up their sense of themselves as efficient and humane through their "binding out" of dependent children. As the forerunner of adoption, which would not become legal until the 1850s, pauper apprenticeship participated in the nineteenth century's efforts to temper punishments and more humanely care for the defenseless. *Our Nig* deepens our understanding of the paradoxical way in which compelled service not only broke black families and lives but also brokered white middle-class families' relationships to respectability, efficiency, and family.

Binding Out Black Children

As the most extensive account of African American indentured servitude in the antebellum era, *Our Nig* speaks on behalf of probably thousands of African American children who were "bound out" during the nineteenth century. Given the compromised economic and social status of indigent African American children, it is not surprising that statements about their experiences of, and feelings about, indenture have not received sustained attention. Nonetheless, a handful of black women's narratives from the antebellum era suggest the pervasiveness and sometimes the painfulness of this system.

The spiritual autobiographies collected in William L. Andrews's *Sisters of the*

Spirit suggest the wide influence and nature of child indentured servitude in African American women's life writing. Despite being a tale of a free-born black, the spiritual autobiography of Jarena Lee, *The Life and Religious Experience of Jarena Lee*, begins with a declaration of childhood dependency and potential captivity: "I was born February 11, 1783, at Cape May, state of New Jersey. At the age of seven years, I was parted from my parents, and went to live as a servant maid, with a Mr. Sharp" (27). Likewise, the narrative of Zilpha Elaw's spiritual conversion, *Memoirs of the Life, Religious Experience, Ministerial Travels and Labors of Mrs. Zilpha Elaw*, begins by explaining that after her mother died, "my father, having placed my younger sister under the care of her aunt, then consigned me to the care of Pierson and Rebecca Mitchel, with whom I remained until I attained the age of eighteen" (53). Both Elaw and Lee provide skeletal terms with which to flesh out their experiences; Lee is a "servant maid" and Elaw is "consigned" to the services of other adults. While Elaw explains that her mother died, Lee just tells us that she was "parted from [her] parents," leaving the reader to speculate about the reasons for their separation. As spiritual autobiographies, and not records of material histories, the overarching theological imperative of these texts prevent them from providing any substantial commentary on the motivations and meanings of apprenticeship or how it might have compared to slavery. Instead, they provide fairly conventional narratives of spiritual conversion (as is the case with Lee)—a reprobate heart (27), sin sickness (28), and thoughts of suicide (28, 30)—but not any significant explication of the conditions of physical servitude. Like the "servanthood" to General Winslow that frames Hammon's 1760 account, their references to unfreedom are perhaps purposely ambiguous in order to highlight more emphatically the kind of bondage that is really at stake in these stories: the servitude of people to sin, not of children to adults.

Julia Foote's *A Brand Plucked from the Fire* provides a slightly more revelatory depiction of a black child's indenture. Like those of Elaw and Lee, the narrative begins with a statement announcing an arrangement whereby the young child will become the ward of another family: "When I was ten years of age," Foote remembers, "I was sent to live in the country with a family by the name of Prime. They had no children, and soon became quite fond of me. I really think Mrs. Prime loved me" (18). However, this favorable impression quickly gives way to a more menacing reality. After failing to find baked goods in the attic, Foote is "whipped with a rawhide," an unfortunate rehearsal of the many scenes in which Frado is whipped in *Our Nig* with a rawhide by her mistress, Mrs. Bellmont. Unlike Frado, however, Foote still has the luxury of returning to her biological family, which she promptly does: "It was a long, lonely road, through the woods; every sound frightened me, and made me run for fear someone was after me" (176). When the Primes come to reclaim Foote from her biological parents, they are asked to explain the reason for the child's severe beating, but she is, tellingly, returned to the Primes for another year. What is more, this decision is made, as Foote is sure to point out, "very much against my will" (176). Though Foote has the ability to declare her displeasure with her new living arrangements, she has little power to effect any changes in them.

The probable ur-text of free African American children's displacements and dislocations from their biological homes is the text that opens this chapter, Nancy Gardner Prince's *Narrative of the Life and Travels*. Typically read through the lens of transnationalism for its descriptions of Prince's journeys to Jamaica and Russia, the narrative's first twenty pages are also an invaluable record of the lives of free black children in the antebellum North.[2] According to the text, Prince and her seven siblings live with their mother in Boston, but the integrity of the home is continually compromised by their mother's unstable mental health, insolvent financial condition, and precarious marital status; she is widowed two times by the time Prince is fourteen. Consequently, the adolescent Prince takes on the role of a surrogate mother, trying her best to care for her siblings and provide them with homes. Not before long, however, all of the children, including Prince, live on the fringes of their own family unit and in temporary arrangements with other families. As Prince laments, "We were scattered all about" (9).

The first time Prince references her own specific physical location in the narrative, after the death of her first stepfather, Money Vose, she informs the reader that she is "in Captain F. W. Sargent's family" (8), probably working as a domestic servant. This situation is apparently unexceptional, as Prince reveals that "at the age of eight" she had already "left [her] mother's house" (17). Though she returns home after Vose's death to assist her mother, Prince notes that soon afterward she and her brother George "heard of a place eight miles out of town, where a boy and girl were wanted. We both went and were engaged" (9). Likewise, at later points in the narrative, Prince states that she "live[s] with" a "Mrs. John Deland" (16) or that she "live[s] in the Rev. Dr. Bolle's family" (19). Though the full terms of these "living" arrangements are never disclosed, as suggested by the details from this chapter's epigraph, Prince is likely "living" as a servant in these households.

Poor black children appear to have been regularly involved in this domestic economy. This seems to be the case when a "friend" takes Prince's destitute brother John into his/her home (20), and when Money Vose dies the "three oldest children were put into families" (8). Likewise, Prince's sister Lucy resided with a "friend" for eleven months and then "lived in different families until she was about twelve years old" (20). At that point, Prince "put her in the Rev. Mr. Mann's family, at Westminster, for a certain time, thinking it would be best for her" (20). Again, the terms of this "putting in" are not entirely clear, but the entanglements of child care and child labor suggest that Lucy probably engaged in household work in exchange for her board and might have even earned wages. For Prince's other siblings, who were too young to labor for their own keep, their "scattering" often takes the form of being "boarded out" or placed with a family for a fee. As she notes of Lucy before she is able to labor for herself, she "was not nine, and very small of her age" (19). Therefore, she boards her at the rate of a dollar per week as she does her little brother Samuel (19). While her brother John eventually finds "a place where he had wages," she notes that she had to board him out before he secured a paying position (19).

For some of Prince's relations, this "scattering" seems to have most likely taken the form of child indentured servitude. Upon the death of her first stepfather, Prince recalls, "My oldest sister, Silvia, was seventy miles in the country, with the family that brought her up" (9). Though the phrase "brought her up" is hardly definitive, it strongly suggests that Prince's sister inhabited some relationship of child indenture or even informal adoption with this family. The fact that she returns to live with them, even into early adulthood, hints at how intimate this "bringing up" might have been. If antebellum chronicler Caroline Briggs's *Reminiscences* is any indication, to be "brought up" was to be an integral and essentially permanent member of the family. Numbered among the guests at her wedding that she "loved the best" was a "colored girl who [her] mother had 'brought up'" (93). Though she grew up to be a "bad woman," in Briggs's estimation (93), the prominence of this woman in Briggs's memory suggests that to be "brought up" was to build a long-term relationship, one that might even have outlasted the terms of indenture, as appears to be the case with Silvia and her host family. Likewise, of her younger brother Samuel's fate, Prince exults, "Soon the Lord opened the way for little Samuel; Dr. Phelps took him to bring up" (19). Unlike with her other siblings who are in and out of temporary employment, Prince seems to be relieved because Samuel will finally have a permanent home and a more stable environment, at least until he reaches adulthood. As Youcha observes of many colonial apprenticeships, "For very young children the system was more pure foster care than apprenticeship, animated by the expectation that the child would eventually become a useful member of society" (22). If nothing else, the fact that Samuel's new guardian is presumably a white physician at the very least suggests Samuel's improved social and financial situation over the certain poverty he faced by remaining with his biological family.

For the most part, Prince implies that these placements are necessary evils, unenviable decisions made to compensate for the fact that her mother cannot support or maintain herself, much less her children.[3] She flatly (if problematically) states, "Care after care oppressed me—my mother wandered about like a Jew—the young children who were in families were dissatisfied" (17). Prince never elaborates on the nature of their "dissatisfaction," but her sober representation of the trials she faces as a child domestic to a "Christian" family speaks to some of their probable concerns. They might have been overworked, underpaid, and physically broken by their experiences. What is more, regardless of the treatment dispensed by individual host families, the asymmetrical structure of these placements—white, adult, and middle-class host families on the one hand and black, financially destitute children on the other—could easily lend themselves to conditions that were uncomfortably close to lifelong bondage. Faye Dudden writes: "Even though they nominally had a choice, black families would have been more likely to see their members forced into service not just temporarily but indefinitely, pressed by the kind of poverty that afforded no pretense of obliging" (34). Caught between the rock of class and the hard place of race, the distinctions between ward, orphan, adoptee, domestic, slave, and captive must have been disturbingly unclear for poor children of African descent.

Prince's mother might have been inclined to agree. On at least one occasion, albeit influenced by "one of her spells of insanity," she attempts to retrieve one of her children from a host family (20). And as is the case with her son "living in Essex," at least some of the children attempt to return to her. Despite the benevolent narratives of white guardianship and charity that suffuse Prince's account, the children's various placements, as probably was the case for many African American children, was likely marked by varying and overlapping feelings of relief, resentment, excitement, anxiety, safety, and subjugation.

The First Story: A Respectable New Hampshire Family

If child indentured servitude had the potential to fracture African American families and constrict the lives of its children, it also had the potential to consolidate claims to respectable middle-class identity and whiteness. A consideration of the historical figures from Milford, New Hampshire, that compromise the "Bellmonts" of *Our Nig* reveals the provocative ways in which child indentured servitude benefited white families. Similar to the ways African American disenfranchisement and bondage abetted Cherokee conceptions of themselves as civilized, urbane, and progressive, black indentured servitude in New England, I would argue, galvanized northern white families' claims to efficiency and decorum.

The archival research of Barbara A. White has shown that Nehemiah Hayward and Rebecca S. Hutchinson, the historical counterparts of John and Mary Bellmont, were exemplars of New Hampshire polite society and respectability. Hayward males, in particular, defined their identity and freedom through their ability to buy, use, and sell tracts of land; the Haywards were one of the first families to own land in Milford. Nehemiah Hayward Sr., for example, made "frequent land transactions and participated in local affairs" (White, "'Our Nig'" 29). It is from these significant acquisitions that Nehemiah Jr. inherited this land and home from his father, enabling the setting for the "two-story white house, North" that defines Frado's servitude. Like his father, Nehemiah Jr. occupied himself with "buying and selling small parcels of land" (29) and generally making a decent name for himself. Undoubtedly, such ownership put them in good stead for positions in town and county life. Nehemiah Sr. was a "surveyor of highways" and "fence viewer" (a job in which he delimited the borders of property), and Nehemiah Jr. was a constable and member of the Committee to Examine Bridges. Perhaps "wish[ing] to appear as solid citizens," White speculates, father and son even purchased a church pew, even though their particular religious beliefs appeared to be nominal (29). At any rate, Nehemiah Hayward Jr., like his father before him, played an active and respectable role in Milford town life, and moreover, their material possessions bolstered and solidified their position in the town's social hierarchy.

Even more so than her husband, Rebecca S. Hutchinson Hayward, the "she-devil" of the text, was a woman also "born to social prominence" (White, "'Our Nig'" 29). A descendant of the famed colonial heretic Anne Hutchinson, Rebecca Hutchinson hailed from "one of the most distinguished families in Milford" (29). Hutchinson's maternal grandfather was Milford's first settler and her paternal grandfather was a town founder and veteran of the Revolutionary War (29). Though she is described as an inveterate racist in *Our Nig*, Hutchinson and the entire town had deep connections to abolitionism. Rebecca S. Hutchison was second cousin to the famed Hutchinson Singers, one the most famous and influential abolitionist singing groups in the antebellum era. As they "tuned [their] voice for the cause of freedom," they traveled throughout the New England states raising money for the protection of fugitive slaves and awareness of the need for antislavery (35). Though Rebecca never espoused an explicit commitment to the goals of abolitionism, her family's deep connection to the movement suggests the kind of collateral capital Hutchinson had in terms of the ways she was viewed with respect to her treatment of blacks. Described as "an abolitionist stronghold and station on the Underground Railroad" (38), Milford held one of the largest antislavery rallies in its history in 1843 (35), just a year after Wilson was probably released from service at the Bellmonts.

This apparent devotion to African American uplift, at least publicly, is also a story that the family probably told about itself to others. As James tells Frado after one of Mrs. Bellmont's many vicious beatings of Frado, "I assured her that mother's views were by no means general; that in our part of the country there were thousands upon thousands who favored the elevation of her race, disapproving of oppression in all its forms" (Wilson 42). James frames his mother's beliefs and behavior as idiosyncratic, inconsistent with the humanitarian antislavery work for which Milford had become known. However, as Wilson's title emphatically asserts, "slavery's shadows fall even there" (1), showing us that James seriously misunderstands the range and depth of northern antiblack racism. Wilson is even more emphatic when she later describes her release from indenture and how she is "maltreated by professed abolitionists" who "didn't want slaves at the South, nor niggers in their houses, North. Faugh! to lodge one; to eat with one; to admit one through the front door; to sit next to one; awful!" (71). Northern racism was rampant and vicious, yet the Haywards, at least as represented in the form of the Bellmonts, clearly saw the North as essentially raceless and thus free of racism.

Far from understanding their use of Frado's labor as a potential act of exploitation, then, the Haywards/Hutchinsons might have seen their indenture and treatment of Wilson as effecting the benevolent rescue of a neglected child. Carol Singley argues that one way in which Frado's absorption in the Bellmont family can be read is as a protoadoption narrative, even if it is a failed one (134). Particularly if we read child apprenticeship as a form of "foster care" (Youcha 20), it is not difficult to see how the Haywards might have interpreted Wilson's servitude as an ultimately beneficial experience. Wilson suggests her awareness of her host family's claim to this kind of narrative at several moments. When Frado first arrives at the house, Jack teases Mary about the likelihood that she will soon begin to see Frado as her own personal servant and thus, implicitly, as a member of the family: "If she should stay, it wouldn't be two days before you would be telling the girls about *our* nig, *our* nig!" (16). Jack's invocation of the possessive "our" hints at the possibility that, albeit under the sign of property or dependence, Frado may become a legitimate part of the family, integrated enough to be mentioned in lighthearted conversations with Mary's female companions. A recognition of this possibility is, in part, what animates Mrs. Bellmont's attempt to darken Frado's light skin by exposure to the sun; Frado's appearance might not only accord her a racial identity that is uncomfortably close to whiteness but also a familial identity that compromises the integrity of the Bellmont name. Drawing on these tensions, Wilson's decision to identify the author of her text as "Our Nig" ironizes and parodies the allegedly caring and adoptive relationship the family claimed to have with her.

The influence of the Bellmonts' narrative of adoption and benevolence can also be seen in Wilson's framing of Frado's eventual release from indenture. Upset that Frado is unwilling to stay on after her time has been served, Mrs. Bellmont asks a neighbor, Mrs. Smith, to explain to Frado "how ungrateful it would appear to leave a home of such comfort—how wicked it was to be ungrateful!" (65). Mrs. Bellmont's ability to call on a neighbor to vouch for the family's good intentions suggests that the story of altruistic rescue was one that made sense to the family and to the wider community, particularly one that prided itself on its antislavery leanings. One even imagines that the well-to-do and respected Haywards probably liked reminding Wilson of their decision to keep and (even informally) indent her. Repeating this story made sure that she understood she was fortunate to be included in the family, if only as a live-in servant. Furthermore, it allowed them to believe that they were not brutal exploiters of a child's labor but rather munificent and empathetic caretakers, who had accommodated an indigent black child essentially abandoned at their front door.

The Second Story: Sickening Service

In contrast to the "first story" offered by the Haywards/Hutchinsons, *Our Nig* offers an alternative account of Wilson's childhood and early adult life in Milford, New Hampshire. Refusing the moral economy in which Frado owes the Bellmonts for their boundless and disinterested charity, Wilson asserts that it is the Bellmonts who are indebted to Frado for her many years of uncompensated and arduous labor. This narrative deconstructs the fictions of middle-class respectability, race blindedness, familial adoption, and social benevolence that the Haywards and other white New England subjects likely reported and believed. It offers a second story. The appropriateness of this phrase is suggested when Frado is mourning James's impending death and the narrator intones that Frado "dared not be seen below [downstairs] in tears; so she choked her grief, and descended to her usual toil" (53). As Lois Leveen has argued, "Spatializing hierarchies of power" define the geographic terrain within the "two-story white house North" (561). Accordingly, on the first floor, Frado cannot claim her pain or experience; her grief must be contained in order to preserve the official narrative of benevolence propagated by the Bellmont family. To "descend" to the first floor then is to conceal her interior life and personal suffering. But on the second story, where her tiny, L-shaped room is situated, Frado finds a temporary respite from the restrictive regimes of the house. Allegorizing these spatial metaphors, Wilson's "second story" offers a critique of the Bellmont's supposed benevolence and decency by showing her breakdown, her "descent" into infirmity.

The word that most conspicuously manifests this deterioration comes in the penultimate and actually climactic chapter of the text: "Still, an *invalid*, she asks your sympathy, gentle reader" (emphasis added, 72). In her pioneering study of the figure, Diane Price Herndl writes that the invalid signified "a state of weakness or a predisposition to illness" (*Invalid Women* 1). Aligning with this picture of chronic ill health, Frado is plagued by bouts with fatigue, immobility, and pain. "Improved in health" at one moment, she is racked by a "severe sickness" at another (68). Extending from the previous definition, invalidism also suggested irremediable infirmity and that the subject was outside the arc of medical rehabilitation. Maria Frawley writes, "To have become an invalid was to have moved out of medicine's narrative of promise, a trajectory marked by diagnosis, treatment, and cure" (5). Toward this end, the town physician tells Frado's companion, Aunt Abby, "she may never get well" (67). Along with being an expression of the physician's increasing authority in the antebellum era, the doctor's prognosis underlines the fact that Frado is beyond redemption.

In relying on what Herndl calls the "sentimental trope of illness" that we see in antebellum best sellers like *Uncle Tom's Cabin*, *The Lamplighter*, and *The Wide, Wide, World* (Herndl, "The Invisible" 558), Wilson took a considerable risk. The capacity to withstand pain, as Debra Walker King has pointed out, has often been framed as the natural role of black subjects, a myth that renders invisible the suffering of African American people. Proslavery defenders contended, in fact, that freedom literally sickened African Americans since black bodies were naturally suited for slavery. Elaborating on this point, Douglas Baynton cites the conclusions of antebellum physician Dr. Samuel Cartwright, who coined the term "dyaesthesia aethiopis," a "mental disease" peculiar to blacks who went mad from a lack of proper white guardianship (562–63). When read in the light of such theories, the portrayal of sick African Americans in the North could consolidate arguments that blacks were healthier and happier in slavery, an anxiety that surfaces when Wilson asserts that she did not wish to "palliate slavery at the South" by "disclosures of its appurtenances North" (3). At the same time, if Wilson glossed over her sufferings and illnesses in the North, she put herself in danger of contributing to the myth of what Mary Louise Kete calls a "New England beyond race and outside the reach of slavery's shadows" (111).

Internal evidence from the text suggests that Wilson might have ultimately insisted on her identification as sick and disabled, despite these concerns, because she had been accused of unfairly profiting from public relief. Completing her indenture sometime in the mid-1840s, Wilson found herself in the novel position of having to be completely self-sufficient after twelve years of violent and incapacitating servitude. The novel probably memorializes this anxiety when Frado wonders "if she *could* succeed in providing for her own wants" (emphasis in the original, 64). Consistent with this representation, Wilson had to return to the Hayward house due to failing health and poor job prospects only months after her release. A final expulsion by the Haywards and subsequent marriage to and pregnancy by counterfeit fugitive slave, Thomas Wilson, led to her complete destitution just four or five years after her indenture ended. Consequently, Wilson and her son would spend much of the 1850s living at the Milford County poor farm, what was considered "indoor relief," or with families whose expenditures were reimbursed by the town, which was called "outdoor relief" (White, "She Devil" 46–7). However, such "relief" was not provided without grumbling, if not outright hostility. On at least one such occasion, Frado's white benefactress, Mrs. Hoggs, "reported her to the physician and town officers as an impostor. That she was, in truth, able to get up and go to work." What is more, this might have been a perception that had been manufactured by certain members of the Hayward family, as evinced by Mrs. Bellmont's declaration that "I doubt if she is much sick" (66) when Frado initially returns to the house after her first attempt at providing for herself fails.

Dependent on town resources for more than a decade and apparently accused of being a swindler by one of her benefactresses as well as the family that had "brought her up," Wilson might have conceived of *Our Nig* as a final refutation of the argument that she was able-bodied, if not vigorous, while she lived on public assistance. Although claiming disability is almost always a fraught enterprise, as Simi Linton has argued (*Claiming Disability*), it nonetheless allowed her to counter the claim that she was (like her unscrupulous husband) a loafer and a charlatan. Moreover, it would enable her to identify the true source of her sickness as emerging not from blacks' unfitness for freedom but from the brutal treatment she received in the Hayward house. Indeed, the abrasive titling and identification of the author of the text as "Our Nig"—a phrase not calculated to excuse white cruelty but to expose it—suggest that Wilson's motives were not just economic but psychic. In short, claiming disability might have been her only way to prove that she was not a calculating free loader but someone who had essentially been crippled by racism and who deserved compensation.

The scant, but growing, body of evidence that is available about Wilson's post–*Our Nig* life suggests that an emphasis on sickness might have also served her well in later years. Shortly after her son died in February 1860 (just months after the publication of the "experiment" written to save him), Wilson moved to Boston and eventually became a prominent figure within its Spiritualist movement, serving as one of its only African American "trance physicians" (Ellis and Gates 250). In this capacity, she regularly delivered speeches to Spiritualist audiences, founded and directed a Spiritualist "school" for children, and conducted private séances for the remainder of her life (Ellis and Gates 239–42, 246–47). This level of activity would have, seemingly, been impossible had Wilson maintained the level of debility she claims in her narrative. However, Henry Louis Gates Jr. avers: "Though the description of Wilson as a chronic invalid in both the testimonials and the text of *Our Nig* would make it difficult to believe she survived until 1900, such recoveries were not unknown, and a career in spiritualism was not infrequently launched from a sickbed" (Gates and Ellis xlix). Historian R. Laurence Moore explains that Spiritualists "accepted sickness, suffering and self-sacrifice as part of the natural lot of women," adding that "a long illness" could frequently abet "the career of a successful medium" (203). While it is tantalizing to conjecture about this aspect of Wilson's biography, there is still much that we do not know about Wilson, much less her health status and its relationship to her later career in Spiritualism. But what these slight biographical details suggest is that curing sickness, as opposed to suffering from it, was Wilson's preferred mode of self-presentation in her post–Civil War years. As early as 1868, Wilson advertised herself as having the ability to remedy "chronic diseases" with "great success" (Ellis and Gates 250). The 1870 census listed her as "Dr. Hattie Wilson" (Foreman xlviii) and depictions of her in Boston's Spiritualist press represented her as a "trance physician" (Ellis and Gates 250) and "healing medium" (237). Read in this light, Wilson's illustration of invalidism in *Our Nig* might have been her first foray into determining and deploying the social value of sickness in a life that would be defined by multiple relationships to categories of health.[4]

But in 1859, instead of declaring her indomitable health after years of overwork and ill treatment, the thing to do would be to affirm emphatically the lingering and long-lasting effects of a sickness that had begun in childhood and that now debilitated her in adulthood. Such a story of a stolen, if not perverted, childhood would have had particular resonance with what we now know to be the overwhelming readership of *Our Nig*: white middle-class children in neighboring New Hampshire towns. Sold in the context of Wilson's door-to-door hair elixir business, *Our Nig* was purchased by adults but given as gifts to children from the ages of eight to fourteen (E. Gardner 12). *Our Nig* is a text that speaks to the experiences of children and how racialized and gendered abuse can cripple young lives. Crucial to this project is detailing the fact that Frado arrived at the Bellmont house healthy and happy, in a state that was unsullied by work and abuse. By showing that Frado exhibited the characteristics of an energetic and optimistic child before and even for the first years of her indenture, Wilson makes it clear that "hard labor" and "unkindness" under her host family were the main culprits for her injuries, and thus her years of dependency on the public's coffers were completely justified.

The Spirited Child

A very particular conception of childhood emerging in the antebellum era made the story of her incapacity especially poignant. As the research of Karen Sánchez-Eppler in *Dependent States* and Robin Bernstein in *Racial Innocence* has shown, childhood became associated with innocence and exuberance during the first half of the nineteenth century. Wilson uses the terms of this new social order to underline the ways that the Bellmonts are faithful to an antiquated and, in fact, debilitating model of child rearing: they treat Frado as an object of labor instead of love. However, as an embodiment of what Lisa Green calls the "disorderly girl" (142), Frado's natural environment is amusement and sociality, not routines and arduous tasks.[5]

Toward this end, our first introduction to Frado, Sánchez-Eppler points out, is not by way of her name but by way of scenes of "potent" and "valuable" mischievousness (*Dependent* 44). Like the incurable Pearle in *The Scarlet Letter* or the incorrigible Topsy in *Uncle Tom's Cabin*, Frado's childhood antics signify a rambunctiousness that Wilson will later contrast with her exhaustion and depression in early adulthood. "Time levied an additional charge upon [Frado's father]," the narrator explains, "in the form of two pretty mulattos, whose infantile pranks amply repaid the additional toil" (10). Too, when Seth, Frado's common law step-father, insists Frado would be a good candidate for binding out, Mag replies that the child is "such a wild, frolicky thing, and means to do jest as she's a mind to; she won't go if she don't want to" (12). As such, Frado is not just an impetuous child but the definition of antebellum childhood: independent, emotive, and unyielding. This initial presentation of Frado anticipates the many other "infantile pranks" as well as acts of spontaneity that will mark her characterization throughout much of the early part of the narrative: her overnight disorientation and stay in the woods, her setting of a fire in her teacher's desk, her balancing act on top of the roof, and her encouragement of the dog to lick her plate at the dinner table. Frado is not concerned with practical consequences but only childlike amusements.

The iconic scene of Frado's childlike yet risky playfulness is her dunking of the sheep. In order to get back at a "willful" sheep, "who always persisted in being first served," Frado baits the animal by placing an empty plate of food near the edge of a cliff. The headstrong sheep, of course, rushes after the plate, and Frado moves the dish before he is able to stop himself, sending the sheep flying into the river below. As the narrator reminds us, the scheme is a dangerous one for Frado, for if she should "loose her footing, she must roll into the stream, and, without aid, must drown" (31). But as a fearless and incorrigible child, Frado is not concerned with such sober realities. Mr. Bellmont embodies a more solemn perspective, speaking "seriously to the child for exposing herself to such danger," while Frado "hopped about on her toes, and with laughable grimaces replied, she knew she was quick enough to 'give him a slide'"(31). The scene just as importantly establishes her physical strength and agility. Able to give the sheep "a slide," Frado can dodge the sheep swiftly and effortlessly. This physical vigor is underscored by the fact that when Mr. Bellmont confronts her about the potential danger of her ploy, she merrily hops on her toes, suggesting a literal springiness in her step. Wilson underlines this vitality by sandwiching this episode between two scenes of Frado's brutal beating (scenes that I gesture toward later). Such a placement indicates that Frado retains, at least at this early point in her indenture, her essentially childlike humor and health, as confirmed by the paragraph's closing sentence: "Strange, one spark of playfulness could remain amid such constant toil; but her natural temperament was in a high degree mirthful" (31).

Wilson tempers this rambunctiousness, perhaps fearing the full "potency" Sánchez-Eppler identifies, by emphasizing Frado's childlike naïveté, which Robin Bernstein more specifically calls obliviousness, "the performance of not-noticing," of being unconscious of the "social categories of class, gender, and . . . race" (6). Frado's misrecognition of her abandonment by her indigent white mother and her black lover, Seth, provides the quintessential example of this unawareness. Sitting upstairs in her cramped "L" chamber, Frado muses on the redemptive possibilities of her new situation: "She remembered the conversation of her mother with Seth, the words 'given away' which she heard used in reference to herself; and though she did not know their full import, she thought she should, by remaining, be in some relation to white people she was never favored before. So she resolved to tarry, with the hope that mother would come and get her some time. The hot sun had penetrated her room, and it was long before a cooling breeze reduced the temperature so that she could sleep" (Wilson 17). In Frado's "little mind," the return of her mother is still a realistic possibility, and buoyed by this prospect she "resolve[s] to tarry." But such a resolution only exposes her ignorance of her lack of choice, the painful truth that her decision to enter the house was ultimately not hers and that her ability to leave will not be hers either. To be sure, some part of her consciousness recognizes her actual predicament, that she has, in fact, been "given away," but her condition as a child does not allow her to process this idea fully. Trapped in "a state of holy ignorance" (Bernstein 6), she cannot admit that her mother will never return and cannot perceive that the Bellmonts intentions are not to "favor" her but to exploit her. Though some critics have read this language of purposeful action ("resolved to tarry") as a sign of Wilson's desire to assert Frado's child agency (Leveen 568; Sánchez-Eppler, *Dependent* 46), the episode seems more calculated to express Frado's childlike naïveté. Underscoring this point, Wilson carefully shows that while upstairs Frado daydreams of new opportunities and an eventual family reunion, downstairs the Bellmonts calculate her labor. Mary exults that Frado "came just in the right time" since their other servant, Bridget, has just left, and Mrs. Bellmont soberly adds, "I'll see what she can do in the morning" (17). Reading her integration into the house as a kind of benevolent adoption, Frado cannot see that her placement in the unfinished attic is actually a parody of child development and black uplift, misinterpreting the "L" chamber as a sign of love, when it is actually one of labor. Anticipating the suffocating and debilitating effects of Jacobs's garret in *Incidents*, her tiny living quarters stifle her to sleep. As Holly Blackford notes of such scenes, children drifting off to sleep often signify young minds and bodies that are unable to process the seriousness of their adult situations, even as their "liminal consciousness" enables them to glimpse the actual conditions in which they live (143). Frado is likewise an unsuspecting child, whose drowsiness makes her temporarily open to the reality of her abandonment even as it lulls her to sleep with the fantasy that she has found a safe, if provisional, home.

Aligning with this picture of obliviousness, the next day, Frado is more intrigued by the incredible novelty of her surroundings than the remarkable amount of her work. Making good on her promise to see what Frado can "do," Mrs. Bellmont indoctrinates her into the household's daily grind: feeding the farm animals, washing dishes, raking hay, and eating in the kitchen, supplemented by a few slaps on the head and verbal insults for good measure. Reflecting on the day's events, however, Frado is anything but discouraged. "She found some attractions about the place," Wilson explains, "and retired to rest at night more willing to remain" (18). Like the innocent child protagonist of Sarah S. Baker's *Bound Out*, a fictional account of white indentured servitude, Frado is too credulous to suspect that her host family could mean her anything but kindness.[6] As a child, she is too mystified by the "attractions about the place" to see the true nature of her condition. Read in the context of such "attractions," the title page's reference to the "two-story white house" smacks of a child's initial impression of a foreign and seemingly impressive structure. Perhaps as she walked up to the Hayward house for the first time, the six-year-old Wilson felt a strange mixture of fear and interest on seeing the white house, and this initial reaction suffused and demanded its pivotal placement in her characterization of her indenture. As an innocent antebellum child, living under mean circumstances with her destitute mother, the grandness of a two-story white house forestalls her ability to recognize the terrible turn her young life has taken. But we are not meant to judge or impugn her for this; she is an innocent, oblivious child, and we cannot expect more of her.

The Exploited and Abused Child

Having established that Frado entered the Bellmont house as an innocent, spirited, and healthy child, Wilson shows how indentured service breaks the child's spirit and body. Through detailed scenes of Frado's living, dietary restrictions, labor, and abuse—what Prince calls "hard labor and unkindness" (11)—the narrative shows the child's slow but steady descent into a sickly adulthood. Frado's "room" is the quintessential emblem of such unhealthy development. Described as an "unfinished chamber over the kitchen, the roof slanting nearly to the floor," the lopsided room prefigures Frado's own premature transformation into an "invalid." Just as Frado is never allowed to become "finished," so the room remains an incomplete and thus apparently deficient space. At six years old, she is already too tall to enter the doorway, and Jack has to instruct her to lower her head so as not to bump her head on the ceiling (17). He foresees that "the child would soon out grow those quarters" (17), but Mrs. Bellmont tellingly retorts, "When she *does*, she'll outgrow the house" (17). Leveen suggests that "the statement constructs the house as something that she must earn not solely through her labor but also by embodying physical confinement, by denying herself full adulthood and restricting herself enough to fit within the racially- and class-constructed spatial limitations imposed upon her" (565). Such a predicament literalizes the profound irony of Frado's position in the Bellmont household. When her labor is required, Frado must "[twist] herself into all shapes," as the narrator notes in another context (45), but when it is not, she must shrink back into an unnoticeable and essentially invisible child. Fallen through the rabbit hole of racialized pauper apprenticeship, Frado must labor but not grow, understand but not feel, ultimately exist but not live. Joined in an undesirable metonymic relationship with her unfinished room, Frado is destined for what the novel presents as a catastrophic disability.

The rationing of food is an important part of this program of underdevelopment and ill-treatment. As Dudden notes of the differences between "help" and "domestics," help typically ate the same foods and at the same table with their employers, but "domestics" ate apart from the families they served, underscoring their designation as a separate social class (36). Situated even below a domestic, Frado neither gets to consume food in the same place as the Bellmonts nor has the luxury of enjoying it. On her first day in the house, she is instructed that she must eat in the kitchen while standing "and must not be over ten minutes about it" (17). Extending Leveen's analysis of racialized space, we might add that restrictions regarding food allegorize Frado's exclusion. Literally not allowed a seat at the table, Frado is an exile living inside the home. In a later scene, we learn that Frado has a "selected diet" (38), though the specific food items she is denied are never revealed. The rationing and prohibition of food becomes a quite literal way in which the Bellmonts check the growth of the girl's body and reinforce her estrangement from the family.

Wilson explicitly invokes Frado's child status in order to underscore the deleterious consequences of this treatment. Explaining Frado's value to the house after just a year, the narrator reveals, "Her labors were multiplied; she was quite indispensable, although but seven years old" (18). The conspicuous inclusion of Frado's age signals not only that Mrs. Bellmont ignores "the recognized limits associated with a laboring body," as Santamarina has suggested, but that she disavows the recognized limits associated with a black child's laboring body. The supreme figure of this disavowal is the pickanniny, a figure that was gaining increasing purchase around the time of the publication of Wilson's *Our Nig*, Robin Bernstein explains. Usually described as extremely dark, thick lipped, and with impossibly large eyes, their defining characteristic was their immunity to pain: "When threatened pickaninny characters might ignore danger or quake in exaggerated fear; when attacked, they might laugh or yelp, but in either case, they never experience or express pain or sustain wounds in any remotely realistic way" (35). Such a definition lays bare the denial of black child sentience at the heart of Mrs. Bellmont's contention, "You know these niggers are just like snakes; you can't kill them. If she wasn't tough she would have been killed long ago" (49). Contrasting with the economy seen in Frado's preindenture home—in which Frado practices "infantile pranks" and her father performs "additional toil"—the Bellmonts require that Frado perform both a child's "infantile pranks" (as seen in the Spirited Child section) as well as an adult's "additional toil." This exponential increase of Frado's labors outstrips the relatively infinitesimal addition of just another year to her life. Though Frado's growth works by steady addition, the Bellmonts' desire for her labor is governed by racist, erratic, and exploitative multiplication.

As the account progresses and Frado matures, the narrator continues to call attention to the disjuncture between the prolific growth of Frado's chores and the more modest advance of her age. Mary is "installed" as "housekeeper" while the adult Bellmonts visit James, and consequently Frado must "do all the washing, ironing, baking, and the common *et cetera* of the household duties, though but fourteen" (35). This reference to Frado's liminal fourteen-year-old status rehearses the almost identical strategy employed earlier by Nancy Prince in her narrative, when she recalls, "I was a poor stranger, but fourteen years of age, imposed upon by these good people" (53). Though the formal category of adolescence would not emerge until the late nineteenth and early twentieth century (White, *Growing Up Female* 9), both Prince and Wilson appear to appeal to a nascent sense that young adults are not quite equal to the demands of fully grown-up labor. In both instances, white benefactors and employers corrupt the category of an innocent childhood by obligating growing bodies to perform adult work, obligations that are later revealed to slow and even stunt the child's proper development.

Exemplifying this logic, Frado's tiny, still-developing body is regularly pasted against a backdrop of impossibly large, overwhelming objects. Note, for example, the first time Frado must wash the dishes. After already performing a full day of work, Wilson explains, "A large amount of dish-washing for small hands followed dinner" (18). The notable contrast between Frado's "small hands" and the "large amount" of dishwashing animates the pathos of the passage. Frado's child body is not equipped to handle the adult-sized work the Bellmont house requires. She has, in fact, to be "placed on a cricket" to complete the task (17–18). Though a seemingly harmless household item, the footstool demonstrates how the house's economy contorts the child's body in unnatural and unhealthy ways. A parody of the ethics of prosthesis, it elevates the child only so that she can better sustain the Bellmonts' middle-class comforts, not so that she can better meet her own desires. Such scenes anticipate the aesthetic imperatives of the documentary photography used to condemn child labor in the early twentieth century, epitomized by the work of Lewis Hines.[7] Just as Hines positioned lonely, besmirched children against a backdrop of serious, inflexible, and overwhelming machinery, Wilson's representation of the diminutive Frado perched on a cricket accentuates the delicate boundaries of the child body. Frado is a lovable, innocent, and fragile child, but the Bellmonts violate such boundaries and compel her to do more strenuous work.

To this picture of child labor, Wilson adds child abuse. As the adult narrative voice of *Our Nig* laments, "Manual labor was not in reality her only burden; but such an incessant torrent of scolding and boxing and threatening, was enough to deter one of maturer years from remaining within sound of the strife" (37). Lyman Cobb and other antebellum reformers specifically organized their reformations of school instruction and home discipline around the termination of such a program of "scolding and boxing and threatening."[8] Eschewing the move toward what Richard Brodhead calls "disciplinary intimacy," or control through love, Mrs. Bellmont does not rule through affection but through physical tyranny.

The first and most emphatic episode of this perverse education is the one that contextualizes Frado's dunking of the sheep. When Frado refutes Mary's false claim that Frado intentionally pushed her into the river, she is viciously beaten by Mary and Mrs. Bellmont. For such "tale-bearing," (52) Frado receives her first lesson in the Bellmont brand of discipline: "Mrs. B. and Mary commenced beating her inhumanly; then propping her mouth open with a piece of wood, shut her up in a dark room, without any supper" (20). Recoinoitering the use of food as a site of Frado's abuse, the rough wood is a sorry and sick substitute for the meal Frado is denied. But the wood just as powerfully suggests the physical pain Mrs. Bellmont and Mary inflict. As Elaine Scarry has argued, the recognition of someone else's suffering is an almost impossible task because pain, unlike many other emotive states, is "wholly without objects" (162). But through the wood-block, Wilson gives physical shape to the amorphous and inexpressible feeling of pain. Read as a species of what Scarry calls "analogical verification" (14), the inclusion of the wood block makes available an object that is both visible and intelligible to others. Conveniently benign and domestic, it illustrates Mrs. Bellmont's transformation of a seemingly harmless and everyday object into an "instrument of torture," as the text calls another piece of wood inserted into Frado's mouth (52). Straining and stretching the limits of Frado's child body, the wood concretizes Frado's paradoxically invisible but unmistakable suffering. Such scenes also rehearse other moments in which Frado is situated at the center of spectacular moments of violence and silencing, such as when she is gagged with a towel for confessing her eventual sickness (46). As Cynthia Davis and others have suggested, these representations of penetration and violation likely stand in for other forms of physical violence, specifically rape (397).[9]

But Frado's physical abuse is not always this spectacular; she also finds herself on the receiving end of more pedestrian but nonetheless menacing acts of aggression. Underscoring the notion that Frado is "under her [Mrs. Bellmont] in every sense of the word" (24), Frado receives many of her attacks from Mrs. Bellmont on her head and ears, as a small child might. On her indoctrination into the regular household labor, she experiences "frequent blows on her head" (18). Failing to retrieve the proper amount of wood, Frado earns a "box on her ear" (24). Contemplating if she should rescue Frado from one of Mrs. Bellmont's "storms," Aunt Abby desists for fear that she would "only bring reserved wrath on [Frado's] defenceless head" (25), probably in both literal and figurative senses. Even in one of the many poems that Wilson uses to embellish her chapters, the speaker references a victim's "unsheltered head," again using the vulnerability of the head as a symbol of Frado's exposure. As with the child's exposed and frostbitten feet, these isolated body parts illuminate the dissection and abuse of Frado's child body that the Bellmont household practices, emphasizing Frado's suffering but also her smallness.

Wilson presents Mrs. Bellmont as not only using her child body as the occasion for abuse but also her child consciousness. In the scene where Frado is beaten for her failure to find a "little wood," it seems likely that Mrs. Bellmont demands that she complete a purposely vague task so that she can abuse her in the name of instruction. Telling Frado to "get some little wood to make the fire burn," Mrs. Bellmont appears to revel in the linguistic undecidability of her instructions, watching Frado flail in the sea of the statement's possible meanings. Indeed, to get a "little wood" could suggest quite a few interpretations, such as to get an individually tiny piece of wood, to get a small amount of several wood pieces, or to get a quantity of wood of any quantity or size (as in, "I will get a little dinner before bed"). The scene reflects the opposite of good instruction.

Just a few moments before, the narrator notes that Frado had been taken out of school because her education was "completed" after three summers of schooling, making Frado somewhere around ten. In this scene, then, Mrs. Bellmont is not only antimother but also antiteacher, as she either fails to see that the child cannot properly interpret her conflicted idiomatic expression or that she purposely refuses to qualify her statement so that Frado can complete her task successfully. Indeed, as best her ten-year-old self can, Frado obeys the rules of logic, patiently working her way through each of the passage's possibilities to find the proper size and/or amount of wood Mrs. Bellmont desires. Reflecting the workings of a child brain, Frado first interprets the scene literally, "bringing the smallest she could find" (24). Mrs. Bellmont quickly rebuffs her with a "box on her ear" and sends Frado out again. Having rejected Frado's first offer, the narrator invites us into Frado's thought process, "Of course, the second must be a trifle larger" and "she well knew it" (24–25). The insertion of the word "of course" signals that Frado's thinking is not faulty; she is working through the problem in a systematic and logical fashion, despite undeserved slaps and bumps. However, Mrs. Bellmont is displeased with this offering as well and "'taught her' with the raw-hide, sending her for a third time for 'little wood.'" Wilson's decision to place "little wood" in quotation marks points to her fully adult awareness that "little wood" could mean several hard to distinguish things, the ambiguity of which Mrs. Bellmont relies upon to torment the little girl. Furthermore, the fact that "taught her" is also quoted highlights Wilson's awareness of the specifically pedagogical foundation on which the scene rests. As backward and abusive teacher, Mrs. Bellmont refuses the pedagogical model of discipline through love espoused by Cobb and other social reformers. Instead, she teaches, rather ineffectively Wilson might add, with "boxes on the ear" and, when that fails, the rawhide and crushing kicks.

In stark contrast, Miss Marsh, Frado's teacher for three summers, is a model of Christian sympathy and progressive instruction, evincing what Eve Allegra Raimon calls the "best ambitions of the movement for universal schooling" that characterized the antebellum era (172). When the other children begin to taunt Frado, she "reminded them of their duties to the poor and friendless, their cowardice in attacking a young innocent child; referred them to one who looks not on outward appearances, but on the heart" (19). The narrator notes that "those kind words" are "the most agreeable sound which ever meets the ear of sorrowing, grieving childhood" (19). Though ostensibly directed to Frado's classmates, such advice is clearly meant for the callous Mrs. Bellmont. In physically beating and psychologically tormenting Frado, she is not only the coward who abuses the "young innocent child" but the unsympathetic instructor who berates an already struggling pupil. Consolidating this picture of Mrs. Bellmont as ruthless teacher,

Mrs. Bellmont loses all self-restraint and mercilessly attacks Frado after she returns for the third time without bringing "little wood," becoming "enraged" at Frado's seeming incompetence and "kicked her so forcibly as to throw her upon the floor" (25). Frado's abuse from Mrs. Bellmont is thus partly physical as well as psychological, and each form of abuse contributes to her eventual loss of the emotional buoyancy and physical stamina that she evinced as a "spirited child."

Merging into Invalidism

Such treatment eventually takes its toll on the developing girl. Shadowing the tale of how Frado "merged into womanhood" (64) is the story of how she merged into a debilitating and chronic illness. The most salient sign of Frado's sickness is her inability to remain upright, to maintain the "standing attitude" that Mrs. Bellmont had instituted from Frado's first day in the house. The first such scene occurs when the adult Bellmonts go to visit James, and Mary is left as the superintendent of the house. Mary is not only unwilling to labor but incompetent to do so. Being "very imperfectly acquainted with" the requirements of housekeeping (36), she is a symptom of the house's failed domestic economy. It is in this context that the text first reveals, "Nig was taken sick! What could be done? The *work*, certainly, but not by Miss Mary. So Nig would work while she could remain erect, then sink down upon the floor, or a chair, till she could rally for a fresh effort" (36, emphasis in the original). The narrator's quick, sarcastic, and italicized response to her own question ("the *work*, certainly") underlines the ever-present pressure of work in the calibration of her sickness. Her rejoinder makes it clear that it is excessive and premature labor that makes Frado ill, making it virtually impossible for her to stand. The image of Frado "sinking down," both physically and figuratively, is a posture Wilson invokes throughout her claim for Frado's disability. "She was at last so much reduced," the narrator points out elsewhere, "as to be unable to stand erect for any length of time. She would *sit* at the table to wash her dishes" (46). Frado's "sitting" here is a parodic and pathetic rehearsal of the repeated and comfortable sitting Mrs. Bellmont does in the parlor or sitting room. Unlike Mrs. Bellmont's reclining, however, Frado's prostration is forced by her increasingly poor health and yet always interrupted by the Bellmonts' demand that she work harder. On "one of her sickest days," the narrator laments, "she attempted to drag her weary limbs along, using the broom as support" (36). Like the cricket, the broom materializes Frado's need for a prop, an object to lean on, even as it identifies and recapitulates one of the primary sources of her disability: her uncompensated and exploitative domestic labors. Abusive labor literally takes Frado down.

Wilson presses Frado's sick claim further by emphasizing that Frado must take care of the sick while she is sick, a move suggested by Prince when she notes that she had to return to care for her mother while she herself was very ill. Substituting Bellmont family members in place of the figure of Prince's sickly mother, Wilson dramatizes how Frado nurses other characters even though she is in desperate need of medical attention herself. The most extraordinary instance of this paradox is Frado's around-the-clock care for the Bellmonts' son James, who foreshadows the invalidism that will eventually debilitate Frado. After leaving the family home and marrying a woman from Baltimore, James becomes chronically ill, returning to the house "feeble" and "lame" (37). As with Frado's poor health, the precise nature of James's condition is vaguely specified; we only know that he has ambulatory difficulties: "He could not walk far from the house for want of strength" (41). But as the primary "mover" in the house, James's care and movement, which is superadded to Frado's usual regimen of labor, falls disproportionately on her. "He was helpless and nervous;" Wilson explains, "and often wished change of position, thereby hoping to gain momentary relief. The calls upon Frado were consequently more frequent, her nights less tranquil. Her health was impaired by lifting the sick man, and by drudgery in the kitchen" (45–46). Despite the fact that Frado is represented as essentially worshipping James, Wilson suggests that James is a critical site of labor and thus bodily injury. Wilson's representation of "lifting the sick man" and "drudgery in the kitchen" in parallel grammatical constructions ("by lifting" and "by drudgery") points to James's care as yet another source of impairment. Such a situation provides a bitterly ironic fulfillment to Frado's earlier wish in the attic that her life in the Bellmont family would bring her into a more "favorable" position to white people. As Dudden notes, illness in a family frequently necessitated the hiring of more help or increased labor for those who were already there (31). Accordingly, Frado's responsibilities multiply when James arrives: "She must now *milk* the cows, she had then only to drive" (30, emphasis in the original). Though "representing one's self as an invalid puts into play a whole structure of care, attention, responsibility, and privilege" for white heroines (Herndl, *Invalid* 9), Frado receives no such support. The sickness of the people around her increases her own toil despite the fact that she is already ill.

The effect of such an immobilizing, persistent, and untreated sickness is that it will outlast the terms of her service. In freedom, Frado experiences "three years of weary sickness" that "wasted her" (67). In keeping with Frado's continued cycles of sickness, when she is able to work, it is not for long: "What seemed so light and easy to others, was too much for Frado" (67). This sickness is compounded by Mrs. Bellmont's refusal to acknowledge her exclusive role in Frado's decline and to provide help. Though "all felt that the place where her declining health began, should be the place of relief," (66) Mrs. Bellmont refuses to allow Frado admission back into the house. Moreover, Mrs. Bellmont's declarations that "we shan't pay you for doctoring her" and that "you may look to the town for that" (66) show the ways she has absolved herself of all responsibility for Frado. But Wilson insists otherwise: "Yet she felt sure they owed her a shelter and attention when disabled" (67). In contrast to Mrs. Bellmont's and Mrs. Hoggs's already stated indifference if not callousness to Frado's plight, figures like Mrs. Thorn, the embodiment of white, Christian benevolence Thomson mentions, provide the kind of support that Mrs. Bellmont withholds. Mrs. Thorn is described as "like a mother" to Frado and thus some compensation for the mother who abandoned her. Unlike Mrs. Hoggs, who accuses her of faking disability, Mrs. Thorn recognizes true sickness when she sees it. It is she who realizes that Frado's childhood has been stolen, that she never had that "happy period."

Wilson ultimately argues that her fellow New Englanders have the power to practice Thorn's "mother love" by purchasing her book. Switching from the voice of the sympathetic speaker to that of the more urgent autobiographical narrator, Wilson pleads in the preface, "Deserted by kindred, disabled by failing health, I am forced to some experiment which shall aid me in maintaining myself and child without extinguishing this feeble life" (3). *Our Nig* is Wilson's experiment, a mish-mash of child autobiography, autopathography, and servant narrative crafted to demand assistance, what she elsewhere calls "sympathy" and "aid," to make readers appreciate the pain of racialized and gendered abuse and, ideally, resist its prerogatives. If they do so, they can lift Frado and her destitute child up, even in a world that constantly threatens to knock them down. The cricket, the kitchen table, and the broom are all perverse manifestations of such prosthesis, reminders that Frado's life now constitutes a lack that must be compensated for by acts of elevation and benevolence. The interwoven and compensatory narratives of childhood, servitude, and disability in *Our Nig* are crucial to claiming such assistance. They make it clear how Frado was transformed from a spirited and healthy child into a debilitated adult, and, moreover, in the face of a family and a world that would not offer her support, the responsibility rests with the reader to provide her and her child with much-needed assistance.

Rethinking Infirmity, Reclaiming Disability

Such an analysis might suggest that *Our Nig* only conceives of disability as loss and other disabled characters as extensions of Frado's need for compensation. However, sickness is not only conceived as deficiency. Working against the ideology of ability and problematizing the deficit model of infirmity, *Our Nig* also authors a narrative in which bodily debility and difference are conceived as acceptable and potentially valuable. Reflecting what Thomson calls an "accommodation model" of disability, in which "bodily differences become markers of exceptionality to be claimed and honored" (18), *Our Nig* normalizes difference and infirmity. Particularly through "invalid" white characters like Jane and James, Wilson gestures toward, though does not fully inhabit, a redemptive vision of physical anomaly found in later African American women's writing, such as the unapologetic and (likely) self-amputating Hannah Peace in Toni Morrison's *Sula*. Moreover, by designating Jane, James, and Frado as "invalid," Wilson suggests alliances between infirm subjects across race, class, and gender lines, even as her figuration of sickness also illuminates the potentially manipulative nature of dependency, particularly when somatic impairment is paired with racial and class privilege. Read in these ways, the text is not just revelatory of how the meanings attached to disability shape *Our Nig* but also how *Our Nig* shapes more nuanced understandings of disability.

Consider the crucial fact, for instance, that Frado's most ardent supporters are "invalid." Though the preface imagines that Wilson's "colored brethren" will form a "faithful band of supporters and defenders" (3), it is the ill Bellmont siblings, Jane and James, who most consistently fulfill this function, especially during the years of her indenture.[10] The "invalid daughter" (14), Jane, provides emotional support for Frado and develops a bond with her that appears almost sisterly. Upon Jane's marriage and departure from the house, the narrator bemoans the fact that "another light" has been taken from Frado (34). Jane's return and subsequent exodus elicits a similar lamentation: "Thus vanished all hopes of sympathy or relief from this source to Frado" (61). As the only other Bellmont daughter living in the house besides the bellicose Mary, Jane is essentially Frado's white, middle-class double, dependent as she is on the care of Mrs. Bellmont and thus subject to her whims and aggressions.

Likewise, the "invalid" James represents an indispensable advocate for Frado. Playing the Eva to Frado's Topsy, James is the sentimental white protector whose illness and death signifies his moral purity but also the corrupted nature of those who are able-bodied. As he is in male form, however, James's connection to Frado borders on (big) brotherly love to sexual attraction, as in the many scenes where Frado appears to take the place of James's wife, Susan. Whatever the nature of their relationship, James is a powerful protector of Frado. He, in fact, is the only white character specifically to articulate Frado's abusive treatment as a function of her race: "I have seen Frado's grief, because she is black" (4). First introduced as an able-bodied white subject, James becomes critically ill after his marriage, returning home "feeble" and "lame" and "so changed Frado wept at his appearance" (37). Despite this description, the narrator explains that to Frado he is "a shelter" (38), a word, significantly, that reprises the "shelter" that Wilson notes the Bellmonts owe Frado. What Mrs. Bellmont denies, James provides. Among his many interventions, he chastises his mother for beating Frado, allows Frado to hide in his room, lobbies for her ability to attend church services, defends her good name to the family, and hides her from his mother's wrath. To be sure, James's protections only work while he is a resident in the house and alive and is also undoubtedly abetted by his status as a male Bellmont, but it is also clear that his status as a "feeble" and "lame" man does not diminish either his desire or ability to advocate for Frado. In fact, as a dependent and sickly Bellmont son, his construction as "invalid" might have consolidated his power to effect his wishes in the house. As Herndl notes of white invalid women, their dependency consolidated their claims to other people's labor and wills; likewise, James seems to derive the authority to help Frado, in part, from his debility.

Wilson's decision to recruit the "invalids" Jane and James as Frado's sympathizers and defenders suggests an implicit critique of able-bodied figures in the text and fictions of able-bodiedness and appearance more generally. Able-bodied characters are, in fact, more prone to deceive and hurt. The counterfeit fugitive slave lecturer, who marries and abandons Frado, for example, "was a fine, straight negro, whose back showed no marks of the lash, erect as if it never crouched beneath a burden" (70). Wilson's letter writer, Allida, likewise describes him as "well-formed and very handsome" (73–74). Such invocations of the symmetrical, fully functional, and pristine body enjoin readers to suspect that seemingly healthy subjects have a greater capacity for corruption. Further, Samuel's smooth and erect back implies that bodies that are fully functional might have maintained their integrity precisely because they have displaced the "burden" of labor, reproductive and otherwise, onto others. Just as Samuel's impregnation of Frado distends and burdens her body, Mrs. Bellmont cripples Frado by displacing the house's labor on to the child, allowing her to remain healthy and whole while everyone around her appears to succumb to sickness.

More generally, the text argues that appearances deceive and thus somatic "abnormality" is not an appropriate index of interior states, consistent with a sentimental economy that at once calls attention to difference but then reintegrates it as insignificant. The ideal mate for Jane is named George Means, which the money-minded Mrs. Bellmont incorrectly reads as a sign of his meanness (32), but the incorrect choice bears "sinister, blue eyes," a refutation of the sentimental association of blue eyes and good character. In a similar way, Frado's school teacher, Miss Marsh, tells her classmates to look past Frado's exterior and see her inside, illustrating that genuine goodness is a function of invisible traits that cannot be made manifest on the surface of the body. Mrs. Moore, too, can see beneath Frado's skin color and recognize that she has a sincere heart. This is, of course, complicated by the fact that Frado is a product of an interracial union, what the text calls a "mulatto" (68), and thus her pigmentation is a very poor indicator of bodily difference and abject blackness. But inasmuch as the biracial figure constituted another species of stigmatized identity, *Our Nig* urges readers to be skeptical of the good intentions and idealized bodies of normate subjects. Just because Jane and James, and by implication Frado, are invalid, it does not make them any less worthy; in fact, they may be even more morally upright.

These pairings of racially and medically "invalid" characters imply that Frado's later resistance to Mrs. Bellmont at the woodpile may have parallels to, and even precedents in, Jane's and James's defiance of Mrs. Bellmont. On a first reading, the narrative seems to suggest that the passive-aggressive Mr. Bellmont is directly responsible for Frado's resistance to his wife, reminding the reader of his "advice" to Frado just before Mrs. Bellmont and Frado's standoff at the woodpile. However, Mr. Bellmont's instructions to Frado are hardly liberatory and are more properly described as, at best, "mealy-mouthed" (Gates and Ellis xxx). Telling Frado that "when she was *sure* she did not deserve a whipping, to avoid it if she could (58)," his orders are contradictory and cryptic. As Xiomara Santamarina points out, Mr. Bellmont tells Frado to "avoid" a beating "if she could" but says nothing about how to do so or that she should withhold her labor from Mrs. Bellmont (92). In fact, his specific directive is that she not behave in a way that is "saucy or disrespectful" (58). Refusing both Mrs. Bellmont's order to get wood and Mr. Bellmont's request that she behave subserviently, Frado uses insolent, if not violent, language and gestures. The narrator recalls: "'Stop!' Shouted Frado, 'strike me, and I'll never work a mite more for you'; and throwing down what she had gathered, stood like one who feels the stirring of free and independent thoughts." Another example of what Joanne Braxton calls "sass"—a form of "wit" and "verbal warfare" (30)—Frado's challenge to Mrs. Bellmont not only resists her exploitation but does so in a way that expresses her personality and vivacity, an emerging sense of womanly pride. The force of her verbal aggression is complemented by her "throwing down" the wood, the object that had previously gagged and silenced her. Frado thus refuses the violently enforced silence orchestrated and implemented by Mary and Mrs. Bellmont in earlier scenes. What is more, Frado's refusal to carry the wood compels Mrs. Bellmont to pick up the stack that Frado discards and dejectedly follow her back to the house. To be sure, this moment is not as conclusive as Douglass's idealized fight with Covey; the narrative openly concedes that the ambivalent effect of the standoff is that Frado had the "usual amount of scolding, but fewer whippings" (59). Douglass, on the other hand, is never struck again and, just as importantly, goes on eventually to manifest the individual, able-bodied freedom and life for which his narrative has been venerated. But within the more modest and realistic terms of Wilson's narrative, in which long-lasting resistance does not just require individual effort but also systematic, structural, and cooperative change, Frado achieves a distinct triumph.

Jane and particularly James, I would submit, offer more likely archetypes for such complicated, dependent, and incomplete resistance. Consistent with the focus of disability studies on vulnerability and dependence as constitutive parts of identity and resistance, Jane does not have to defy Mrs. Bellmont once and for all time for there to be meaningful resistance. With the help of Aunt Abby and Mr. Bellmont, for example, Jane actively resists her mother's injunction not to marry her "boy-favorite," George Means (32), and to instead choose the wealthy suitor, Henry Reed. Though Jane initially capitulates because she "had not strength to oppose" her mother's injunction (32), Jane eventually coordinates her own deliverance. Recruiting Aunt Abby to her side, the two eventually precipitate a showdown between George and Henry that brings Henry to the house in protest of the "late coldness" of Jane to him (33). These events elicit Mrs. Bellmont's anger and indignation, creating such a "storm" that Mr. Bellmont is finally compelled to intervene (34). If we recall from the many scenes of Frado's abuse, it is clear that Mr. Bellmont only intercedes when conditions reach a fever pitch. Drawn into action, he communicates Jane's feelings to both Henry and George and secures Jane's union with the latter. In this way, Jane initiates and orchestrates her own redemption, as Frado will later do at the woodpile. To be sure, there is an "after clap" (59) when Jane must "brave her mother's fury" (34), but Jane effectively challenges her mother's claim to the destiny of her body, setting a possible precedent for Frado.

Especially given the fact that the narrative reveals shortly after the woodpile scene that Frado had "merged into womanhood" (64), there is also the equally powerful suggestion that Frado's resistance might be linked to a developmental narrative of a young girl's growing independence suggested by Jane. As a young, white, middle-class woman, Jane's defiance of her mother falls within a familiar narrative of antebellum girls' confrontations with their mothers. In order to become a woman, as signified by her transition from daughter to wife, Jane must pass through the charbydis of her mother, the "she-devil." As an "invalid," to be sure, this process becomes slightly more complicated, but it is essentially no different from having her aunt and father intervene on her behalf, as even able-bodied girls would have needed assistance in negotiating this transition. The narrative uses the exact same phrasing to describe the moment at which Mag Smith falls from grace: "As she merged into womanhood," Mag is "unprotected, uncherished, uncared for," and the narrator explicitly links this neglect to her sexual transgression. Having no mother even to challenge, like Frado, she cannot help but make an ill-advised decision. This "merging" is thus a crucial time in a young girl's life and can lead to liberation, as is the case with Jane, or dissipation, as is the case with Mag. Likewise, Frado's defiance of Mrs. Bellmont appears to be a redaction of this developmental story, aligning Frado's refusal of Mrs. Bellmont's claims and attacks on her body as part of (white, middle-class) antebellum women's refusals of their mother's rules. Consolidating the many earlier moments when Frado is an uncontrollable and "disorderly girl," Frado has learned to channel that rambunctiousness to challenge her (anti)mother-figure. This moment is complemented by other moments, such as when Mrs. Bellmont attempts to intimidate Jack's wife, Jenny, and Frado successfully intervenes on Jenny's behalf: "Frado succeeded in managing the affair so that Jack came to the rescue" (64), the narrator notes. As with her invalid "sister" Jane, Frado is repeating, then, albeit with pointed racial and class differences, the story of a young girl who must come of age by standing up to her mother's rule. Frado appears to be defiant like her older, invalid "sister" Jane.

James represents an even more aggressive model of resistance. The emblematic example of this resistance is his termination of Mrs. Bellmont's ruthless program of food deprivation. As detailed above, Mrs. Bellmont strictly circumscribed the way in which Frado could eat, that she should not have as much as the other family members, that she should eat in the kitchen, that she should eat while she was standing, and that she should not be "ten minutes about it." However, after James returns to the house after his sickness, he defiantly tells his mother: "Now, while I stay, she is going to sit down *here*, and eat such food as we eat" (38). The uncannily similar reactions of Mrs. Bellmont to James's audacity suggest how the narrative compels a reading of James's defiance as a preparation for Frado's. While the narrator notes that after James's declaration, "she feared to oppose where she knew, she could not prevail" (38), the narrator notes after Frado's defiance: "It was characteristic of Mrs. B. never to rise in her majesty, unless she was sure she should be victorious" (59). Modeling each other so closely, these passages imply that Frado replicates a resistance to her mother that she sees in her beloved James. The likelihood of this reading is confirmed by the fact that the chapter begins with the family dispersing after James's funeral, which is to say that Frado has lost her most effective defender. It becomes gradually apparent that, in fact, the "last light" has left the house. Frado is beaten violently after the funeral, but the timing of Frado's rebelliousness would appear to link it to the absence of her ability to rely on James's defense or even his succor. James thus represents an "invalid" model of what Frado could do, and what she necessarily must do, now that he is gone.

But any attempt to read Jane and James as Frado's unproblematic invalid allies, if you will, is complicated by the ways in which their dependency and class position secure, if not abet, Frado's subjection. An examination of what appears to be one of the most celebratory invocations of invalidism gestures toward some of these tensions. For most of the fifth chapter, Wilson describes Jane's courtship by and eventual marriage to George Means. Within the moral economy of sentimental fiction, it is important to remember, no calling was higher or more essential for a middle-class woman than marriage (Welter 170–71), so Jane's ability to marry is tantamount to her definition as a "true woman." Reflecting on Jane's prospects for finding a mate, the narrator remarks: "Although an invalid, she was not excluded from society. Was it strange *she* should seem a desirable companion, a treasure as a wife?" (32). Deconstructing the affiliation between physical impairment and social stigma—one of the central imperatives of disability studies—the narrator's question presumes that Jane has inherent merit, despite her somatic difference. What is more, Jane's individual will-to-belong is not the source of her value; that impulse comes from outside her person, from those who deem her "a desirable companion, a treasure as a wife." This is an important distinction. As Linton explains of traditional views of impaired individuals, "Disabled people are to be acted on, shaped, and turned out as best as can be done to fit into the existing social structure" ("What Is" 518). In contrast, the passage implies that Jane is fine the way she is, absolving her of the burden of making herself over into something that might be found acceptable by society's standards. Equally important, more than just arguing that Jane should be included in social institutions, the narrator's question figures the invalid body as an object of desire. Two suitors pursue Jane (are "desirous of possessing her" [32] in the admittedly problematic language of the narrative), and their forceful competition for Jane's affection is meticulously described throughout the chapter, underscoring her value in the world of the text. As John Ernest contends, *Our Nig* is structured around "economies of identity": exchanges of services, objects, affections for material or social returns ("Economies of Identity" 425). Figured as "treasure" within the heterosexual economy of eligible, middle-class, white northerners, Jane has her choice between two apparently healthy men and can exchange her consent to marry (and dowrie) for a union that will consolidate her identity as a respectable, white female. To be clear, her invalidism appears to frustrate, at least initially, the kind of choice she is able to make, as "she had not strength to oppose" her mother's choice of an unwanted lover, the blue-eyed Henry Reed. But, at her own behest, her aunt's and father's interventions secure her desired mate. The narrator sums up the episode by noting, "A free, voluntary choice was of such importance to one of her health" (34). As an "invalid," Jane is not only desirable; her wishes will be protected.

Such sympathetic representations of white female invalidism signify ambivalently on the condition of the "invalid mulatto" (68), Frado. One the one hand, the notion that Jane might be included in society and deemed a "treasure" appears to articulate Wilson's subversive valuation of Frado as "treasure." Wilson declares the sexual attractiveness of free black women through the more acceptable commentary on an invalid woman's subject position. The likelihood of this reading is suggested by Wilson's discussion of Frado's marriage prospects in the almost identical kind of language she employs to depict Jane's courtship. Using the same interrogative style, the narrator asks, "Was it strange she should attract her dark brother; that he should inquire her out; succeed in seeing her; that he should toy with her shining curls, feel proud to provoke her to smile and expose the ivory concealed by thin, ruby lips; that her sparkling eyes should fascinate; that he should propose; that they should marry?" (71). Both scenes reflect difficult moments when Wilson tackles taboo romances, an "invalid" woman (even if white) who attracts two suitors and a black woman who charms a free black lover. They present instances of "strange love," if you will, as indicated by Wilson's explicit denial of how "strange" each episode would have been. However, the representation of a free black woman as eligible bachelorette and independent sexual subject would seemingly have occasioned even greater trepidation. Wilson's apprehension about such a narrative is borne out by the terseness of the description of Frado's courtship, only about a paragraph, when compared to the proliferation of rhetorical questions, totaling eight in such a short space (compared to the one used for Jane). If we imagine that these questions are meant to disarm the reader, compelling them to assume an affirmative response that was by no means self-evident, the explosion of rhetorical questions would seem to point to a kind of narrative anxiety on Wilson's part, an anxiety about declaring black women's agency and desirability. Read in light of these concerns, Wilson's earlier and elaborated description of Jane's courtship feels like, in part, a practice run for the much more difficult description of Frado's courtship. It allows her to comment on Frado's attractiveness and desirability through a less volatile figure, the "invalid" Jane. Though admittedly brief, the passage is incredibly indulgent, providing the most sustained description of Frado as a sexualized physical body, complete with luscious ringlets, sparkling eyes, and succulent lips. Read as the extension of Wilson's description of Frado as one who had "merged into womanhood," the passage might be understood as a muted affirmation of Frado's sexual status, in a world that only wanted to see her as medically and socially in-valid.

On the other hand, Wilson's declaration of Jane's favorable marriage prospects might be read as an indictment of Frado's less favorable ones, the fact the she is not "treasured" like her white middle-class doppelganger, Jane. For while Jane has the ability to choose between the proverbial "two offers" of marriage from comparatively wealthy men, a staple subplot of nineteenth-century domestic fiction, neither the fictionalized Frado nor the historical Wilson had such a luxury. Frado's marriage leads to an unexpected pregnancy and abandonment by her husband, and, at the time of the publication of *Our Nig*, Wilson had not only been abandoned by her husband, she was also left destitute with a child that she had to deliver at the Milford County poor farm. Unlike the poverty-stricken "invalid mulatto" Frado (68), Jane is screened from the social effects and economic consequences of her medical condition by her racial status and class position. Reflecting on the disparities between Jane's and Frado's marriage prospects, Jennifer James and Cynthia Wu conclude that "the popular nineteenth century sentimental novel's presentation of disabled bodies as objects inspiring care and pity" is essentially "nullified if that disabled body is black" (7). In this light, Wilson's designation of Jane as a "treasure" signifies as a critique of "society's" exclusion of black females as worthy of care and desire. There is no Mr. Bellmont or Aunt Abby to intervene on Frado's behalf to help her select the proper suitor. Even the denigrated Mag Smith, from whom the townspeople suspect "to get some awful disease" (7), is named a "treasure" but only because her whiteness is a prize to the African Jim within the racial economy of the antebellum North. As an "invalid mulatto," Frado cannot attain such heights; she is barred from the sign of even the semirespectable woman. Between Frado and Jane, there exists a formidable boundary—whiteness and class—that cannot be elided by their seemingly common invalidism. Therefore, it is not entirely surprising when Jane offers Frado the opportunity to live with her after her indenture, and Frado reveals that "she felt disposed to flee from any and every one having [Mrs. Bellmont's] similitude of name or feature" (61). Frado's potential domestic service to Jane, even though both are "invalid," threatens to reproduce Frado's exploitation.

James presents an equally problematic ally for Frado. This is no clearer than in James's attempt to "comfort" Frado after a particularly rough beating. Reprising the narrative that Mary Louise Kete identifies in which the North is exempt from racism, James tells Frado that "mother's views were by no means general; that in our part of the country there were thousand upon thousands who favored the elevation of her race, unpitied, friendless, and utterly despised; that she might hope for better things in the future." Casting Mrs. Bellmont's behavior as exceptional, James fails to see the institutional forces that limit Frado's opportunities. When read in tandem with Wilson's later comments that antislavery whites "didn't want slaves at the South, nor niggers in their houses, North," the bitter irony of James's words becomes readily apparent. Though well-intentioned, they deceive Frado by denying her true condition in the North and offering her the dangerous illusion that hard work will ultimately lead to equal treatment in some unspecified "future." As Leveen observes, his and other white family members' "benevolence to Frado enacts her imprisonment" (569). Despite his invalidism, and maybe even because of it (since his sickness and class status requires Frado's labor), James is just as capable of crippling Frado as his able-bodied and tyrannical mother.

As such, *Our Nig* is a conflicted text, embodying both compensatory and accommodating models of claiming disability. Reflecting an awareness of the cultural power of disability and the agency of disabled subjects, it argues for the humanity of people with somatic differences. But even as it claims disability as that which legitimizes black suffering and that which articulates a source of power, it also shows how differently raced and classed individuals with disability can hamper black subjects from achieving full humanity. In keeping with this somber picture, the final image we have of Frado is as chronically ill, an "invalid" even, but yet laboring toward sustaining herself and reclaiming her son. The narrative thus begins, continues, and ends in sickness. Resisting both sentimental death and romantic recovery, Frado lives inside her invalidism and fashions a troubling yet productive narrative, one that both depends on the sympathy of the disabled subject and exposes that subject's limits.

Feeling Wrong

I want to close this chapter by considering the implications of Wilson's exploration and appropriation of disabled service as metaphor and metric of black suffering. These implications might be thrown into quick relief by looking at Diane Herndl's comments about the meaning of sickness in white women's nineteenth-century sentimental fiction. She argues that in these texts ill women have three options: further sickness, recovery, or death. But, in a footnote, Herndl outlines another, though less likely "fourth narrative alternative": "The woman can just remain sick. But if the narrative is *about* her illness, then such an outcome is a resistance to resolution; if nothing happens in regard to her illness, then there is, by definition, no story. For there to be a narrative about the *illness*, illness cannot be an ontological state. . . . For the story to 'work,' there must remain the narrative tension between whether [the protagonist] will die or get better (if not well)" (*Invalid* 223). Though *Our Nig* is precisely "about" illness, it eschews the romantic possibility of recovery or the sentimental escape of death. In a very real way, as suggested by its hazardous publication history, there is "no story" here; it does not "work." It is a text that consciously fails to abide by the narrative rules and sentimental economies that defined antebellum writing. At the same time, it is also this fundamental brokenness that so powerfully animates its critique. Its "sick" representations invalidate the fictions of black (child) inhumanity, white autonomy, middle-class privilege, female community, and the able body that would subjugate poor, female children of African descent.

In this light, critics' various characterizations of *Our Nig* as a text defined by "a whole series of conflicts" take on renewed meanings (Piep 179). More than just an enigma of the text, its unique ability is that it foregrounds the necessity of dependence, lack, and sickness. Such a vision renders invalid sentimental economies that champion good feeling and able-bodiedness as the only outcomes for meaningful fiction. As the narrator of *Uncle Tom's Cabin* famously instructs the reader in that text's final chapter, "There is one thing that every individual can do,—they can see to it that *they feel right*. An atmosphere of sympathetic influence encircles every human being; and the man or woman who *feels* strongly, healthily and justly, on the great interests of humanity, is a constant benefactor to the human race" (Stowe 404). Unlike Stowe's program, with its ethics of healthy good feeling, Wilson's advice to her reader is not to feel right but to feel wrong. She urges her audience, of middle-class white children as it were, to realize that the only "cure" for a sick society is the recognition of mutual dependency and the hierarchies of infirmity that structure it. Eschewing fantasies of independence and imperviousness, *Our Nig* insists that a truly sympathetic economy is one that affirms difference and dependence. As a "free" black woman in the antebellum North, such was the life she inherited but also the one she interpreted. In claiming disability, her conflicted, unconventional narrative is a testament to the enduring relevance of dependence, servitude, and sickness to figuring and facing black life.

5
Savage Moors, African Companies, and Mulatto Explorers

North African Captivity in *The Narrative of Robert Adams*

In order to show that the "white slave can sink as low in the scale of humanity as the black one" (Garrison 6), famed antebellum abolitionist William Lloyd Garrison makes a telling reference to Barbary captivity in his preface to *Narrative of the Life of Frederick Douglass*. Quoting from a speech made by Irish statesman and political activist Daniel O'Connell, Garrison reasons that the identical responses of both blacks and whites to the hardships of bondage prove black people's humanity. O'Connell asserts: "No matter under what specious term it may disguise itself, slavery is still hideous. *It has a natural, an inevitable tendency to brutalize every noble faculty of man*. An American sailor, who was cast away on the shore of Africa, where he was kept in slavery for three years, was, at the expiration of that period, found to be imbruted and stultified—he had lost all reasoning power; and having forgotten his native language, could only utter some savage gibberish between Arabic and English, which nobody could understand, and which even he himself found difficulty in pronouncing. So much for the humanizing influence of THE DOMESTIC INSTITUTION!" (6). As theorized here, the invocation of North African slavery is simultaneously a barrier to the achievement of respectable personhood as well as a pathway to it. One the one hand, Barbary captivity transforms rational subjects into "gibbering savages." Consistent with the etymology of the word "barbary"—which from the Latin, *barbaria*, means "land of barbarians" (*OED*)—the Barbary captive returns unable to utter any language intelligible to refined people and even to himself. Working within an inherited Enlightenment framework in which speech and the manipulation of language signified intelligence and humanity, the American sailor's ignorance of his "native tongue" suggests his estrangement from the most basic requirements of civilized life. On the other hand, Garrison frames the debilitated condition of African Americans under the regime of chattel slavery as a distinctly human response. Read as a form of bondage that is perceived as particular to whites, Barbary captivity shows that European Americans have a similar capacity for degeneracy and, thus, black people's low place in the "scale of humanity" is dependent on their unfortunate circumstances, not on their allegedly innate depravity. The passage substitutes one fiction of naturalness for another, exchanging the natural certainty of African American inferiority for the "natural" and "inevitable" consequences of slavery on "every noble faculty of man." Though the final sentence from O'Connell's speech mocks the "humanizing influence" of American chattel slavery, Garrison's allusion to O'Connell's story affirms the "humanizing influence" of Barbary captivity tales.

North African slavery might seem like a curious rhetorical space from which to assert black people's humanity, but this move was hardly unprecedented. The first piece of antislavery literature in America, colonial jurist Samuel Sewall's *The Selling of Joseph*, made the connection between white slavery in Africa and the subjugation of people of African descent in this way: "Methinks," Sewall argued, "when we are bemoaning the barbarous Usage of our Friends and Kinsfolk in *Africa*: it might not be unreasonable to enquire whether we are not culpable in forcing the *Africans* to become Slaves amongst our selves" (11). US senator Charles Sumner's *White Slavery in the Barbary States* likewise observed: "The conscientious man could not plead in behalf of the emancipation of his white fellow-citizens, without confessing in his heart . . . that every consideration, every argument, every appeal urged for the white man, told with equal force in behalf of his wretched colored brother in bonds" (83). Recognizing the brutalities committed against white slaves in North Africa, it would seem, could convince people of the immorality of black slavery. According to one of Abraham Lincoln's biographers, this was also the Kentuckian's reaction as a young man after reading James Riley's bestselling Barbary captivity narrative, *An Authentic Narrative of the Loss of the American Brig Commerce*; it "undoubtedly left an indelible impression on Lincoln's mind in regard to race superiority and the moral wrongs of slavery" (McMurty 135). Most often, however, accounts of Barbary captivity were actually used to defend "the peculiar institution." Archibald Robbins, who was a companion of Riley aboard the shipwrecked *Commerce*, wrote in his version of the affair: "These Africans, of every name and feature and complexion, take delight in enslaving each other" (91), rehearsing the well-worn argument that slavery and oppression were endemic to people of African descent and, thus, hardly worthy of protest. Reflecting what Paul Baepler calls the "semiotic plasticity" of the genre (31), stories of Barbary captivity could express various and even incongruous opinions about black personhood.

The biographical account of Robert Adams's enslavement in western North Africa, of which the abridged title reads *The Narrative of Robert Adams*, occupies a singular position within this catalog. Based on the adventures of a "mulatto" sailor (17), it constitutes the only sustained narrative of Barbary captivity about the life of a person of African descent. His captivity placed him among the ranks of the seven hundred American sailors who were captured between 1785 and 1815 by the Barbary states of Tangier, Algiers, Tunis, and Tripoli (Allison 110). These principalities had been attacking European vessels off the coast of Africa and in the Mediterranean at least since the seventeenth century (Baepler 3) and took an estimated twenty thousand British and Irish captives from the seventeenth to the mid-eighteenth centuries alone (L. Colley 56). American independence made US shipping vulnerable as the British treaties no longer protected American vessels (Baepler 7–8). The single largest attack was the seizure of the USS *Philadelphia* in 1803, a decisive turning point in America's war with Tripoli (1801–5). The *Philadelphia*'s attack resulted in the abduction of over three hundred American seamen, the attempted rescue of which is memorialized in the Marine Corps Hymn line, "To the shores of Tripoli" (Allison 28, 230).

Except for Adams's tale, representations of black American captivity in Barbary come to us in the form of fragmentary accounts found inside white captives' reports. As Bernard Lewis explains, the availability of white slaves (from the Caucasus, Circassia, the Crimea) diminished in the early nineteenth century, thereby reenergizing the centuries-long trade in black Africans throughout the Islamic world (73). If the narrative of Daniel Saunders is any indication, the scorching Sahara sun might have been the least of these black seamen's worries. According to Saunders's *A Journal of the Travels and Sufferings*, African American sailor Juba Hill was separated from his white companions to be sold as a slave by his Arab abductors. Significantly, Hill's white crewmates did not protest his bondage but instead pledged to "defend [them]selves" to the death if the Arabs should try to take one of them (18–19). Robert Allison surmises: "Black captives had the additional burden of exclusion from the solidarity of other captives, of being treated differently not so much by their captors as by their fellow Americans" (121). Hill's encounter with Barbary captivity suggests the painful irony of American-born blacks who had escaped or avoided slavery in the United States only to find themselves bound in Africa.

For reasons I will expand upon below, Adams's text presents a starkly different picture of black bondage in Africa, one in which he receives better treatment, not worse, than his fellow captives and in which any sense of a black American racial consciousness is suppressed. As such, his narrative is less useful as an index for some universal "black experience" of Barbary captivity and more valuable as one very specific example of what might happen when a mixed-race figure is injected into a narrative of "white slavery." Abducted by Moors after his ship bilges off the coast of Mauritania in 1810, Adams was initiated into what Robert Allison might describe as "a life of brutal nomadic egalitarianism" (Allison 111), drinking camel's urine, sleeping in the desert sand, and trekking under the oppressive heat of a midday sun. Eventually, he found his way to Morocco where he was ransomed by the British consulate, but not before allegedly joining a hunting party in search of African slaves, traveling to the interior of North Africa, and even entering into a nearly fatal sexual affair with one of his Arab master's wives. Picaresque stories like that of Adams, fusions of colonial fantasy, anti-Islamic propaganda, and maritime autobiography, contributed to the thriving print industry for Barbary captivity tales in the late eighteenth and early nineteenth centuries, as evinced by texts like Royal Tyler's satirical novel *The Algerine Captive* and William Ray's autobiographical *Horrors of Slavery*.

Adams's 1816 London version of his journey, the first of several that were produced in the nineteenth century,[1] was solicited and organized by the Committee of the Company of Merchants Trading to Africa, also known as the African Company. Simon Cock, the secretary for the company, was largely responsible for the construction and shape of the narrative, which he composed from his many interviews and interrogations of Adams. The account is also the product of various reports and commentary provided by the British vice consul in Morocco, Joseph Dupuis, who ransomed Adams, and other anonymous members from the African Company. As related by Adams and processed by his cadre of interlocutors, the story was designed to make a singular scientific claim: Robert Adams was the first Westerner to visit the famed and then still-uncharted city of Timbuktu. In order to further this claim, the text's editors added a lengthy introduction, detailed map of Adams's travels, numerous explanatory notes, and multiple appendices. Relying on the expected synergies between captive experience and geographical knowledge that David Lambert has identified, the African Company used Adams's story of Barbary shipwreck and abduction to certify its speculations about the unexplored hinterlands Africa and thereby make a name for itself in the budding knowledge industry concerning the continent's interior. Wholly invested in this project, the story has very little to say about Adams's blackness or how it might have textured his experience or understanding of Barbary captivity. As Charles Hansford Adams has observed, "Adams's race is deliberately muted" because it threatens the African Company's claims to scientific legitimacy and international respectability (xliii).

My reading suggests that the erasure of his blackness was insistent but imperfect. His transformation into and temporary occupation of identities like the Christian crusader, accidental explorer, and even honorary white were, if anything, too convincing, and Adams's editors, at crucial moments, attempt to take back the authority that the Barbary captivity narrative bestows on him. This equivocation is evident in the flurry of contradictory epithets that the narrative uses to try to pin down his racial and ethnic identity: "very dark," "light," and even having "features and dress" that "resembled those of an Arab" (47, 89, 15), all of which were calculated to ration out the favorable impression of Adams as reliable and objective but not quite white. This explosion of qualifiers suggests that slavery in North Africa had the capacity to destabilize the sanctity of whiteness and challenge the inferiority associated with blackness, a possibility suggested by Garrison's use of O'Connell's speech in the opening paragraph of this chapter. Hardly constituting an abolitionist polemic, Adams's *Narrative* nonetheless installs an intransigent, mixed-raced figure at the center of its story of African conquest. In the process, it shows how Barbary captivity narratives could fund European's pursuit of imperial knowledge and African exploration, even as they undermined the stability of racial categories and white privilege.

The African Company: Trading in Captivity

The back story of the African Company reveals the changing moral and financial value of African captivity, broadly conceived, in the early nineteenth century. In the previous century, the African Company had been involved in the business that characterized much of England's relationship with West and Central Africa in the eighteenth century: the Atlantic slave trade. As the research of Charles Hansford Adams reveals, the company was, in fact, responsible for "20% of the British slave trade to the New World between 1690 and 1800" (xxiv). However, with the abolition of the British slave trade in 1807, the African Company was compelled to frame its relationship to the "dark continent" in more benevolent ways and find a more forward-looking business model. With his fantastic tale of captivity and travels to the interior of Africa, Adams presented the African Company with a practical way to do so. Instead of trading in the souls of African people, they could now trade in knowledge about Africa. Since the beginning of the slave trade, Philip D. Curtin observes, Europeans hungered for reliable information about the geography, resources, and conditions of the continent, for the practical purposes of colonization as well as for the intellectual project of mapping the world (9–27). The literary conventions and geographical settings of the Barbary captivity narrative furnished a way for the embattled company to enter into this conversation as well as distance itself from its seedy past.

The Association for Promoting the Discovery of the Interior Parts of Africa, or the African Association, epitomized the balance between scientific authority and moral credibility the African Company needed. Backed by founding members like Sir Joseph Banks, Britain's most accomplished natural scientist, and William Wilberforce, its exemplar of antislavery earnestness, the association sought the intellectual mastery of Africa but tempered it with "genuine humanitarian desire" (Heffernan 206). Around the turn of the eighteenth century, it sponsored a bevy of white explorers' ventures into Africa's interior: John Ledyard, Daniel Houghton, Frederick Hornemann, Jean Louis Burkhardt, and, most famously, Mungo Park (207). Park had become an international celebrity, and the success of his *Travels in the Interior Districts of Africa*, the record of his first African adventure, was crucial to this international esteem (Pratt 74).

With *Narrative*, the African Company hoped to attract some of this attention toward itself. This is probably why the text lists Sir Joseph Banks, among other prominent members of the British scientific and imperial community, as one if its auditors and guarantors and, as Charles Hansford Adams has suggested, notes that Adams experience might be useful to "the expedition actually on foot" by Major Peddie (Cock 208), referring to a recent expedition sponsored by the crown's Colonial Office. These statements imply that Robert Adams was actually the successor to the fabled Park since his narrative was the next account of exploration into the African interior. Adams's chance stranding in North Africa, however, was in no way tied to efforts of the British Colonial Office, and the Colonial Office did not recognize the African Company as a legitimate peer (Adams xxix). Nonetheless, the African Company imagined itself as contributing to new scientific knowledge, and Adams's tale was crucial to securing their position within the new governmental hierarchy.

If it was to be believed, Adams's account did more than just put the African Company in the same circle as the African Association and the Colonial Office; it set them apart. In maintaining that Adams had visited the renowned city of Timbuktu, *Narrative* boasted a feat that not even the inestimable Park could claim. As Frank Kryza explains in *The Race for Timbuktu*, ever since the Malian emperor Mansa Musa's fourteenth-century frolic through North Africa bearing gold bars carried by thousands of attendants, Timbuktu stood as the transcendental signifier of economic power, cultural authority, and exotic knowledge (xiv–xv). During its heyday in the fifteenth century, the city was in truth an actual crossroads of Moorish trading routes as well as a hub for Islamic learning and political power (Saad 42), but what Michael Heffernan calls the "Timbuctoo craze" (212) persisted well into the nineteenth century, even after Frenchman Renee Caillee entered the city in 1828 and reported its impoverished condition (210–12). Adams's narrative confirms the persistence of the European fantasy. "At a time when the civilization and improvement of Africa," an appendix in the narrative confesses, "and the extension of our intercourse with the natives of that long-neglected country, seem to be among the leading objects of the British government and nation,—and when, with these views, great exertions are making to procure information respecting the interior of that vast and unknown continent; the following account of Tombuctoo, and the trade and navigation of the Niger, may perhaps prove not altogether uninteresting" (125). If "geography was the science of imperialism, *par excellence*," as David Livingstone has argued (160), then the African Company was performing an enormous service for England's dream of empire with its narrative about "that vast and unknown continent."

Perhaps even more importantly, the production of Adams's narrative was vitally necessary for the company's continued financial support. Just days after the completion of Adams's manuscript, Cock would go before parliament to defend the company's expenditures for the previous years (Adams xxvi). It is highly likely that Cock and the other members of the African Company conceived of Adams's narrative as a means to persuade British authorities that they had quit their traffic in human beings and had begun to deal in more respectable goods. What better way to effect such a transformation than in a narrative that sympathized with the brutal treatment of an American "mulatto" in slavery? Given these motivations and high stakes, it is not entirely surprising that Cock, Dupuis, and one other unidentified editor of *Narrative* situate the account within an elaborate editorial apparatus. It is organized into "Introductory Details Respecting Robert Adams;" "A Map of Adams's Travels;" an "Advertisement to the Map;" the narrative itself; "Notes and Illustrations of Adams's Narrative," "Concluding Remarks," and two appendices, one of which further elucidates the relationship between Adams's discovery and previous explorers, namely Mungo Park. Adams's voice is essentially lost in these sections. As a result, the four chapters that constitute the narrative itself, a trifling forty-one pages, dwarfs in comparison to the eighty-two pages given to the notes and various addendums. The opening words of the narrative reproduce this imbalance. The first chapter heading reads: "Discovered in London—Examined by the African Committee respecting his travels in Africa" (4). As indicated by the word "discovered," it is the African Company who makes the first find, not Adams, and with their prompt "examination," they begin the meticulous process of sifting through the raw materials of his lived experience to produce a coherent and usable narrative. Adams's name is not even mentioned in this initial description, but the labor of "the African Committee respecting his travels in Africa" is duly noted. As a symptom of the entire narrative, this opening chapter description illustrates the formidable control the African Company exercises over *Narrative* and, implicitly, Adams's representation.

Competition in Cunning

Given the conditions under which Adams's account was produced, it is easy enough to read Robert Adams as the flimsy puppet for the African Company, the dumb cipher of their desire for colonial discovery and conquest. The "Introductory Details" note that Adams rendered "simply the facts" (11) and offered "plain and unpretending answers" (9). Dupuis also notes that he told his story with "the greatest simplicity" (16). The extensive notes attached to the narrative go even further, asserting that too much stock cannot be placed in Adams's specific recollections since they are from a "rude sailor cast upon the wilds of Africa" (79). Such descriptions clearly suited the African Company's purposes, as they framed the sailor as an uncomplicated and unlearned man who did not have the will or wherewithal to deceive or even embellish.

But though he might have been illiterate, Robert Adams was hardly ignorant. Internal evidence from the narrative strongly suggests that he was fully aware of the stakes of his story and how telling it in a particular way could benefit him. Cock's "Introductory Details Respecting Robert Adams" immediately introduces the reader to the favorable terms of Adams and Cock's storytelling arrangement. As soon as the destitute sailor revealed his first bit of information, the account notes that Cock busied himself with "equipping [Adams] with decent clothes, of which he stood particularly in need. He was also supplied with a trifle in money, as an earnest of the future recompense which was promised to him, provided he would attend regularly every day until the whole of his story should be taken down" (10). As long as Adams had a provocative story to tell, his situation would be rendered "comfortable," whether in the form of "decent clothes," monetary payments, a place to live, or other material boons. Having spent months on the cold, damp London streets in November, hungry for food and desperate for shelter, Adams perhaps knew that he had to rely on the only commodity he had, his incredible story. Reflecting on Adams's knack for self-interested storytelling, Anne Fabian calls him "the very model of the deferential beggar" (34). He knew that the "truth" of his account was paradoxically made apparent by the simplicity and apparent unwillingness with which he told it. Frederick Douglass would later find this truth out when he was discouraged from being too articulate on the antislavery lecture circuit as it elicited suspicion that he had not really been a slave (Ripley 136). In order for the testimony of persons of African descent and former captives to be taken seriously, it had to appear sincere without being too sophisticated.

One way Adams might have walked this tightrope would have been by allowing his questioners to lead his responses. In his detailing of his methodology, Cock admits that Adams only provided details in response to specific questions, "that he related scarcely any thing without his attention being directed to the subject by a special inquiry" (11). In one section of the "Introductory Details," Cock begins three successive paragraphs with statements that indicate the nature of these inquiries: "Being questioned how he came to have so minute a recollection of the exact number of days"; "On asking him how he could venture to speak with confidence on the precise number of miles"; and "When asked how he came to observe so minutely the *directions* in which he travelled" (12). Perhaps using these interrogatives as signposts, Adams might have shaped his story, in a kind of call-and-response—multiply learned from sailors' yarns or the African American folk tradition—to these pointed queries.[2] One can imagine with each telling of the narrative, Adams might have gained more confidence and begun to understand what parts of his story were credible and what parts were not, based on the way that his interlocutors responded to him. Likely blending details from what he had experienced with what he heard from his acquaintances, Adams fashioned a narrative that was at least partly based on what his audiences wanted to hear. In those silences that spoke humility and plainness to the African Company, Adams might have been stitching together the previous, present, and perhaps even future versions of his captivity tale.

This hypothesis helps to explain the fact that Adams was responsible for helping to produce multiple, and distinctly different, versions of his narrative. Relative to the London version, one of the most distinct versions that Adams related was the first-person account he delivered in Cádiz, Spain, which was redacted by Samuel Storrow; this version was eventually printed in an 1817 edition of the *North American Review*. Entitled "Interior of Africa," the Cádiz account follows essentially the same chronological episodes of the London version—the shipwreck, the capture by Moors, the residence at Timbuktu, return to Barbary captivity, and ultimate redemption—yet it lacks much of the detail and contradicts several of the main points of the London narrative. For example, the Cádiz version notes that the captain of the *Charles* simply died from starvation and heat exhaustion (Storrow 148), but in the London version he is brutally murdered by Moors (Cock 29–30). Even more consequentially, the belligerent Bel Cossim family takes center stage in the London tale (a fact I expand on below), but they are completely absent from the Cádiz account. When the two are compared side by side, the London account appears more cinematic and calculated to encourage sympathy for Adams, while the Cádiz version appears written in a kind of shorthand that reveals little of Adams's courage and idiosyncrasies.

Adams also delivered another version of his captivity to British vice consul Joseph Dupuis, a version that Dupuis argued Adams related to him directly after he was ransomed from slavery in Mogadore, Morocco. Comparing the Mogadore and London versions, Dupuis explains, "The chain of events is uniformly the same; but I think he entered more into detail on many points, in the relations which he gave to me" (Cock 17). Convenient for Dupuis, Adams delivers the most complete narrative of his experiences to him, granting him the power to supplement and even amend information from the London narrative. What is evident from these dissimilar versions is that not only did each editor probably put their own personal spin on Adams's tale but that Adams probably told a slightly and purposely different tale to each listener.

Dupuis alludes to this possibility when he remarks on Adams's deliberate exclusion of a witchcraft episode that was present in the Mogadore version: "It seems strange that Adams should have omitted these extraordinary stories (and almost these alone) in his [London] Narrative; for he frequently expressed to me, a firm belief that the Negroes were capable of injuring their enemies by witchcraft" (Cock 83). Dupuis explains this oddity by arguing (among other things) that Adams simply grew tired of having this story questioned and thus simply left it out to avoid embarrassing questions. But if Adams grew weary of repeating fantastic stories, then he certainly would have been unable to stomach the repeated questioning and outright suspicion that his tale of Timbuktu elicited. Dupuis, however, does not suspect Adams of any cunning and attributes Adams's omission to his "good sense" and "very allowable discretion" (Cock 84). The more likely explanation, of course, is that Adams tailored his story according to the effects he wanted to achieve and according to who was listening.

Based upon their reading or hearing of these various versions—and the dramatic differences between them—contemporary reviewers of Adams's tales arrive at the quite reasonable conclusion that Cock, Dupuis, and others try hard to ignore: that Adams consciously told different versions of his story. As opposed to describing him as an "ignorant sailor" as Cock does (111), they describe him as a calculating storyteller who was quite aware of the consequences of his narrative. The editor of the Cádiz version, Samuel Storrow, is most plain spoken when he asserts that Adams carefully crafted each iteration of the narrative in order to please his audience. "His inducement to frame a story was apparent," Storrow supposes, "as by means of it he had acquired a currency and temporary livelihood, which he had sufficient shrewdness to anticipate at the commencement" (Sparks 180). Likewise, "a gentleman of respectability" from Tangier, having reviewed the various discrepancies between Adams's various captivity accounts, comes to the conclusion that "Adams was shrewd, observing, and of a retentive memory" (181). Both of these critiques were included in Jared Sparks's scathing evaluation of the London and Cádiz versions in his American nationalist periodical, *North American Review*. Bent on contesting the authority of all things British, it is possible that *North American Review* might have been overstating the case. Nonetheless, the discrepancies the journal points out underline an important and inescapable truth: the man known as Robert Adams was a careful crafter of his various captivities and identities. Aboard the *Charles*, in fact, he went by the name of Benjamin Rose and only started presenting himself as Robert Adams after his captivity had ended. Sailors fabricated names while at sea for any number of good reasons, perhaps, as may have been the case with

Adams, to escape an enslaved past or to avoid an enslaved future. Indeed, his invention of the figure of Rose, a name evoking the New Testament tale of divine resurrection, and Adams, a surname suggesting the Old Testament story of human creation, suggests that he had few qualms about authoring alternative identities.

While Ann Fabian concedes that Adams intentionally sculpted his narrative according to the desires of his interlocutors, she concludes that "what he could not know was what his tale meant" (34). I suspect, however, that after several weeks of being paraded in front of the members of the British intelligentsia and political elite, Phillis Wheatley–like, Adams grew increasingly aware, if he was not already, of the growing value of his story, especially to this particular community of people. They were willing to give him food, clothes, lodging, and even the means to get back to America, if that in fact was where he was from and where he ultimately went. So while we may never know exactly how successful he was in influencing the final version of the published narrative, there is little doubt that he also shaped his narrative toward his own ends. Playing the role of the servile Babo to Cock's and the African Company's myopic Captain Delano, Adams appears to be more than the blank conduit for the power of his white benefactors. He was an active shaper of his narrative and its representations.

The Narrative of Robert Adams: Berths and Transformations

When we get to the narrative proper, the picture of Adams that emerges is one that is made legible by way of the motley crew of foreigners that surround him. Per the conventions of the Barbary captivity narrative, captives' faith in themselves as well as in divine intervention was tested as they faced off against racial and linguistic aliens. Meeting the Other in some fantastic "contact zone," a space of "coercion, radical inequality, and intractable conflict" (Pratt 6), captives then passed through a series of corporal challenges akin to the gauntlet of Indian captivity narratives: "Their skin peels off in sheets under the African sun, their mouths swell shut from drought, their bones are broken by vicious masters, and their stomachs shrink as they wait for their next ghastly meal" (Adams xlvi). This precipitates psychological, national, and spiritual crises through which the sufferer has to preserve "his moral integrity, doing what is necessary to survive and ultimately escape, while resisting the constant temptation to descend into to his captors' depravity or accept their false religion" (xlvi). As the account of a biracial figure filtered through a white amanuensis, Adams's account complicates this model by investing the protagonist with a racial difference that both mimics and mocks the challenge to, and recomposition of, captives' identities.

As in James Riley's narrative, this process of cultural immersion is set in motion by the narrative of a shipwreck off the coast of Africa. Like a metaphorical womb in contraction, Adams's ship, the *Charles*, strikes the reef at three in the morning: "The vessel bilged," the opening chapter reveals, and subsequently, "the cargo was almost entirely lost" (Cock 28). When the ship ruptures, this forces the crew to chuck everything overboard: wine casks, guns, flour, anchors, muskets, powder, essentially constituting an afterbirth of the vessel's material goods and life-sustaining supplies, its placenta. The men swim ashore to safety in a fantastic water birth in which "no lives [are] lost" (28). The first sight the captives see is a perversion and parody and fulfillment of white maternal affection. "The Moors were straight haired, but quite black," the account recalls. "Their dress consisted of little more than a rug or skin around their waist, their upper parts from their knees downwards, being wholly naked" (28). With their "straight hair" but "quite black" skin, these men will serve as taboo models of masculinity for the shipwrecked men. While their "straight hair" suggests European features, their black skin indicates debased African characteristics. As opposed to forming a bond with them based on their common enemies and anxieties, as Dana Nelson has noted of the formation of white fraternal relations, the narrative suggests that the Moors are the enemies and aliens that make the fiction of white masculine identity real. The most sensational signifier of the Moors' alien difference comes in a terse four-word sentence: "The men were circumcised" (28). It was not until the late nineteenth century that circumcision would come to be seen as hygienic and natural in both England and America. In the early nineteenth century it was interpreted as painful and abnormal (Darby 5; Gollaher 5). The sentence is thus a mixture of the fear of, and secret desire for, exotic difference. Perhaps flapping on the coastal wind, the flimsy "rug or skin" that hides the Moors' genitalia is easily flicked aside, exposing to the already frightened European and American males the circumcised penis. The Moors are thus freakish amalgams of typically opposed racial and national identities that will guide the shipwrecked men into a similarly perverse masculinity. Just as the slave Luke's master in Harriet Jacobs's *Incidents* is meant to signify a "disgraced wreck of manhood" (192), the shipwrecked men on the coast of North Africa are potential "wrecks of manhood." Like Luke, they will soon be stripped of their clothing and compelled to do the bidding of their defiled captors. "On the landing of the Captain and crew," the narrator explains, "the Moors stripped all of them naked" (29), a scene that foregrounds the captives' imminent violation and transformation.

In the form of a Frenchman who accompanies the Moors—"a young man in appearance a Frenchman, but dressed like a Moor" (29)—they see a representation of the potential of their identities to change. A former captive like them, the Frenchman now "associated, and ate and slept with the Moors" (29). Though the Frenchman protests to the contrary, the narrative notes that "Adams was of the opinion that he had turned Mohammedan" (29). Association with their Islamic captors will eventually lead to a religious transformation, a conversion that is made even more frightful by the fact that, like the Frenchman, they may not even recognize their own altered condition, the fact that they were once something else. As the narrator later observes of newborns in Timbuktu, "The infants are at first of a reddish colour, but become black in three or four days" (226). Implicitly, the statement seems to ask, how long will it take before Adams's cultural gestation in North Africa replicates this biological model? Particularly for the ambiguously racialized Adams, if African-born infants become "black" in three or four days, how long will it take American born and even mulatto captives? Moreover, in the midst of this motley crew of Moors, Mohemmadans, and the converted Frenchman, what is the status of the mulatto and what would conversion mean?

The narrative provides a window into this complex and unstable world and a way to calibrate the status of the mixed race figure in relationship to it. In the second appendix and the final addendum of the document, "Population of Western Barbary," Dupuis provides a Europeanized schema of racial being that organizes the inhabitants of North Africa, given the narrative's "frequent indiscriminate use of the names of *Arab* and *Moor*, in speaking apparently of the same people" (136). Making no pretense to presenting North Africans as they might see themselves or in the nuanced and differentiated way that many studies have,[3] the appendix admits that it is written from a Western perspective. As Dupuis tellingly notes of the name of the Moors, "This name is only known to them through the language of the Europeans" (141). But since Dupuis's survey employs a "broad brush," as Charles Hansford Adams observes (xlii), it also provides a useful way to figure Adams's racial difference in relationship to the racial hierarchies and assumptions that structure the world of the text.

The appendix approaches the "three great classes" of North Africa: "Berrebbers, Arabs, and Moors." Of this triumvirate, the Arabs are clearly atop the racial hierarchy, as is made clear by the reference to their courageous mode of warfare and pseudo-European facial features. As the descendants of fifth-century invaders of the North African coast, the Arabs work more by "open violence than by treachery" (Cock 141) and also have "fine features and intelligent countenances." Those "fine features" inevitably correspond to the requirements of white and Anglo-American beauty: "strait" hair, large "piercing" eyes, and "noses gently arched" (140). These desirable phenotypical features are, of course, an indication of desirable emotional characteristics; as compared to the debased Berber, the Arab is more "noble and magnanimous" (140). Clearly taking his cue from early nineteenth-century racist pseudosciences, Dupuis equates the Arab's

Anglo-Saxon bodily features with similarly racialized dispositions. He is quick to note, however, that aside from these saving graces, "It is impossible to say anything in his favor." Even so, having something akin to the "noble savagery" of Native Americans, they are seemingly the best of the North African worst. This is in stark contrast to the "Berrebbers," who appear to fall a distinct rung below the Arabs and who are noted as the original inhabitants of North Africa. Though many of their features might be understood as "handsome" (137), they are more significantly characterized by a "malignant and ferocious expression" (137). Accordingly, the Berbers appear to be the most violent of their North African counterparts, "guilty of the most atrocious acts of treachery and murder" (138). As opposed to open warfare, their "usual mode of warfare is to surprise their enemy, rather than overcome him by an open attack" (139). They are a cowardly set of people, Dupuis suggests. Finally, the Moors are offered as the descendants of the first two groups as well as black Africans. Since they are a mixture of "the two other classes" (136), they occupy some indistinct relation to both the Arabs and Berbers but clearly fall below the Arabs. Below these factions are groups that Dupuis does not even bother to mention in the "three great classes," such as the "prolific" numbers of black Africans, who are "continually increasing by fresh arrivals from the countries of the Soudan" (143), and the Jews, who are only given a parenthetical note (136).

Though they are never explicitly listed as an official "class" of people, Dupuis hints at the potential relationship between "mulattos" and the inhabitants of North Africa. Dilating on the characteristics of the Arabs, Dupuis avers: "The colour of those [Arabs] who reside in Barbary is a deep but bright brunette, essentially unlike the sallow tinge of the Mulatto. The Arabs are more or less swarthy according to their proximity to the Negro states; until, in some tribes, they are found entirely black, but without the wooly hair, wide nostril, and thick lip which peculiarly belong to the African Negro" (140). According to Dupuis's classificatory order, the mulatto is a symptom of social disease and taxonomic disorder. Although the Arab is a religious, national, and cultural abnormality, he is unmixed and, therefore, at least identical with himself. In contrast, mulatto subjects, such as Adams, are marked by a "sallow tinge," which is the expression of dilution or sickness. This reading is confirmed with the second mention of the word "mulatto" in the account's editorial matter. Of the "discreditable" unions between Arabs and Berbers, and Moors derived from black Africans, Dupuis notes: "These matches entail on their offspring the Negro feature and a mulatto-like complexion, but darker" (143). Put another way, the mulatto is the product of unlicensed encounters, the product of forbidden relations and crossed racial boundaries. In both uses, mulatto is read as a kind of stain, a deformation, a mixture that corrupts the original. Though not quite as bad as a "Negro"—

with his wooly hair, flared nostrils, and pronounced lips—mulattos apparently fall well short of the Arabs and probably below the Berbers as well. They appear to be most like Moors, who are a promiscuous fusion of the Arabs and Berbers, the two "classes" who sit atop the North African chain of racial being. Lending credence to this thesis, Dupuis asserts that Adams's complexion is similar to the Moors of Fez, whose pigmentation is "quite as light as that of Adams" (89). According to the logic of the appendix, the mulatto, in fact, is merely the Moor turned inside out. While some of the Moors have dark skin and white features, mulattos have light skin and black features (as was the reputed case with Adams). Moors and mulattos are thus perverse racial cross dressers, joining together and intensifying the stigma of already despised and denigrated groups.

All of these observations lead to an important but veiled truth governing the racial thinking of the text: the mixed race figure Adams is likely viewed by Cock, Dupuis, and the members of the African Company as being just as degenerate as his North African captors. In relationship to the "three great classes," he is probably no better than the Arabs and Berbers, only a slight step above the black Africans, and uncannily similar to the "half-breed" Moors he encounters on the coast. At the same time, Dupuis, Cock, and the other agents of the African Company must use, and to some extent, value Adams's experience and opinions if the narrative is to work. Within this framework, *Narrative* presents a paradoxical opportunity for the mulatto Adams to rehabilitate his image by being a captive to Moors and black Africans. In the counterintuitive logic of the Barbary captivity narrative, to be bound by someone is to be morally and culturally superior. The captive is spiritually authoritative, and the captor is morally abject. Inasmuch as Anglo-American whiteness is read as a function of moral, cultural, and spiritual identities, the Barbary captivity narrative could also render the mulatto Adams as metaphorically and literarily white, elevating him above his nearest rivals in the North African chain of racial being. The mutability of these identities ultimately trouble their seeming integrity and singularity. As Cassandra Jackson notes more generally of biracial figures we could also note more specifically of Adams's depiction in his narrative, which is that they work to "call attention to the constructedness of blackness and whiteness" (6). In this way, the burden of "preserving" whiteness under the duress of foreign captivity could become an ironic opportunity to reinvent it.

Insupportable Heat, Hard Slavery, and Fragile Racial Identities

The racialized schemas of the appendix are borne out in the invocations and illustrations of racial, ethnic, and religious groups in the narrative proper. In chapter 1, and then in chapters 3 and 4, Adams's captivity consists of his abduction and largely hostile treatment by Islamic masters. Throughout these sections, Adams is not constructed as a disposable black man, as Juba Hill is in Saunders's captivity tale, or even as the tainted mulatto figure, as the Moors of Fez are in Dupuis's sketch of Barbary inhabitants. Rather, he is a sympathetically drawn and courageous "white man." Underscoring this provisional status in North Africa, Adams is paired up with a European companion at the beginning of his journey. "About this time," the narrative reveals of his initial capture by the Moors, "John Stevens arrived," a Portuguese and white shipmate of Adams from the *Charles*. Everywhere his shipmate goes, so does Adams, and just as importantly, they experience the same treatment, suggesting that Adams is essentially read as white in his travels. Referring to Adams and his Portuguese mate, for example, the narrative notes that the "party" was made up of "eighteen Moors and the two whites" (32). Likewise, when the Moors, Adams, and the Portuguese boy are ransomed from Timbuktu, the list of the redeemed reads, "10 Moorish traders," "14 Moorish prisoners," "1 slave," and "2 white men," the latter entry referring to Adams and his European companion (49). Serving as Adams's doppelganger, Stevens highlights the valuation of Adams as essentially white in the context of Islamic captivity.

Adams's response to the stifling heat becomes a typical way in which the narrative materializes this new, if temporary, racial identity. While the Moors do fine under the heat, the captives are stripped of their clothing and cannot bear the elements. The narrator explains: "Being thus exposed to a scorching sun, their skins became dreadfully blistered, and at night they were obliged to dig holes in the sand to sleep in, for the sake of coolness" (29). At another moment, the narrative laments, "They suffered severely from exposure to the scorching sun, in a state of almost utter nakedness" (53). The blistering of the skin suggests the physiological and corporal transformations hinted at when the sailors first meet the circumcised Moors. If they continue to bake in the African sun, the account implies, they might too become, like the Moors, "straight haired, but quite black," an apparently hideous amalgam of European-American hair and African pigmentation. Recalling a standard moment in Barbary captivity narratives where North African captors easily endure the heat, the European subjects collapse under the oppressive heat of the sun. In *The Glory of Goodness*, Cotton Mather's 1703 sermon about several colonists' Algerine captivity, the speaker effuses, "Their Strength must have been the Strength of Stones, & ther Flesh of Brass" because the climate was "so hot" (62). *Narrative* uses a similar method in its description of the inhabitants of Timbuktu, thereby conflating the hardiness of the Moors with that of black Africans. "The natives of Tombuctoo are a stout, healthy race, and are seldom sick," the narrator intones, "although they expose themselves by lying out in the sun at mid-day, when the heat is almost insupportable to a white man" (225). Adams's provisional whiteness is ironically supported by the "insupportable" heat. He is a de facto "white man" for his inability to suffer the heat as the "stout" and "healthy" natives of Timbuktu do. Paradoxically, this lack of stamina on the part of Adams and his other captives is not an indictment against their virility but a mark of their intellectual superiority. To invoke O'Connel again, it is what "naturally" happens to delicately made white subjects under slavery. Since their bodies are supple things that cannot endure the strain of the African sun, moments of vulnerability and corporeal failure paradoxically prove their authentic humanity, similar to how Frado's sickness under child indentured servitude suggested her sentience. But in stark opposition to Wilson's narrative project, the image of fainting captives here buttresses the imperial fantasy that the native Africans will labor quite easily under the sun. As the surrogate white colonizer in this colonial dream, Adams is the frail white observer whose only appropriate job is to manage the indestructible natives, no doubt from the shady relief provided by an umbrella or nearby tree.

At other times, *Narrative* establishes Adams's whiteness and respectable identity through unfavorable comparisons between him and his Moorish captors. In a quintessential example of what Jacob Rama Berman refers to as the "arabesque," or the deployment of stereotypical images of Arab people in order to define white identity advantageously (16), the account describes the Moors as an essentially spineless bunch when they are enslaved by indigenous Africans. Of their "prison" at the black African encampment, *Narrative* notes: "The place of confinement was a mere mud wall, about six feet high, from whence they might readily have escaped (though strongly guarded), if the Moors had been enterprising; but they were a cowardly set" (33). Though the Moors behave confidently and decisively as captors, when they are reduced to captives, they are afraid to tackle even the most trifling of obstacles. In late eighteenth-century parlance, they might be said to lack the "virtue" that was seen as essential for all self-respecting and self-governing men (Frustenberg 1310).

In contrast to this effeminate rabble, Adams makes several heroic escape attempts, particularly after he is transferred back to the Moors after their ransom from Timbuktu. Like the antebellum slave narrator, Henry Bibb, he is a master in the "art of running away," using his various errands for his captor as an opportunity to flee. While serving as a slave to Hamet Laubed in Vled Duleim, Adams is sent on an errand to fetch water from a well; though he "signifie[s] his consent," he is "determined to make his escape" and flees to Wadinoon (54). After an amorous affair between Adams and one his master's wives, Adams again "[makes] his escape" and flees to a neighbor's tent (56). Having been sold to another Moorish master, Boerick, and then transferred to his associate, Abdallah Houssa, who promises to take Adams to Wadinoon for redemption, Adams again runs away. Impatient for his freedom, Adams cannot wait for another person to deliver it for him. The narrator explains, "As the time hung very heavy on his hands, and he saw no preparation for their departure for Wadinoon, and his anxiety to reach that place had been very much excited by the intelligence that there were other Christians there, he took every opportunity of making inquiry respecting the course and distance; and being at length of the opinion that he might find his way thither, he one evening determined to desert; and accordingly he set out on foot alone" (58). Unlike his cowardly Moorish captors, Adams does not suffer captivity easily. Taking "every opportunity" to find the way to Christian relations, he escapes his Islamic master once he realizes that his manumission is not eminent or even likely. Without camel, horse, or any other means of transportation, Adams will "set out on foot" and "alone" to secure his freedom. Recalling Hannah Dustan's trek through the New England "wilderness" after the violent dispatch of her Abenaki captors, Adams uses only his feet to navigate the path to freedom. Like her, he is a lover of freedom and cannot remain in captivity for long, despite the costs.

When he does not have the ability to flee his Moorish masters, Adams actively refuses to labor for them, demonstrating his bravery and defiance. Upon learning that Hamet Laubed does not plan on redeeming him in Suerra or Mogadore, the narrative reports, "Adams resolved not to attend any longer to the duty of watching the goats and sheep" (53). This act of insolence results in Adams being struck with a "thick stick" (53), but as opposed to merely accepting this indignity, "he resisted, and took away the stick" (53). Though this attempt to defend himself promptly leads to a "severe beating" by a throng of mostly Moorish women, such scenes reflect Adams's refusal to succumb to his "Mohammedan" masters, even in the face of violent retribution.

Adams's tenacity in the midst of similar adversity is most elaborately staged through the text's rendition of his captivity to the belligerent and religiously intolerant Bel Cossim family. The representation of this family is contextualized by the specifically religious mandates of Islamic slavery. According to historian Paul E. Lovejoy, the Islamic slave trade emerged as an outgrowth of Islamic holy wars and eventually spread throughout several regions, from Saudi Arabia to the Middle East, India, and North Africa (16). It was grounded in the belief that if foreign slaves would convert to Islam, then they would be freed or at least be eligible for emancipation. It is in this sense that Lovejoy characterizes it as a "religious apprenticeship for pagans" (16). Noticeably absent from the Cádiz version of his captivity, Adams's trials with the Bel Cossim family consolidate his identity as a resistant Christian male subject who refuses to countenance Islam. The first opportunity to demonstrate this steadfastness comes when Hameda Bel Cossim, his master's son, desires him to work on the Sabbath day and Adams refuses. In response, "Hameda struck him on the forehead with the cutlass, and gave him a severe wound over the right eye." In turn, "Adams knocked him down with his fist" (61). Adams's retaliation instantaneously precipitates his attack by several nearby Moors who beat him till "he was almost killed" (61). Though in less poetic and measured terms, the depiction of Adams's resistance to the Bel Cossim family anticipates Frederick Douglass's recollection of his heroic refusal of the slave breaker Covey in his *Narrative*. Like Douglass, who "repell[s] by force the bloody arm of slavery" (Douglass 50), Adams too uses physical resistance to oppose his master. Moreover, just as in Douglass's narrative, such violent disobedience renews a "sense of [his] own manhood" (Douglass 50). To be sure, Adams never successfully overpowers his attacker as Douglass does; nonetheless, his steadfast and physically aggressive model of resistance demonstrates his courage and endurance.[4]

The Bel Cossims' reaction to Adams's defiance further bolsters his image as an embattled Christian martyr. In response to Adams striking his master's son, Hameda's mother, Moghtari, verbally chastises him, and along with Hameda's father, tells Adams that he must kiss Hameda's hands and feet in order to avoid further discipline (62). The staging of Adams's refusal and subsequent punishment powerfully frames Adams as a faithful Christian in the midst of an ungodly and uncivilized people. The narrator explains: "Adams then stated to him, that he could not submit to do so; that it was 'contrary to his religion' to kiss the hands and feet of any person; that in his own country he had never been required to do it; and that whatever might be the consequence, he would not do it. Finding he would not submit, the old man ordered that he should be put in irons, and accordingly they fastened his feet together with iron chains, and did the same by his hands" (62). More than any other moment in the Barbary captivity portion of the narrative, this scene composes Adams as a resilient and courageous Christian crusader. Kissing the feet of another person is "contrary to his religion." Significantly, this is one of only a handful of moments in the text in which Cock chooses to use what is presented as Adams's actual language, as indicated by the quotation marks in the above passage.[5] The choice to insert Adams's exact words (or even to present them as such) underscores the significance of Adams's rebelliousness. Cock deploys Adams's language as a means of underscoring Adams's commitment to Christian doctrine at the point at which that subject position receives its most strident attack. In his refusal to kiss the hands and feet of his master's son he is refusing the transformation into a North African subject, a traitor to and defector from Christianity and presumably white civilization, embodied in the Frenchman encountered on the beach after his shipwreck. Charles Hansford Adams asserts: "In [Adams's] refusal to submit to the inhumanity and degradation of his master's demands, Adams stands for individual dignity. Bel

Cossim's only principle is greed, and his professed religion is a sham" (xlviii). Equally important, the passage encodes not just his resilient religious identity but also his national one, for "in his own country" Adams would have never been required to perform such an act. Though wrecked on the shores of a land of perverse masculinity, Adams will not use his body for purposes that his national identity will not allow. *Narrative*'s portrayal of Adams's steadfast refusal, even in the face of incredible bodily harm, thus reiterates his spiritual, national, and racial identity as a Christian, American, white male. As John S. Jacobs is imprisoned for his refusal to submit to Norcom, and thus metaphorically kiss Norcom's hands and feet, Adams is chained and imprisoned for his refusal to submit to his Islamic masters. As with John Jacobs, the iconography of the carceral is invoked to underscore Adams's suffering as well as his masculine endurance. His literal binding by the Bel Cossim family—hands and feet chained together—binds him to his readers' affection. Replicating and anticipating the movements of sympathy in antislavery writing, Adams's tied hands tie him to his readers, link him to their affections, and chain him to their compassion. Serving as a paradoxical link to his white and European American readers, the iron chains bind him to readers who mourn the bondage and poor treatment of a Christian subject who refuses to accede to the perverse demands of Islamic slavery.

After more than a week in this condition, the narrator reveals, "Moghtari came to him again, urging him to do as required, and declaring that if he did not, he should never see the Christian country again; Adams, however, persevered in turning a deaf ear to her entreaties and threats" (62). Adams's "deaf ear" allows his cry for national citizenship and religious affiliation to be heard. His "perseverance" is precisely what is made clear in this scene; Adams is not one who will turn "Mohammedan" or bow to Islamic power but will stay true to his nation and God. Adams is kept in this condition from June until August, to the point where his "sufferings having reduced him almost to a skeleton" (62). Provocatively, while Adams is a "mulatto" in England or America, with its corresponding "features and complexion," Adams is a "skeleton" in Barbary, that is, mere white bone. Put another way, he literally loses his flesh here, removes the tainted skin that signals his identification with the Moors and black Africans. Through his skeletal form, he is ironically and paradoxically a "white" subject. A striking metaphor for, and example of, the (de)racializing imperatives of narratives of North African captivity, Adams's reduction to a "skeleton" speaks to the insistent production of white identity typical of North African captivity narratives. Like the Adamic "bone" of Genesis, it authors the white subject presumably already existing within Adams. In turn, Adams's status as "mulatto" is elided in these scenes as he is "reduced" and reconstituted as a sympathetic white subject.

The narrative consolidates and concludes its rendition of Adams's exceptional Christian character by contrasting it with the untimely conversion of two of Adams's shipmates. Unlike Adams, Williams and Davison do not have the religious fortitude or national fidelity to remain Christians and, implicitly, Anglo-Americans: "As the Moors were constantly urging them to become Mohammedans, and they were unceasingly treated with the greatest brutality, the fortitude of Williams and Davison being exhausted, they at last unhappily consented to renounce their religion, and were circumcised" (63). Bringing the narrative full circle, Williams's and Davison's circumcisions certify the conversion that had been predicted on the beach, that culturally if not physically they would retain the "straight hair" of Europeans but become culturally and spiritually "black" like the Moors. More to my point, serving to negatively define Adams's identity, the apostasy of Williams and Davison prove that Adams is a dedicated Christian; nothing will deter him from keeping his faith, national identity, and physical constitution. After his shipmates convert, the narrative describes Adams as "the only remaining Christian at Wadinoon," which forces him to be a "more especial manner an object of the derision and persecution of the Moors" (63). In this way, the narrative frames Wadinoon as the ex-slave narrator Henry Bibb frames his sufferings in the deplorable Louisville workhouse. Similar to Bibb's pronouncement that "in such company, and under such influences, where there was constant swearing, lying, cheating, and stealing, it was almost impossible for a virtuous person to avoid pollution" (Bibb 94), Adams strikes the pose of the solitary man holding on to his salvation in the midst of Christian apostates. Unconverted by the transformations and contaminations of North African captivity, he remains uncircumcised and true to his religion. So though North African captivity is supposed to be a challenge to the religious and racial identities of European American subjects, *Narrative* actually consolidates the white Christian identity that Adams would have probably been denied outside North Africa.

From a Captive to a "Curiosity"

Adams's abduction by indigenous Africans shows alternative models of whiteness in Barbary captivity. Instead of being held by Moors or Arabs, Adams is held by Africans, a racial proximity that foregrounds his reputed whiteness but that also requires the text to become more tightfisted with the authority it necessarily grants Adams. These depictions reveal continuities with as well as stark differences from the kinds of power Adams generates in his Islamic captivity sections.

This fictional representation, if only obliquely and in fantastic form, emerges out of the historical facts of lineage slavery, a system the narrative suggests when it notes that Adams had become a slave to "Negroes" (Cock 32). Most similar to what we have seen with the pre-Columbian slavery practiced by southeastern Native Americans, lineage slavery was not based on race but on familial relationships. Such slaves were first taken as prisoners of war, for example, but they were not understood as a category of people that were fundamentally distinct from other Africans (Lovejoy 13). As a result, the line between captive and captor could eventually be crossed by becoming a part of the local kinship system through intermarriage, childbirth, and communal living. "In this setting," Lovejoy explains, "people had slaves along with other types of dependants, but society was not organized in such a manner that slavery was a central institution. These were not slave societies" (13). After the intervention of European demand for slaves in the Atlantic slave trade, the line between free and unfree became more pronounced, as was also the case with the southeastern Native American practice of slavery.[6] Lovejoy writes: "The pull of the [Atlantic slave] market had the effect of pushing indigenous forms of slavery further away from a social framework in which slavery was another form of dependency in societies based on kinship relationships to a system in which slaves played an increasingly important role in the economy" (18). Though it did not necessarily maintain a belief in the fundamental inferiority of slaves, as came to be true in European slavery, indigenous African slavery had nonetheless transformed from a marginal system in tribal life to a central one by the early nineteenth century. In this way, Adams finds himself, if only by implication, entangled in the same kind of bondage that Africans brought over on the Middle Passage would have initially encountered as well as in domestic African slavery.

The narrative presents this form of bondage as categorically more favorable than Islamic slavery. In contrast to his rough treatment under his Moorish and Arab captors, Adams is treated as a prize in his section on Timbuktu, chapter 2, the longest chapter of the entire narrative. Moving from the position of a debased captive among the Moors, Adams is a cherished "curiosity" in Timbuktu. While their former Moorish captors are taken to prison, Adams and his Portuguese double are taken to the house of the Timbuktu elite (35). As opposed to the Cádiz narrative in which the natives "manifested no desire of knowing any thing further of me or my country" (Storrow 157), Adams is depicted as practically a celebrity in the London version. "For some time after their arrival," *Narrative* explains, "the Queen and her female attendants used to sit and look at Adams and his companion for hours together" (Cock 35). The account further maintains that "neither Adams nor the Portuguese boy," says Cock, "were ever subjected to any restraint while they remained at Tombuctoo. They were allowed as much food, and as often as they pleased; and were never required to work" (47). Significantly, Adams is not free or able to leave Timbuktu, either from not knowing how to or not being given permission to do so. It is only after a period of six months, when a band of traveling Moors ransom Adams, Stevens, and the imprisoned Moors for an unknown quantity of tobacco, recalling Mary Rowlandson's ransom fee, that he is able to leave Timbuktu. It is for this reason that Charles Hansford Adams argues that Adams constitutes a form of "human merchandise" in Timbuktu, simultaneously having bodily freedom to roam the city and yet having clear monetary value as a white ward in the all-black state (xii). As such, Adams experiences the mildest captivity depicted in the account, hovering somewhere between a political prisoner and a houseguest.

The narrative's invention of this relatively mild captivity permits and prompts Adams's detailed description of Timbuktu. As one who is free to roam the city, Adams's role as fact finder, the narrative wants us to believe, is not hampered by the usual limitations of captives, such as the immobile Moors, for instance, who stay locked in a "prison" for the entire six months. In fact, his position as a guest in the "king's" house means that he has access to information and details to which only an insider or friend of the ruling authorities might be privy. The narrative rationalizes an "ignorant sailor's" discovery of a five-hundred-year-old geographical mystery by an appeal to one of the fundamental realities of captivity: bound subjects must go where their captors take them.

This use of the power of what David Lambert terms "enslaved knowledge" (51) finds a historical corollary in the case of Scottish geographer James MacQueen. MacQueen was the first European to identify the directional flow of the Niger (50), a geographic holy grail for Western explorers (B. Gardner 8). As he admitted and, one might even say, paraded in the preface to his seminal *A Geographical and Commercial View of Northern Central Africa*, both his interest in and pioneering contributions to African exploration could be significantly attributed to the Mandingo slaves he oversaw on a Grenadan plantation (Lambert 49). Hearing MacQueen read from Park's *Travels to the Interior Districts of Africa*, one of his bondspeople noted their familiarity with the region and another even revealed that he had helped Park navigate the Niger (49). MacQueen represented this as a turning point in his life that spurred him to further scientific investigation and discovery. These surprising bonds between captivity and scientific authority would define MacQueen's entire career and life, as related in an 1870 obituary written by the Royal Geographic Society (successor to the African Association): "The information obtained through this intelligent boy [an enslaved Mandingo child] was afterwards of great use to Mr. Macqueen, when he was engaged in bringing together all that was known about the geography of the Niger, a subject on which he became a leading authority" (qtd. in Lambert 51). Considered an "arm chair" or "speculative" geographer, MacQueen never set foot in Africa (48), but because of his largely unmediated access to, and indeed control over, African-born bondspeople, he was able to establish a preeminent reputation as a "leading authority" on African exploration.

Similar to MacQueen's use of Grenadan bondspeople's geographical expertise, the African Company built their case for international respectability and scientific authority on the specialized knowledge of Africa that a survivor of Barbary captivity might acquire. Confirming the applicability of the Barbary captivity to this model, one of the many written sources James MacQueen used to flesh out his speculations about North African geography was James Riley's best-selling Barbary captivity narrative, which also contained information about Timbuktu and the African hinterland (Lambert 57). Along these same lines, the African Company needed the imprimatur of direct experience and contact to legitimize their assertions. Providing first-hand experiential knowledge, Adams's urgent story of Barbary captivity allowed the African Company the direct, fieldwork model of geographic investigation that would come to dominate the discipline in the nineteenth century (Lambert 49) and thereby strengthen their claim to intellectual credibility.

Fertile Land: Cultivating Whiteness in Timbuktu

Heavily leaning on this authority, chapter 2 of Adams's account contains sundry, if fantastic, descriptions of the rituals, vegetation, political life, and the many details that would have interested early nineteenth-century Westerners about the famed "emporium of Africa." These descriptions underwrite his identity as a rational and objective Western subject. Functioning like a biblical Adam, he re-creates Timbuktu in the image of Euro-American places and patterns. As William Boelhower notes of early European maps, they reflected "an interpretive gaze that objectifies the eye of the beholder and offers an identikit of his desires and possibilities" (51). Adams and the African Company thus do not record a map of Timbuktu, as much as produce one from available models and forms.

The account's take on the obligatory question of the features of the Niger provides one such example. "The river," the narrator explains, "is well stored with fish, chiefly of a sort which Adams took for the red mullet: there is also a large red fish, in shape somewhat like a salmon, and having teeth; he thinks it is the same fish which is known in New York by the name of 'sheep's head'" (222). Note the presence of the "same fish" that are found in New York, as well as the fact there are others that look "like a salmon" and "the red mullet," suggesting that Adams remembers only what he has already seen. Seeming more like the Hudson on which Adams was allegedly born, the river is merely a duplicate of what Adams and his readers might have already known. Though the account is factually negligent and historically untrue, it strikes a pose that is representationally honest, that of rendering foreign lands in the language of home.

Styling Adams as a colorful ethnographer of the people of Timbuktu, the narrative's description of a Timbuktuan dance sets him up as a rational observer of strange and foreign customs. Anticipating the rendition of an eccentric "Indian frolic" that Henry Bibb delivers in his slave narrative, the passage casts Adams as an authority on indigenous African cultural forms. In one of the many footnotes provided by Dupuis, a footnote recorded in the extensive notes to the narrative taken from Dupuis's Mogadore version of Adams's captivity, a traditional African dance is described in this way:

> The following was the nature of the dance:—six or seven men, joining hands, surrounded one in the centre of the ring, who was dressed in a ludicrous manner, wearing a large black wig stuck full of cowries. This man at intervals repeated verses which, from the astonishment and admiration expressed at them in the ring, appeared to be extempore. Two performers were playing on the outside of the ring; one on a large drum, the other on a sort of guitar. They did not interrupt the singer in the ring during his recitations; but at the end of every verse the instruments struck up, and the whole party joined in loud chorus, dancing around the man in the circle, stooping to the ground and throwing up their legs alternately. (84)

A seeming mixture of colonial fantasy and the actual improvisational dynamics and call-and-response that generally characterize West African dance,[7] the description consolidates both Adams's and Dupuis's sense of themselves as authorized redactors of African cultural practices. They make value judgments (the clothing is "ludicrous") as well as substantive claims about the effect of the song leader's verbal instructions on the audience. As before, foreign elements are made accessible through the familiar iconography and cultural referents of the white European American observer, as in the fact that the unidentified and unidentifiable instrument is "a sort of guitar." The specificity of the details provides the aura of facticity and Adams and Dupuis emerge as unexpected experts. As Native Americans were being displaced in North America through the Civilization Act of 1817 and other unofficial programs of assimilation, the African continent was being readied for its measured and deliberate mapping by European powers (Livingstone 166–76). In both cases, the representation of simple, strange, and crude Native Americans and black Africans facilitated the removals and annihilations of identity attendant to colonial conquest. Paving the way for African removal and expropriation, Adams and Dupuis prove themselves adept at this kind of literary disenfranchisement through their representation of allegedly "indigenous" dance. They fashion themselves as respectable through the alleged savagery and vulgarity of Africans.

The text's description of Adams's accompaniment of an elephant hunting party quickly puts into relief his elevated status in the city. *Narrative* remembers the elephant hunt as a consolidation of racial difference and hierarchies. "Upon the occasion of the elephant being killed," Cock informs the reader, "The Negroes were greatly delighted: and Adams frequently laughed with them, at the recollection of their appearance as they stood around the dead carcase [*sic*], all laughing and shewing [*sic*] their white teeth at once, which formed a ridiculous contrast with their black faces" (40). The passage reinforces the exalted aesthetic value of the white subject and the category of whiteness more generally in North Africa, particularly as the native blacks pathetically skin their teeth, which only emphasizes the difference of their hyperbolically dark faces. Though Adams is said to exhibit racially questionable "features and complexion" in the "Introductory Details," he is essentially white here, at least next to the black Africans of Timbuktu. His laughter at the contrast of their faces and teeth elide his disparaged pigmentation and facial features. He is imagined as self-evidently and uniformly white in contrast to the dark creatures who feast on the elephant. In miniature, the contrast of their "white teeth" and "black faces" mimics the production of Adams's whiteness in the midst of the apparently all-black city. Like the proverbial drops of black concentrate mixed with white paint in *Invisible Man*'s paint factory, the purest whiteness comes from blackness in Timbuktu as well. Adams's conditional whiteness is made all the more apparent and recognizable due to the blackness around him.

Moreover, the elephant hunt allegorizes the search for whiteness that is at the center of the text's description of the famed city. One of the many points that Adams's detractors criticize the London narrative for is its claim that the elephants of Timbuktu, at least based on the aforementioned tale, have four tusks. Significantly, in the manifest of items the African Company claimed it would now trade in as opposed to human beings—rice, indigo, cotton, palm oil, timber, and gold—ivory is also mentioned. Hence, it would seem that *Narrative* advances this point considering the economic boon four-tusked elephants would suggest for European colonization. To be fair, though, Cock parts ways with Adams on the matter of the four tusks and blames his deficient memory; he states it is clearly a "mistake" (79). But more than just commercial profit, the four-tusked and thus ivory-rich elephant also communicates the idea that whiteness, in literal and metaphorical ways, can be found in high quantities in Timbuktu. Like the great Melvillian search for the sperm whale in *Moby-Dick*, the elephant hunt has whiteness and masculinity at its core. He and his fellow hunters sit around and eat the flesh of the animal, feasting on this dark animal that produces whiteness out of its face. In consuming it, they imbibe its operations, but the unfortunate "Negroes" can only take its darkness while Adams draws on its whiteness. Ironically, even as the Africans' "black faces" allegorize the creation of this relative whiteness, they cannot participate in it. Conveniently, black Africans can lead Adams to an accessible and prolific whiteness, but they cannot be transformed by it. Since the elephant is also an infant (though "an immense size, the natives said it was a young one," the narrator explains [40]), its identity is in flux, as is the captive Adams's. The consumption of the baby elephant abets his achievement of racial purity, defining him against the blackness around him. In a laconic sentence reminiscent of the narrative's brief note on the Moors' circumcised penises, the account notes of the baby elephant: "The legs were as thick as Adams's body" (40). The elephant occupies a metonymic relationship with Adams; he too is in formation and is a "dark" entity that will produce whiteness.

This picture of Africans as childlike savages with hyperbolic and uncomely racial features contrasts sharply with, but also unnervingly anticipates, the construction of African blacks found in the accounts of African American explorers. Since Paul Cuffee in the late eighteenth century, African Americans had been traveling back to Africa. The formation of the Society for Colonizing Free people of Color in the United States in 1816, which eventually came to be known as the American Colonization Society (ACS), furnished a practical, if highly controversial, way in which this dream was realized. Sponsored by both antislavery whites, who desired a convenient way to address the calls for freed blacks' enfranchisement, and proslavery whites, who feared the wrath of African American rebellion, the program was almost unanimously rejected by black Americans, who saw it as a means to banish them (Fairhead et al. 8–9). Despite its conflicting constituencies, the ACS facilitated the emigration of some thirteen thousand blacks to what eventually became the republic of Liberia (10). Of this number, a handful of émigrés made journeys into the African interior and provide a useful counterpoint to Adams's account's minstrel-like rendition of Timbuktuan natives.

Free-born black George Seymour was one such explorer. Though originally opposed to the colonization movement, Seymour became one of its most vocal proponents, relocating himself and his family to Liberia in 1841 and encouraging many others to do so, particularly blacks in his hometown of Hartford, Connecticut (Fairhead et al. 32). Seymour's change of heart was likely encouraged by the rapid success he achieved in business and politics after moving to Liberia, establishing a school, cotton and coffee farm, blacksmith shop (33), and missionary settlement (40) as well as serving in the Liberian House of Representatives (39). Indeed, it was likely as a businessman and government official that Seymour eyed the expansion of the colony's commercial, political, and religious influence into the African interior. This goal was the expressed purpose of his 1858 expedition, along with fellow émigrés Levin Ash and William Taylor, to the prosperous but remote town of Musadu (41), which resulted in *The Journal of George L. Seymour to the Interior of Liberia, 1858*, a chronicle he addressed and dedicated to Liberia's expansion-minded president Stephen A. Benson.

Unlike the African Company's representations, Seymour's account clearly wants to draw a dignified picture of black Africans. "We saw industry, cleanliness, economy, and mechanical genius," he notes of his first encounters, "far surpassing any land ever seen among the natives of the coast" (Seymour 127). Reversing the racist logic of what Anne McClintock calls "anachronistic space," in which Europeans move forward through African space but backwards in historical time (40), Seymour's progression into the African hinterland reveals technological mastery and agricultural sophistication. At almost every one of his stops, he identifies the number of looms, livestock, produce, earthen goods, and other manufactures particular to the town. At Quanyer, he emphasizes the "daily market for oil, rice, peas, corn, cotton, and snuff" (Seymour 139). At Boo, he points out the community's full measure of "rice, corn, cassava, ground-peas, etc., all of which looks as thriving as if it was land from which heavy timber had been cut" (143). In Seymour's handling, the African interior epitomizes abundance and industry not apathy and indigence.

Combating the colonial myth of "Africans' purported lack of hygiene" (A. McClintock 226), Seymour celebrates the natives' steadfast commitment to cleanliness. Of the Mandingoes, he remarks that "they and their children are very cleanly," and of the inhabitants of Quanyer, "the people are very clean in their cooking. They have covers to all their pots; and they wash them clean" (Seymour 139). Seymour's journal thus uses its clear commercial interest in untapped markets and manufactures to mount a defense of African respectability, similar to Olaudah Equiano's re-creation of his idealized African childhood in *Interesting Narrative*. Created for an audience of Liberian émigrés, but also for an international audience of potential naysayers, Seymour's *Journal* attempts to position Africa and Africans in the best possible light, especially to American blacks ambivalent about colonization. Perhaps with a promise of the benefits of diasporic reunion, Seymour highlights the continuities between black culture in Africa and in the United States: "Head handkerchiefs are very common in this part of the country, no doubt the fashion went over from Africa to America" (130). Africa, even if inaccessible by thousands of miles, is really home for African Americans, and black emigration and exploration redressed this strained relationship.

But even as Seymour's report cultivates a nascent, pan-African solidarity, it also exposes the many fissures within the Americo-Liberian community as well as between black colonizationsts and the surrounding native populations.

The colony was made up of several competing, overlapping, and highly color-conscious groups: the white governors who initially headed the colony, light-skinned and mixed-race blacks who dominated the government up until 1870, seemingly darker-skinned blacks who controlled agriculture, West Indian blacks who vied with blacks from various American states, Africans who had been rescued from slave ships and resettled in Liberia, and indigenous Africans who cast their lot among the immigrants (Fairhead et al. 20–23). Seymour, Ash, and Taylor were apparently mixed race and could have had ties to other light-skinned émigrés, who were alternatively seen as (depending on who one asked) highly intelligent, excessively self-important, or sickly mongrels (19–20). Apparently seizing on the opportunity to settle the debate, the narrative is sure to point out the instant celebrity, and authority, these light-skinned adventurers achieve as they move inland. At the town of Zanga, the narrator recalls, "They have great curiosity to see us, and, not being accustomed to mulattoes, some regard us as dead men come to life" (Seymour 132). Black Liberian settlers of all shades, it should be noted, were perceived as white by natives because of their European language, dress, writing, and religion (Fairhead et al. 29). According to Seymour's chronicle, these associations facilitate their easy passage through the various towns and no doubt lubricate their commercial negotiations with their leaders. At the city of Solong, Seymour notes that they received extraordinarily kind treatment because they were the "first civilized men in this part of the country" (Seymour 133), a muted allusion to the magical properties accorded to mulattoes. At the city of Blackabelley, the reception is even more spectacular: "Two or three hundred people flocked around us, to get a good view, and formed a complete circle" and when they are about to leave "many ran to the wall, near the gate, to get a view of us; for it is evident that we were the first civilized men they had seen" (140). As elsewhere throughout the literature of European-American travel and captivity, "civilization" is a euphemism for racial and religious superiority, as when Seymour declares that the natives are models of hard-work, and all that is needed is "good religion and civilization to complete their happiness" (132).

This feeling of colonial entitlement is manifest in several scenes where Seymour enjoys a panoramic view of the African landscape from a mountaintop. From the summits of Mounts Jane, Roberts, and Benson—all mountains Seymour takes the liberty of christening with the names of members of Liberia's elite—Seymour surveys the African creation and, God-like, pronounces that it is good. As he recollects of Mount Jane's peak, "From the top, the prospect is beautiful" (143). Though Seymour's journal attempts to rehabilitate the image of Africans in European-American exploratory and missionary literature, it also betrays the same hierarchal values, literally placing the colonizers on top.

But if the African Company's fantasy of physical domination and intellectual mastery is set in motion by the logistics and language of captivity, Seymour's wistful African adventures come to a screeching halt with the introduction of bondage. Proceeding from Wosodo without its absent "king's" approval, Seymour and his companion, Levin Ash, are attacked by what appear to be foot soldiers sent by Wosodo's spurned ruler or what might have been renegades from a neighboring town (Fairhead et al. 46). Consequently, Seymour is lacerated on the shoulder and hand, and Ash has to abandon Seymour in order to save his life (Seymour 152). This episode precipitates the end of their journey, and apparently the narrative, as it rapidly proceeds to the rather trite conclusion that "we should have waited for the king, and given him a good present" (154). In the few pages left of the narrative, we learn that Seymour makes it back to Wosodo, but Ash is eventually captured and held hostage for more than a week. He is stripped, tied, and nearly sold to another band of Africans for a gun (153). Earlier in the narrative, Seymour had basically dismissed the threat of African slavery, noting that it was "mild and patriarchal," a practice that could easily be eradicated with the Liberian government's intervention (131). However, here, the imperial fantasy of a homogenous mass of interior and inferior peoples ready to prostrate themselves for the mulatto strangers runs into a much harsher reality: the various and competing inhabitants of Africa's interior will make no special allowances for those of black ancestry, mixed race or not. Far from being "mildly" treated, Ash escapes from his would-be enslavers "looking wild and much exhausted, having suffered very much" (153).

Ultimately, Seymour's *Journal* provides a much more vexing picture of the black encounter with African captivity than Adams's text. Besides highlighting the pervasive racial and cultural elitism that animate both white and black accounts of exploration, it illustrates the limits of intraracial relations under the umbrella of colonization. Seymour, in fact, would die at the age of forty-one, in no small part due to the lingering effects of the wounds he received from his 1858 attack (Fairhead et al. 47). So as much as his account challenges the myth of African inferiority, suggested by white-sponsored captivity narratives like Adams's, it also problematizes the notion of pan-African solidarity and suggests the real problems that occurred when Americo-Liberian blacks tried to impose their wills on the peoples and land of the African interior.

For quite different reasons, the African Company's fantastic account of white-sponsored African exploration and domination runs into difficulties as well. Toward the end of the Timbuktu chapter, the narrative begins to summarize the natives' view of their captives, particularly their view of the Moorish captives as opposed to that of the "two whites," the Portuguese boy and Adams. While it notes that Moors frequently visit the city, it notes this of the "whites": "*Adams could not hear that any white man* [*sic*] *but themselves* had ever been seen in the place; and he believes, as well as from what he was told by the Moors, as from the uncommon curiosity which he excited (*though himself a very dark man, with short curly black hair*), that they had never seen one before" (47, emphasis added). This scene exposes the complex and often contradictory tensions animating the articulation of Adams's racial identity. From the lips of the natives themselves, Adams's claim and the African Company's desire is confirmed: Adams and his Portuguese companion are the first Western subjects to enter the city of Timbuktu. The testimony of the Moors as well as the "uncommon curiosity," which the captives inspire, proves the singularity of their achievement, just as Seymour and Ash's wild receptions prove them to be the first "civilized" people in the backcountry of Liberia. But significantly here, and no place else in the entire text, Cock is careful to insert that Adams is a "very dark man, with short curly black hair," an observation that confounds the claim that he is the first "white man" that the natives of Timbuktu have ever seen before. Of all the descriptions of Adams's racial identity, beside the designation that he is the son of a "mulatto" woman (Cock 17), this is the most detailed; furthermore, this is the only one to make specific reference to his "darkness," the distinction that almost universally organizes the differences between Adams and the Moors and Arabs he encounters throughout his captivity. Certainly, it is this "dark" complexion, spelled out in the appendix on racial distinctions, that the text wishes to disavow. Why would Cock make such a statement, and why would he make it at this point in the narrative? In an account that has tried so hard to suppress Adams's messy racial identity, why highlight it here?

Fearing the transfer of too much authority to the son of a "mulatto," I would submit, Cock reminds readers of Adams's stigmatized blackness. Coming in the final two pages of the Timbuktu section, the passage is an urgent reminder that Adams is of mixed race, with conspicuously distinct black "features" and "complexion," lest the reader become carried away with the many declarations of Adams's whiteness in Timbuktu (vis-à-vis his fainting in the sun, his close affiliation with the Portuguese boy, and his later defiance of his Arab masters). Certainly, as Charles Hansford Adams submits, the "veiling of Adams's blackness" would have facilitated the "political and scientific weight that the Narrative had to bear for the African Company" (xliii). However, Cock had to bracket such considerations because the Timbuktu natives accomplish too seamlessly the production of ethnic chauvinism, scientific credibility, and implicit whiteness that the African Company desired, as evinced in the elephant hunting scene. Though Cock is fine with the Timbuktu natives' misidentification of Adams, he is not willing to let an English and European-American reading audience make the same mistake. Though the prize of discovering Timbuktu is monumental, the ownership and proper distribution of whiteness is clearly an even greater treasure. The fact that Cock was willing to compromise the African Company's achievement in order to do so suggests how much the boon of whiteness, even against the glory of discovering the ancient African city, must have meant. The parentheses that close around the statement that "though himself a very dark man" signify the reins on a horse that might run away from Cock and the African Company. In order to control this loose animal, Cock goes beyond identifying Adams as an "ignorant sailor," the more frequent and acceptable charge that Cock and Dupuis make against Adams, and explains that he is a person of African descent. Recognizing the ambiguity and plasticity in Adams's subject position, Cock wants to be sure that the reader gets the right Adams at this crucial moment of discovery, that they understand how much power and authority to grant Adams and how much more is due to African Company, the true and first "discoverers."

The power of this anxiety is confirmed by way of the lengthy footnote that Dupuis provides explaining the natives' seemingly irrational identification of Adams as white. "I do not imagine," begins Dupuis, "that the curiosity of the Negroes can have been excited so much on account of Adams's colour, as because he was a Christian, and a *Christian slave*, which would naturally be to them a source of great astonishment. The Negroes must have seen, in the caravans from the Barbary states which annually visit the countries of Soudan, and Timbuctoo in particular, many Moors, especially those from Fez, of a complexion quite as light as that of Adams" (89). Dupuis is thus willing to grant Adams's pioneering achievement as a Christian but not as a white subject. Relying on the Muslim versus Christian divide that animated and organized the representation of racial difference in the Barbary captivity narrative, Dupuis attempts to sheathe Adams's ambiguous racial identity in religious terminology. He is not white but merely a Christian. Since the natives would have undoubtedly been used to seeing black slaves through the system of lineage slavery and even black slaves through Islamic slavery, Adams would have been nothing special. Here, of course, Dupuis's note clearly means to contest Adams's presumption of whiteness and to make it apparent that the prize of "white" discovery is still available to other explorers since Adams is of a mixed pedigree. Using different strategies, Cock and Dupuis muster their arsenal of truths related to North Africa and Adams to prove that Adams is black and, thereby, save whiteness for those deemed genuinely worthy of it.

However, this inability to grant Adams the whiteness the natives imagine for him poses formidable problems for the narrative of Euro-American domination suggested by Cock and Dupuis and implicitly the African Company. If what is clearly a "mulatto" for Cock can be understood as "white" by African natives, then what is the foundation of whiteness and the idea of race for that matter in a North African context? In reference to the same passage, Cock identifies Adams as "very dark" (in relation to whites) and Dupuis asserts that Adams is "light as" the Moors of Fez. Far from clarifying Adams's racial identity, the result of these competing classifications is to destabilize the notion of race, at least as a function of color. In a narrative that has repeatedly attempted to play linguistic, religious, national, and racial differences against each other in order to generate sensationalism, sympathy, and authority, its binaries break down in the form of Robert Adams, who is neither white nor black and yet both.[8] Accordingly, Cock and Dupuis scramble to recover the pieces of the crumbling edifice of white identity.

But in trying to preserve this structure for "genuinely" white subjects, it achieves an unintended consequence. It places a "very dark" and "curly haired" man at the center of its most important chapter and at the site of its most important "discovery." When the text should be making its greatest revelation—that the African Company has discovered the route to Timbuktu and it is a haven for white subjects—it makes quite another: an "ignorant" black man has made his way to the middle of Timbuktu before any educated white man could. What is even worse, there is a congress of black subjects at Timbuktu, from the promiscuously dressed "queen" to the bone-wearing "king" and now the "very dark" Adams. Uncannily rehearsing the image of Mansa Musa sitting cross-legged with his gold nugget at the center of seventeenth-century maps of Timbuktu, Cock's will to dispossess Adams of any authority reproduces the black power he strives against. Ambiguous pigmentation and hybrid genres collide to make a "white man" out of a "very dark" man and, consequently, trouble the notion of racial classification. To be sure, the Portuguese boy adds significant legitimacy to Adams's whiteness, but the text's all-too convincing display of Adams's whiteness, even with an "authentic" white subject right next to him, confirms the power of the ruse, the provocative truth that not only have whites discovered Timbuktu but that whiteness has been discovered there as well. It has been exposed as, in part, a fiction based on consent and indistinct skin tone. If we recall, it is here in Timbuktu that Adams makes his observation that the native infants are first born with a "reddish color, but become black in three or four days" (43), suggesting white readers' fear of white subjects becoming black. However, Cock's parenthetical note alerts us to a different and more catastrophic fear: How long would it take for a mulatto to become white, and thereby destabilize the meaning of whiteness, in Timbuktu? If Adams becomes "white," then not only would the slave trade be lost but also lost is the very idea on which it largely depended: the difference, superiority, and alleged singularity of whiteness.

The final achievement of the text here then is not only a privileging of whiteness or blackness but rather a destabilization and reappraisal of both concepts.

While whiteness as privilege is certainly valued in the account's rendition of Timbuktu, it is a whiteness that can be extended to the "very dark," those outside the Euro-American standard of whiteness, and perhaps even to the dusky inhabitants of North Africa. In such a context, Adams is simultaneously an emissary of whiteness as well as its confounder. In imperfectly reproducing the alleged naturalness and inevitability of whiteness, *Narrative* thus debunks race even as it participates and perpetuates the authority reserved for white Barbary captives.

"Very Dark" Captives and the Challenge to Whiteness

Given Adams's ambiguous racial identity and the deconstruction of race in *Narrative*, it is interesting to speculate on the racial identity of the anonymous "American sailor" with which this chapter commenced. Adams's narrative begins by also noting that he was an "American sailor" and similarly explains that, when he returned to "civilization," he spoke a hodgepodge of English, Arabic, and indigenous African languages. According to the appropriately titled "Introductory Details Respecting Robert Adams," Adams demonstrates the same kind of residual effects as the "American sailor" who has been captive in Barbary. "The appearance, features and dress of this man upon his arrival at Mogadore," Dupuis reveals, "so perfectly resembled those of an Arab, or rather of a Shilluh, his head being shaved, and his beard scanty and black, that I had difficulty at first in believing him to be a Christian. When I spoke to him in English, he answered me in a mixture of Arabic and broken English, and sometimes in Arabic only. At this early period, I could not help remarking that his pronunciation of Arabic resembled that of a Negro, but concluded that it was occasioned by his intercourse with Negro slaves" (15). In almost identical language, Adams is the "American sailor" who has returned from North Africa as a half or not even human subject. Owing to the conventions of Barbary captivity narratives, of course, this similarity in phrasing is not wholly unexpected. Nonetheless, in an irony of all ironies, the likeness of the "mulatto" Adams to this presumably white "American sailor" suggests the possibility that O'Connell's and thus Garrison's American sailor may not have been white or did not need to be white. Which is to say, the "proof" that Garrison means to provide that "the white slave can sink as low in the scale of humanity as the black one" may have only proved that black slaves can sink as low as other black slaves. Consequently, Garrison's use of Barbary captivity is merely smoke and mirrors, a light show that relies on the myth of racial purity and difference in order to debunk the myth of racial privilege. Though the "American sailor" is meant to be a representative of every white American male, it is possible that the captivity of one black subject authorizes the humanity of another black subject, pointing to the pointlessness and circularity of all racial taxonomies. Adams is thus the "American sailor," and he is not. He is "light," and he is "very dark." He authorizes others, and he is authorized. He simultaneously follows the rules for bondage and respect and also breaks them, showing their constructed and artificial nature. Due to the happenstances of geography, genre, and ambiguous pigmentation, this "American mulatto" experiences a captivity that is frequently read as the province of whites and in which he is also and consequently read as white. As a whole then, *Narrative* shows the nonsensical, but nonetheless necessary, constructions around captivity that can be used to make (black) humanity legible.

Epilogue

Imprisonment and Domestic Captivity in *The Color Purple*

With an eye toward a restatement of the central concerns of this project, I would like to close by briefly considering Alice Walker's 1982 Pulitzer Prize–winning novel, *The Color Purple*. Set in the rural South of the early twentieth century, the narrative recounts the embattled life but eventual redemption of a fourteen-year-old black girl named Celie, who Walker describes in the preface as a "spiritual captive." While still an adolescent, she is raped and impregnated by the man she believes to be her father, given away in marriage to an abusive stranger, and thereby forced into concubinage and domestic imprisonment. Through Celie's relationship with a series of resilient female figures, however, she learns to appreciate and cultivate her own divinity. One of the figures who helps Celie on this path to redemption is Sofia Butler, a stout, no-nonsense woman who leaves her husband after he attempts to assault her.

A tumultuous sequence of events from Sofia's life foregrounds the value of multiple forms of bondage and unfreedom to appreciating the complexity of black life and culture, then and now. One day while strolling through town, Sofia, her children, and male companion are approached by Miss Millie, the mayor's wife. Apparently fascinated by black people, Millie proceeds to pet and inspect Sofia's children, noting their well-kept appearance and "strong white teef" (85). Turning to Sofia, who she also understands as an object for her amusement, Millie asks her if she would like to be her maid. Not one to suffer fools easily, Sofia responds with a stone-faced, "Hell no" (85). Taken aback by her brashness, the mayor asks her to repeat herself, and Sofia repeats her response, verbatim; at which point, the mayor slaps her. Anyone who knows Sofia knows that the mayor has made an irrevocable mistake: Sofia knocks him out, and a brawl ensues, for which Sofia is ultimately held responsible. When her family finds her in jail, she has a fractured skull, busted eye, distended tongue, broken ribs, and black and blue skin (86–87). Adding insult to injury, when she is finally released from jail (several years later), she is forced to become the maid of the mayor and his wife (100), thereby reducing her to the position of domestic servant that she had so defiantly refused years before. Telling Celie that white people are an "affliction," she begins to document her trials as a live-in maid at the mayor's house, adding that they have her "slaving away." Sofia's "oldest boy," however, objects to her use of this phrase. According to Celie's recollection of the conversation,

> He say, Don't say slaving, Mama.
>
> Sofia say, Why not? They got me in a little storeroom up under the house, hardly bigger than Odessa's porch, and just about as warm in the winter time. I'm at they beck and call all night and all day. They won't let me see my children. They won't let me see no mens. Well, after five years they let me see you once a year. I'm a slave, she say. What would you call it?
>
> A captive, he say.
>
> Sofia go on with her story, only look at him like she glad he hers. (103)

By substituting "captive" for "slave," Sofia's son suggests that even though his mother has experienced brutal mistreatment, mistreatment that he is undoubtedly aware of since he is her "oldest boy," "slavery" would be an imprecise, if not improper, identification of her condition. His comments suggest that there are alternative and even acceptable words that can be used to talk about black suffering and that "captive," among others, might be one of them. Conversely, his interruption also implies that to deny the language of slavery, when that is what is demanded, is likely an equally serious offense.

For this latter reason, I appreciate the contributions of, and am greatly indebted to, scholarship that attempts to calibrate the ways that slavery is a "viable and relevant interpretive lens for meditating on black trauma and suffering in the contemporary era" (Richardson 163), as the work of Riché Richardson has done in the context of novels like *Push* (1996) and the film based on it, *Precious* (2009). By reading these cultural productions through the prism of what Ashraf Rushdy and others have termed neo–slave narratives, such analysis exposes the ways that the logics and legacies of chattel slavery organize modern-day social phenomena and narratives. Even so, many neo–slave narratives provoke much more than the memory of chattel slavery. As I alluded to in my chapter on slave incarceration, Toni Morrison's *Beloved*—perhaps the most iconic contemporary fictionalization of the traumas of slavery—finds its historical basis in the life of Margaret Garner, the fugitive slave who murdered her daughter and was then thrust into Kentucky's Covington jail, the same carceral structure in which fugitive slave Henry Bibb was held. *Incidents* and *Beloved*, in fact, both speak to the role of local, southern penal structures in frustrating black motherhood, not just after slavery but alongside and through it. Oriented toward similar concerns, the research of Dennis Childs shows how *Beloved* imagines technologies of black bondage both prior to antebellum chattel slavery, as in Beloved's "crouching" in the belly of the slave ship and barracoons, and after it, as in Paul D's detention in an Alfred, Georgia, chain gang cage (274).

In the spirit of seeking more textured ways to account for black suffering, in the past and at the present moment, this book offers a constellation of alternative words, narratives, and archives to conceptualize African American bondage. As its focus has been on the antebellum era, a moment in which black people were actually "slaving away," such arguments are especially complicated. It might seem counterintuitive, and almost against the spirit of Sofia's son's remarks, to consider black prisoners, servants, and captives in such a context. But as I have tried to demonstrate, slavery and other kinds of unfreedom were not (and are not) diametrically opposed, even in the antebellum era. Rather, various forms of bondage operated within the first half of the nineteenth century, abetting the power of chattel slavery where that form of oppression existed and informing the nature of black bondage in places where it did not. What is more, people of African descent not only experienced oppression in the form of imprisonment, indentured servitude, and abduction, but they drew on narratives and metaphors of other kinds of captivity to make sense of their pain and even to make sense of their resistance. Jacobs calls on the language of the penitentiary to name her sexual and racial oppression in the context of North Carolina slavery. Bibb calls on the language of colonial Indian captivity narratives to sentimentalize slavery to the Cherokees. Conversely, Harriet Wilson's account of black child indentured servitude in the North is "shadowed" by continuing practices and narratives of chattel slavery in the South. And in Robert Adams's Barbary tale, histories of transatlantic and indigenous African slavery helped to give shape to the experience and representation of North African shipwreck and abduction. Multiple iterations of confinement, captivity, and coercion have thus always and simultaneously defined black life. *Bound to Respect* teases out the interplay of these constrictions. If stories of captivity lean on and link to one another, as suggested by Hammon's tale from the introduction, it should not be surprising that "slaving" helps Sofia to enunciate her imprisonment and domestic captivity in the twentieth century, just as servitude, captivity, and imprisonment helped bondspeople to articulate their trauma in the antebellum era.

As such, the historical experience and literary figures of captivity connect African American autobiographical production and the literature of slavery to a host of phenomenon typically seen as ancillary to black American writing. They reveal, for example, that the slave narrative is a locus for emergent black prison writing. People of African descent were some of the first prisoners in the new American republic, and throughout the antebellum South, blacks were repeatedly thrust into local jails and other penal institutions. No simple line can be drawn between where their slavery ended and where their imprisonment began. Their slavery was their imprisonment, and their imprisonment was their slavery. Bibb's narrative, as well, engages with multiple kinds of slavery in unexpected places. His account underscores the fact that the dispossession of the Cherokee is also a "black" story, and that blacks' captivity in Indian Territory is both consonant with and complicates what it means to be a slave. Moving to the antebellum North, Harriet Wilson tells a story of pauper apprenticeship or binding out, but popular and sentimental narratives of sickness and invalidism enable this project as well, even as the narrative of slavery "shadows" Frado's abuses. The histories of poor children speak to the familial and institutional captivities that black children were experiencing and recounting in the first half of the nineteenth century. Finally, Robert Adams's account alerts us to the international draw of accounts of Barbary captivity and to how the presence of a "very dark" protagonist can redouble and revise the imperial claims of that genre. Literally beyond Barbary, Americans of African descent were exploring the African interior, making them susceptible to some of the same kinds of bondage that led to their forced exportation to the Americas. Blacks were thus writing in, and written in, multiple, overlapping, and ironic discourses of bondage.

Recognizing the diversity and fluidity of such histories, if done sincerely and carefully, will not diminish the relevance of chattel slavery. Rather, the histories and the narratives that grow with and out of them will help us to create a fuller catalog of black diasporic writing and experience. This catalog does not have to be necessarily laudatory or uplifting. If what we hope for in the best of our scholarship is not just that we write eloquently, or that our research will be widely circulated, but that the people, lives, and stories that populate our studies might be illuminated, then a consideration of early narratives of black unfreedom gestures toward this goal. It offers an account of black life that I hope Briton Hammon, Harriet Jacobs, Henry Bibb, Harriet Wilson, Robert Adams, and Sofia Butler—and the many lives they stand in for—might look at and recognize as theirs.

Notes

Chapter 1

1. In Starling's pioneering *The Slave Narrative*, she identifies "the first slave narrative" as *Adam Negro's Tryall* (1703), the court record of a New England slave's freedom suit against his master, John Saffin. Starling names Hammon's account as "the next slave narrative" in the tradition (52). However, most scholars tend to identify Hammon's account either as the first slave narrative or, doubting Hammon's status as a slave, the earliest prototype of the genre. In *The Slave's Narrative*, Davis and Gates begin their bibliography of slave narratives with the *Uncommon Sufferings*, and in "Briton Hammon's Narrative: Some Insights into Beginnings" Foster argues that "its content and form are the direct antecedents of the slave narrative" (179). Similarly, *Call and Response* dubs the account the "forerunner of the African American slave narrative" (Hill et al. 112). *The Oxford Companion to African American Literature* sums up these sentiments when it concludes that Hammon's text is "generally regarded as the first African American slave narrative" (Williams 337). Speaking to the implications of Hammon's account for African American literature writ large, Zafar calls *Uncommon Sufferings* "this first African American narrative" ("Capturing" 28), and Andrews anoints Hammon's narrative "the opening statement of black autobiography in America" (*To Tell* 32). Following these interpretations, Gould places Hammon among the "first black autobiographers" ("The Rise" 12) in his discussion of early slave narrators.

2. Intriguingly, Daniel Vollaro has argued that the Indian captivity narrative portion of Hammon's narrative was likely fabricated, as suggested by the seeming geographical inconsistencies, chronological impossibilities, and lack of cultural specificity with respect to Hammon's "Indians." Vollaro's observations shed light on the many stock elements of Hammon's portrayal of the Florida Natives, but Gagnon's historical analysis convincingly demonstrates how they might have been grounded in the realities of circum-Caribbean life.

3. For a discussion of the limits and shifting meanings of coartacion in Spanish America, see Fuente, "Slaves," and Varella.

4. Havana was the single most important producer of ships for the Spanish empire. McNeill writes: "Beginning in the 1720s, Havana built more durable ships more cheaply than any port in Spain" (173).

5. Among the many consequences of the case, the decision declared the unconstitutionality of the 1820 Missouri Compromise and, in the process, provided the first example of the Supreme Court's nullification of a major federal law. For a comprehensive overview of the facts and legal implications of the case, see Fehrenbacher.

6. Brian Ward notes, however, that Franklin "steadfastly denied" that she had any political motivation or agenda when she performed the song. "For Franklin," he explains, "'Respect' was primarily an appeal for domestic respect which had particular personal relevance in the midst of her tempestuous marriage to manager Ted White" (362). Even so, Ward is sure to note that the song was "musically and lyrically ideal for appropriation as a black rallying cry" (362).

7. See Bloch, Gallay, Bales, Bush, Turner, and Patterson. By grouping these scholars together, I do not want to suggest that there are not real differences between the types of bondage they consider or their approaches to them. Bales, for example, modifies Patterson's definition of slavery as "permanent, violent domination of natally alienated and generally dishonored persons" (qtd. in Bales 279) and more loosely defines a slave as a "person held by violence or the threat of violence for economic exploitation" (280). On the implications of these differences, see Bales's discussion of Patterson's critique of his definition of slavery (xxxv–xxxvi).

8. Exemplars of the first wave include texts like Francis Smith Foster's *Witnessing Slavery* and Charles T. Davis and Henry Louis Gates's *The Slave's Narrative*. The impulses of the second wave can be seen in Carla Peterson's *Doers of the Word* and Claudia Tate's *Psychoanalysis and Black Novels*. Studies like Elizabeth McHenry's *Forgotten Readers* and Lawrence Hogue's *The African American Male, Writing, and Difference* provide a sample of third-wave concerns. To be clear, these waves (as the aquatic language indicates) are not meant to suggest mutually exclusive spheres or an evolutionary progression, as many of these studies overlap with each other and anticipate each other in generative and nuanced ways. Even so, these distinctions suggest the changing emphases that have marked the study of African American literature over the last few decades.

9. For various versions of this narrative, see Angela Davis, *Are Prisons Obsolete?* 28–39 and "Race, Gender, and Prison History"; Franklin, 99–104; and T. Green, 2–4. This is not to argue that scholars have not acknowledged the historical links between antebellum slavery and imprisonment, but to say that those links have been largely conceived as emergent, discursive, and approximate. For example, Tara Green asserts that confinement, which she defines as "the status of individuals who are placed within boundaries," marks "the experiences of black men and women under slavery, during Reconstruction, and within the penal system" (3). At the same time, she suggests that imprisonment, "a physical state of existence when men and women are

sentenced to serve time in an institution because they have committed a crime," better explains life for blacks postemancipation, even while recognizing the continuity between various forms of black subjugation. Not too differently, prison historian Adam Jay Hirsch writes: "One may perceive in the penitentiary many reflections of chattel slavery as it was practiced in the South. Both institutions subordinated their subjects to the will of others. Like Southern slaves, prison inmates followed a daily routine specified by their superiors. . . . And both frequently coerced their subjects to work, often for longer hours and for less compensation than free laborers" (71). While essential, these observations sidestep the question of how literal penal structures were used to punish, contain, and manage bondspeople in the antebellum era.

Chapter 2

1. Deborah McDowell argues that Douglass's depiction of Aunt Hester's and other enslaved women's abuse elides their suffering: "As the *Narrative* progresses, the beatings proliferate and the women, no longer identified by name, become absolutized as a bloody mass of naked backs" (202). Extending this logic, Saidiyah Hartman begins her *Scenes of Subjection* by famously *refusing* to reproduce the scene of Aunt Hester's abuse, cogently arguing that such illustrations "immure us to pain by virtue of their familiarity" and "reinforce the spectacular character of black suffering" (3). Highlighting the emotive functions of Douglass's deployment of Hester's graphic punishment, Valerie Smith observes, "Passages such as these provide vivid symbols of the process of dehumanization that slaves underwent as their lifeblood was literally sapped" (22). Eschewing the passage's affective imperatives, William Andrews reads the scene as a demonstration of Douglass's rhetorical command: "In both the [Captain] Anthony and Hopkins passages, Douglass takes a 'brute fact' (linguistically and morally) like the whipping of slaves and experiments with rhetorical contexts in which to turn that fact to his own expressive account" (*To Tell* 134). Maurice Wallace takes a psychoanalytic tack, reading the revelation of Aunt Hester's "rape" as an expression of Douglass's own fears of sexual violation: "It is the 'terrible spectacle' of his own ravished body in the place of Hester's which sends Douglass hurrying for the invisibility of a hiding place" (87).

2. Jason Haslam, for example, argues that *Incidents* is "not a prison text per se" (49) but examines the ways in which slavery and prisons similarly "construct the subjectivities of their victims" (53).

3. See Burnham, Randle, and Green-Barteet.

4. In *Incidents*, the structure is generically referred to as the "old jail" (25). I owe my identification of it as the Chowan County jail to Jean Fagan Yellin's thorough biography of Jacobs's life and edited version of her narrative. In Yellin's biography, she notes that the "old jail behind the courthouse" was used to detain blacks during the panic created after Nat Turner's rebellion (38). The map included in that text shows one building, but its legend reveals that there are two structures in that place: the "Chowan County Courthouse and Jail." A footnote in Yellin's edition of *Incidents*

further identifies William Grimes as the jailor at the time of Jacobs's uncle's (Joseph) incarceration at the "county jail" (286, fn 8). The most extensive history of the jail can be found in Marc Brodsky's essential *The Courthouse at Edenton*. For more on the intimate connection between North Carolina courthouses and jails, see Watson.

5. See A. Davis, *Are Prisons Obsolete?*, 28–39, and "Race, Gender, and Prison History"; Franklin, 99–104; and T. Green, 2–4. The works of all of these scholars, it should be noted, represent indispensable contributions to an understanding of African American subjugation and confinement, but their periodizations imply that the antebellum era is primarily, if not exclusively, intelligible by way of reference to slavery while imprisonment only matters on a discursive level. Also see footnote 9 in this book's first chapter.

6. To read the stories of contemporary African American women's experiences in prison, see P. Johnson. For a survey of the condition of women in the prison system from the antebellum era to the present, see Dodge. For a provocative discussion of incarcerated women's reading practices in the early twenty-first century, see Sweeney.

7. Jacobs's uncle Joseph, remembered as Benjamin in the narrative, was likely kept in the pre-1825 structure.

8. The Covington, Bedford, and Louisville jails occupy significant positions within the connected histories of antebellum slavery, local jails, and penal reformation. Covington's jail was the one-story building in which the fugitive slave Margaret Garner was allegedly detained after she killed her daughter during a failed escape attempt. At least one contemporary newspaper report (*Cincinnati Daily Gazette*, April 11, 1856) places her in the jail, but there are also dissenting accounts. For my purposes, the fact that it was plausible that Garner could have been detained at the Covington jail (which none of the contemporary reports doubt) points to the regularity with which slaves were detained there and throughout jails in the antebellum South. For more on the Garner case, see Yanuck. The Bedford jail was the structure in which abolitionist Delia Webster was imprisoned for rescuing slaves in 1854. For a more detailed discussion of Webster's detention at Bedford and other Kentucky jails, see Runyon. Besides Bibb, perhaps the most notable visitor (though not inmate) of the Louisville jail and workhouse was Dorothea Dix, the nineteenth-century pioneer in penal reform who inspected both institutions in 1845, six years after Bibb's and his family's detention there. See Dix. For background information on the Louisville workhouse, see Childress.

9. Specifically, Bibb's declaration that "it was almost impossible for a virtuous person to avoid pollution, or to maintain their virtue" in the workhouse implies that sustaining sexual purity, a state that was often metonymically expressed in antislavery writing by the word "virtue," was impractical both inside and outside of the prison. This idea, however, is somewhat mitigated by Bibb's representation of the prison population as overwhelmingly sympathetic to Malinda's distraught condition after Garrison returns her to the workhouse. Even so, this is not to say that her his-

torical treatment by these prisoners and other prison agents was not marked by maltreatment, sexual or otherwise.

Free-born African American hairdresser, Eliza Potter, provides several anecdotes in her memoir about black women's incarceration in what appears to be the Louisville jail and workhouse. Potter herself was detained for three months in the Louisville jail because she aided a Kentucky bondsperson to freedom in 1834 (7). Consistent with this book's thesis about captivity and cultural authority, Potter scholar Xiomara Santamarina argues that the events surrounding her Kentucky imprisonment are indicative of the quality of "her antislavery sentiments and her willingness to help slaves escape" (Potter 201 fn 10). Glossing the religious cast of these "sentiments," Potter reads her incarceration as a proof of spiritual devotion when she boasts, "I was then removed to Louisville, where I was for three months a prisoner, and *this* for doing what I conscientiously felt to be a Christian deed" (7). Potter also tells the story of a freed, New York bondswoman who is kidnapped by speculators and taken to a jail in Louisville for safekeeping, perhaps the same one in which Henry Bibb, his family, and Potter were kept (149). Potter's antislavery views were complex, though, as when she notes that she would not identify herself as an abolitionist (150). Santamarina, who edited Potter's work, explains that "Potter's refusal to identify herself as an abolitionist makes sense in the context of her Cincinnati clients' many commercial links to the South" (212).

10. "Warrant for the arrest of Bill," North Carolina State Archives (NCSA). It is important to note that the names I have given for these sources (i.e. "Warrant for the arrest . . .") are titles I have constructed for the benefit of the reader. The warrants I reference here can be found in the Chowan County Court Records, which often consist of a series of boxes and folders organized by year related to court proceedings. Besides the year, many of these individual items do not have a title or even a general description. Therefore, I have had to invent titles in order to make the information they contain more useful and intelligible. I also recognize that an arrest warrant suggests the intent to capture, but it is not identical to a jail receipt.

11. "Warrant for the Arrest of Edward and Anthony." The case of Edward and Anthony is especially intriguing because the warrant indicates that they were owned by Mrs. Mae Haughton and Mrs. D. Warren, respectively, implying that the services of the jail might have been particularly useful for female slaveholders. This is only conjecture, however, and has not been borne out by my research.

12. In *With Liberty for Some*, Scott Christianson is one of the few critics to acknowledge the significance of Brown's observation (153).

13. See, for example, Lacan's reading of fortresses in "The Mirror Stage": "Correlatively, the formation of the I is symbolized in dreams by a fortress, or a stadium—its inner arena and enclosure, surrounded by marshes and rubbish-tips, dividing it into two opposed fields of contest where the subject flounders in quest of the lofty, remote inner castle whose form (sometimes juxtaposed in the same scenario) symbolizes the id in a quite startling way. Similarly, on the mental plane, we find real-

ized the structures of fortified works, the metaphor of which arises spontaneously, as if issuing from the symptoms themselves, to designate the mechanisms of obsessional neurosis—inversion, isolation, reduplication, cancellation and displacement" (4). Like the fortress described here, I would argue that the Chowan County jail is a site where Norcom banished and contained the tensions and insecurities that organized his subjectivity.

14. This sum, which is only meant to be approximate, depends on the dates and various lengths of time Jacobs's family members were incarcerated. According to Jacobs's biographer, Jean Fagan Yellin, and Jacobs's narrative, it appears that Jacobs's daughter, son, and brother must have been kept in the jail from 29 June to nearly the end of August. The runaway slave advertisement for Jacobs, which appeared the day after her escape, from the *American Beacon* is dated 30 June. In Yellin's biography of Jacobs, she notes, "Upon learning of her escape, he had immediately jailed Hatty's children, her brother, and her Aunt Betty" (46). Since Norcom placed the ad the day after Jacobs's escape, this means that her family might have been imprisoned as early as 29 June. Of her aunt, Jacobs notes that she "was taken out of jail at the end of a month, because Mrs. Flint could not spare her any longer." Consequently, I arrived at this approximate figure by multiplying .40 times 60, and then multiplying by three, and then adding that sum to .40 times 30 to account for Jacobs's aunt's "month" detention. Depending on the exact day in June Norcom imprisoned Jacobs's family members, this number may be off by a few dollars.

15. For a similar account of this event, see John S. Jacob, "A True Tale of Slavery," 214.

16. For more on the close relationship between John Jacobs and George Lamb, see H. Jacobs 314 fn 15.

17. John Jacobs's contention that his friends could see him whenever he pleased contrasts sharply with his sister's relation in *Incidents* that Aunt Betty was not even allowed to enter the jail when the children were imprisoned. This difference suggests either a strategically idealized depiction of imprisonment to diminish his powerlessness in the jail or perhaps genuinely different terms for John Jacobs's individual detention than the imprisonment of his niece and nephew. For more on the differences between Harriet and John Jacobs's accounts of Edenton slavery, see Goldsby.

18. My notion of maternal alienation borrows from the wording and logic of Orlando Patterson's notion of "natal alienation," which he defines as a constituent element of slavery. According to Patterson, "Alienated from all 'rights' or claims of birth," the bondsperson "ceased to belong in his own right to any legitimate social order." He is a "socially dead person" or "genealogical isolate" (5).

19. As Taylor notes: "While Benjamin Rush was an ardent abolitionist, he viewed his anti-slavery activism and his efforts to institute penal reform as unrelated endeavors" (435).

20. At the time of the song's release, Shakur was incarcerated on sexual assault charges of a twenty-one-year-old female (James). My reference to his incarceration in a politicized context is in no way meant to downplay or excuse violence commit-

ted against women but only to point out that imprisonment has been the site of black men's punishment, representation, and expression for quite some time.

21. For more on *Incidents* and the rhetoric of criminality, see Accomando.

22. Also see Foster, "Resisting Incidents," and Garfield" on the problematic sexual frames through which Jacobs was seen and her attempts to negotiate them.

23. As revealed in the preface to *Incidents*, abolitionist Lydia Maria Child helped to organize the order of *Incidents*'s chapters, so we might also read the "X" as a reflection of Child's reservations about revealing the details of Jacobs's sexual life.

24. See Brombert and Cassidy.

Chapter 3

1. Defending the position that Cherokee culture mitigated "many of the harsher aspects of plantation slavery," Theda Perdue calls on Henry Bibb's observation, "If I must be a slave, I had by far, rather be a slave to an Indian, than to a white man" ("Cherokee Planters" 125). In a more extensive treatment of Bibb's views on Cherokee slavery, Tiya Miles concludes, "Bibb demarcated crucial differences between various types of masters and found Indian masters to be the lesser evil" (42). While Miles goes on to observe that "Bibb ran away from his Cherokee master just like the others," she also notes that he "declined to reveal the man's name in his narrative, seeking instead to protect the reputation of the master" (42). On her way to contesting these positions, Celia Naylor acknowledges Bibb's depiction of "mild" Indian slavery in a footnote but concludes, "The brevity of Bibb's time in Indian Territory no doubt informed his particular experiences" (*African Cherokees* 244). Perdue's, Miles's, and Naylor's studies constitute, arguably, three of the most definitive statements on the history and meaning of Cherokee slavery, and all three make use of or acknowledge Bibb's remarks in their discussions. Independent of a reference to Bibb, Indian Territory geographer Michael Doran expresses the logic of benign Indian slavery: "Altogether, the available primary evidence is strong that the Indian slaves enjoyed fairly mild conditions of servitude" ("Negro Slaves" 344). Withholding commentary on the nature of the differences between blacks' enslavement to whites and Natives, *Black Indian Slave Narratives* editor Patrick Minges writes: "Though it is hard to make blanket generalizations about subjects as sophisticated as slavery and the diversity of settings in which it was applied, I do believe that slavery among the American Indians was substantively different from the general practices in the South" (xxii). Historian Monroe Billington rejects the argument that Native Americans were milder masters than whites, observing that "Indian slaveholders apparently were no more or less lenient with their slaves than were white slaveholders" (64).

2. If we consult Perdue's language in *Slavery and the Evolution Cherokee Society*, one of the main sources Naylor identifies for this mythology, the language and ideas suggest a slightly more nuanced argument. Perdue asserts: "Thus relative leniency on the part of masters seems to have been characteristic of Cherokee slavery both before and after removal" (98). Elsewhere, however, Perdue also acknowledges: "At first the

lingering noncapitalistic aboriginal culture tended to make Cherokees relatively lenient masters, but the perceptible differences between them and their counterparts gradually diminished" (144). Just as Tiya Miles is sure to note the differences between the pre- and postremoval practice of Indian slavery, so does Perdue. I do think, to be sure, that Perdue's analysis highlights the leniency of Indian masters, but I do not think that what she argues amounts to a myth, as much as it does a particular emphasis that has unfortunately come to stand in for a general and absolute truth about the way southeastern Natives practiced slavery. Hence, I have no doubt that a narrative of benign Indian slavery existed and exists, but to call it a "mythology" seems to lean too heavily to one side of the debate and, furthermore, precludes a simultaneous consideration of historical and fictive sources for this representation.

3. For more on these connections, see William McLoughlin, *Cherokees and Missionaries, 1789–1839*. For a collection of diary entries from the Moravian missionaries at Spring Place (who were also the neighbors of Cherokee slaveholder James Vann), see Rowena McClinton, *The Moravian Springplace Mission to the Cherokees*, vol. I: *1805–1813* and vol. 2: *1814–1821*.

4. Compare, for instance, the representation of child indentured servitude in black women's spiritual autobiographies. These conversion narratives both obscure and testify to black children's exploitation even as they rationalize it as "instruction" and "protection."

5. During the course of a diatribe against Christian slaveholders, Bibb reveals that his Cherokee owner was a "Bro.," a generic term for a male Christian convert, and possibly a "member of the Presbyterian church" (203). Elsewhere in the narrative, he paints a mild picture of his owner as well as Christianity in Indian Territory. However, Bibb's inclusion of his master in this lambaste suggests an interesting counterpoint to his earlier comments. As he queries of these slaveholders' commitment to their faith: "Is this Christianity? Is it honest or right? Is it doing as we would be done by?" (203–4).

6. I signify here on Louis Owens's argument that white American settler constructions of "Indians" produce a "tricky mirror" that "reflects the Euro-American consciousness back at itself" (17). While whites look into the mirror and see a reflection of themselves in bombastic and wonderful form, Natives look into the mirror from the other side and can only see whites gazing back at them. For Natives, the mirror offers visions of lack and inalienable difference while for whites it offers a surplus of positive meaning and identification.

7. For a consideration of *Blake*'s revision of black nationhood as it relates to its serialized dissemination, see Chiles. Also see Sundquist's seminal discussion of Blake, 182–221.

8. See Speck and Broom.

9. See Drinnon for a more elaborate discussion of Indian hating.

10. See, for instance, the discussion of various Creek dances, or what are referred to as "banga," in the narrative of Lucinda Davis (Baker and Baker 111–12).

11. I allude here to Ralph Ellison's *Going to the Territory*. Ellison was born on March 1, 1914, in Oklahoma City, Oklahoma.

12. As Michael Doran and other scholars have pointed out, removal-related disease was significant in the Cherokee Nation West. Though Bibb never discloses the nature of his owner's sickness, it is possible that it was a function of the "bilious fevers" and other maladies that afflicted removed southeastern Natives (qtd. in Doran, "Population" 497).

13. See Harriet Beecher Stowe's reappraisal of this passage, through the words of George Harris, in *Uncle Tom's Cabin*: "I wonder, Mr. Wilson, if the Indians should come and take you a prisoner away from your wife and children, and want to keep you all your life hoeing corn for them, if you'd think it your duty to abide in the condition in which you were called. I rather think that you'd think the first stray horse you could find an indication of Providence—shouldn't you?" (95).

14. Douglass recalls a similar scene in his 1845 *Narrative*.

15. See MacPherson for a further discussion of the centrality of self-possession to liberal models of freedom and identity.

Chapter 4

1. For a sampling of these various perspectives, see Gates and Ellis, Ammons, Foreman, Sánchez-Eppler, *Dependent States* 40–51, and Singley 119–34.

2. Though I refer to the 1856 edition, Prince's text was originally published in 1850, with a revised edition released in 1853 and then reissued in 1856. For a reading of her narrative in relation to questions of black transnationalism, see Gunning, who argues against the romanticization of transnationalism in favor of a "diasporic subjectivity" (33) that takes into account the importance of the local within foreign spaces and the importance of foreign spaces within the local. An examination of binding out and child domestic service in Prince's writing advances this project by suggesting how her advocacy for vulnerable children in Russia and Jamaica is very much rooted in her New England childhood. Also see Birkle.

3. As suggested by *Our Nig*'s invocation of the "County House" (15), some of Prince's siblings might have been placed in poorhouses or other institutions of public relief. Of a brother who tried to return to their mother and is then sent away by her most recent husband, the narrative reveals that Prince "carried him to Gloucester and left him in the hands of the town" (18). Depending on the state of child welfare in Gloucester and the propensities of local authorities, Prince's brother might have been kept at a local poor farm, but he also might been living with a family that the town reimbursed. In either case, his mother could provide no home for him, and he remained "scattered" like the rest of his brothers and sisters.

4. Although I do not develop this argument here, it is worth noting that Wilson's postindenture hair regenerator business is another signal of her interests in health and sickness. Consider her own testimony from an 1860 ad: "I can say with much

pleasure that when the Regenerator was first applied to my own hair it was very gray, and falling from my head, and my scalp was in a very unhealthy state; but upon a very few applications I discovered a decided change, and soon my hair assumed its original color and health of youth" (qtd. in Gates and Ellis xlvii). Reversing the narrative trajectory of *Our Nig*, Wilson's tonic transforms her hair from "a very unhealthy state" to "its original color and health of youth."

5. Lisa Green understands the figure of the "disorderly girl" as a surrogate for the author Wilson, speaking out brashly where Wilson could not have done so. She argues that the disorderly girl is a call for "correction, usually through an internalization of Christian values" (142).

6. For a more sustained discussion of the connections between *Abby at the Farm* and *Our Nig*, see Singley, 130–33.

7. Though she does not make the connection between Wilson's and Hine's depictions explicit, I credit my sense of the potential linkages between these two figures to Robin Bernstein's discussion of Hines in *Racial Innocence*, 30–33. For a thorough investigation of Hines's photography in its historical context, see Kate Sampsell-Willmann. Similar to the expressed motivation behind the Child Welfare Exhibit in 1911 (to which Hines contributed), part of the objective of Wilson's representations is "to point the way to lift the burdens from childish shoulders—to straighten these bent little backs—to prevent bent little backs for the future" (qtd. in Sampsell-Willmann 82).

8. See, for example, Cobb. In his seventh objection to corporal punishment, one of thirty he provides, he reasons: "When children are whipped they resist the blows, either by an obstinate or stubborn *rigidity* of the *muscular* system, or by a nervous *shrinking* of the whole *vascular* system from fear or timidity; so that, in either case, the delicacy of the skin, from the rigidity of the muscles, or by their great and unnatural *laxity*, is *seriously injured*" (emphasis in the original, 28). He adds, "The delicate skin, most beautifully and wonderfully wrought by our Maker, was never designed to be beaten by a rod *as the skin of a horse is sometimes beaten!* Nothing can be clearer than this to any reflecting and rational mind. The fine, delicate, and sensitive pores of the skin become *callous* and *indurated*, by being beaten" (emphasis in the original, 29).

9. Also see Cassandra Jackson, "Beyond the Page."

10. For a discussion of the unlikelihood of an exclusively black readership, see Ernest, "Economies of Identity" 425. For an alternative reading, see Santamarina, 190n5.

Chapter 5

1. For a complete list of the various nineteenth-century editions of Robert Adams's narrative, see Adams lvii.

2. For more on sailor's language and culture, see Linebaugh and Rediker's discussion of "hydrarchy," 143–73.

3. For various studies on the people that make up North Africa and Central West Africa, see L. Briggs, Gellner and Micaud, Hoffman and Miller, and Ilahiane.

4. In subsequent versions of Adams's account, such as an 1843 reprint edited by Charles Ellms in *Robinson Crusoe's Own Book*, this moment was augmented by an illustration, sensationally depicting an essentially "white" Adams pummeling a significantly dark-skinned Hameda (428). Picking up on the decisiveness of the moment, Ellms or his publisher must have realized the import of such a scene as well.

5. Since he uses the third person, we must presume that Adams actually said it is "contrary to my religion."

6. For a comparative discussion of indigenous African and Cherokee forms of slavery, see Perdue, *Slavery and the Evolution of Cherokee Society*, 44–46.

7. For a sensitive appraisal of indigenous West African dance practices, see R. Thompson.

8. I am alluding to Werner Sollors's study of mixed-race identity, *Neither Black, nor White, yet Both*.

Works Cited

Accomando, Christina. "'The Laws Were Laid Down to Me Anew': Harriet Jacobs and the Reframing of Legal Fictions." *African American Review* 32.2 (1998): 229–45. *JSTOR*. Accessed 15 June 2010. http://www.jstor.org.proxy.libraries.rutgers.edu/stable/pdfplus/3042121.pdf?acceptTC=true.

Adams, Charles Hansford. Preface. *The Narrative of Robert Adams, a Barbary Captive*. By Simon Cock. New York, NY: Cambridge UP, 2005. ix–lxiii.

Allison, Robert J. *The Crescent Obscured: The United States and the Muslim World, 1776–1815*. New York, NY: Oxford UP, 1995.

Ammons, Elizabeth. "Stowe's Dream of the Mother-Savior: *Uncle Tom's Cabin and American Women Writers before the 1920s*." *New Essays on Uncle Tom's Cabin*. Ed. Eric J. Sundquist. Cambridge, UK: Cambridge UP, 1986. 155–95.

Anderson, William J. *The Life and Adventures of William J. Anderson, Twenty-four Years a Slave*. Chicago: Daily Tribune Book and Job Printing Office, 1857. *Documenting the American South*. Accessed 10 May 2011. http://docsouth.unc.edu/neh/andersonw/andersonw.html.

Andrews, William L., ed. *Sisters of the Spirit: Three Black Women's Autobiographies of the Nineteenth Century*. Bloomington: Indiana UP, 1986.

———. *To Tell a Free Story: The First Century of African American Autobiography, 1760–1865*. Urbana: U of Illinois P, 1986.

Awkward, Michael. "The Philadelphia Sound and Family Values." U of Michigan, Ann Arbor. Spring 2000. Lecture.

Baepler, Paul, ed. Introduction. *White Slaves, African Masters: An Anthology of American Barbary Captivity Narratives*. Chicago, IL: Chicago UP, 1999. 1–58

Baker, Lindsay T., and Julie P. Baker, eds. *The WPA Oklahoma Slave Narratives*. Norman: U of Oklahoma P, 1996.

Bales, Kevin. *Disposable people: New Slavery in the Global Economy*. Updated with a new preface. Berkeley: U of California P, 2012.

Bancroft, Frederic. *Slave Trading in the Old South*. Baltimore, MD: J. H. Furst Company, 1931.

Baynton, Douglas. "Slaves, Immigrants, and Suffragists: The Uses of Disability in Citizenship Debates." *PMLA* 120.2 (2005): 562–67. *JSTOR*. Accessed 6 March 2012. http://www.jstor.org.proxy.libraries.rutgers.edu/stable/pdfplus/10.2307/25486185.pdf.

Berlin, Ira. *Generations of Captivity: A History of African-American Slaves*. Cambridge, MA: Belknap P, 2003.

Berman, Jacob Rama. *American Arabesque: Arabs, Islam, and the 19th-Century Imaginary*. New York: New York UP, 2012.

Bernstein, Robin. *Racial Innocence: Performing American Childhood from Slavery to Civil Rights*. New York: New York UP, 2011.

Bhabha, Homi. *The Location of Culture*. New York, NY: Routledge, 2005.

Bibb, Henry. *The Life and Adventures of Henry Bibb, an American Slave*. Ed. Charles Heglar. Madison: U of Wisconsin P, 2001.

Billington, Monroe. "Black Slavery in Indian Territory: The Ex-Slave Narratives." *Chronicles of Oklahoma* 60.1 (1982): 56–66.

Birkle, Carmen. "Traveling and the Discourse of Economy in Nancy Prince's Travel Narrative." *In-Between Two Worlds: Narratives by Female Explorers and Travellers, 1850–1945*. Ed. Béatrice Bijon and Gérard Gâcon. New York, NY: Peter Lang, 2009. 17–33.

Blackford, Holly. *Mockingbird Passing: Closeted Traditions and Sexual Curiosities in Harper Lee's Novel*. Knoxville: U of Tennessee P, 2011.

Blassingame, John W. "Using the Testimony of Ex-Slaves: Approaches and Problems." Ed. Davis and Gates. 78–98.

Bloch, Marc. *Slavery and Serfdom in the Middle Ages: Selected Essays*. Trans. William R. Beer. Berkley: U of California P, 1975.

Boelhower, William. *Through a Glass Darkly: Ethnic Semiosis in American Literature*. New York, NY: Oxford, 1987.

Boggis, Jerri Anne, Eve Allegra Raimon, and Barbara A. White, eds. *Harriet Wilson's New England: Race, Writing, and Region*. Durham: U of New Hampshire P, 2007.

Bolster, W. Jeffrey. *Black Jacks: African American Seamen in the Age of Sail*. Cambridge, MA: Harvard UP, 1997.

Bosman, Julie. "Prison Memoir of a Black Man in the 1850s." *New York Times* 11 Dec. 2013. *Google Search*. Accessed 10 Mar. 2014. http://www.nytimes.com/2013/12/12/books/prison-memoir-of-a-black-man-in-the-1850s.html?_r=0.

Boudinot, Elias. "An Address to the Whites." *Cherokee Editor: The Writings of Elias Boudinot*. Ed. Theda Perdue. Athens, GA: Brown Thrasher, 1996. 65–84.

Bracey, John H., Jr., August Meier, and Elliot Rudwick, eds. *Free Blacks in America, 1800–1860*. Belmont, CA: Wadsworth, 1971.

Braxton, Joanne. *Black Women Writing Autobiography: A Tradition within a Tradition*. Philadelphia, PA: Temple UP, 1989.

Briggs, Caroline C. *Reminiscences and Letters of Caroline C. Briggs*. Ed. George S. Merriam. Cambridge, MA: Riverside Press, 1897. *Google Books*. Accessed 19 Feb. 2012. https://books.google.com/books?id=ltKRAAAAMAAJ&pg=PP8&lpg=PP8&dq=Reminiscences+and+Letters+of+Caroline+C.+Briggs&source=bl&ots=i3B07ongev

&sig=erpz55jTIhfz3E4GNZxj5R-ULtk&hl=en&sa=X&ei=bdDHVPCRG0KXgwTn20PwAw&ved=0CDQQ6AEwBA#v=onepage&q=Reminiscences%20and%20Letters%20of%20Caroline%20C.%20Briggs&f=false.

Briggs, Lloyd Cabot. *Tribes of the Sahara*. Cambridge, MA: Harvard UP, 1967.

Brodhead, Richard H. "Sparing the Rod: Discipline and Fiction in Antebellum America." *Representations* 21 (1988): 67–96. *JSTOR*. Accessed 5 May 2005. http://www.jstor.org.proxy.libraries.rutgers.edu/stable/pdfplus/10.2307/2928377.pdf

Brodsky, Marc. *The Courthouse at Edenton: A History of the Chowan County Courthouse of 1767*. Edenton: Chowan County, NC, 1989.

Brombert, Victor. *The Happy Prison: The French Tradition*. Princeton, NJ: Princeton UP, 1978.

Brooks, James F., ed. *Confounding the Color Line: The Indian-Black Experience in North America*. Lincoln: U of Nebraska P, 2002.

Brown, William Wells. *Narrative of William W. Brown, a Fugitive Slave. Written by Himself*. 1847. *From Fugitive to Freeman: The Autobiographies of Williams Wells Brown*. Ed. William L. Andrews. Columbia: U of Missouri P, 2003. 15–110.

Bruner, Jerome. "The Autobiographical Process." *The Culture of Autobiography: Constructions of Self-Representation*. Ed. Robert Folkenflik. Stanford, CA: Stanford UP, 1993. 38–56.

Brunsman, Denver. *The Evil Necessity: British Naval Impressment in the Atlantic World*. Charlottesville: U of Virginia P, 2013.

Burnham, Michelle. *Captivity and Sentiment: Cultural Exchange in American Literature, 1682–1861*. Hanover, MA: UP of New England, 1997.

Bush, M. L. *Servitude in Modern Times*. Malden, MA: Blackwell, 2000.

Bynum, Victoria. *Unruly Women: The Politics of Social and Sexual Control in the Old South*. Chapel Hill: U of North Carolina P, 1992.

Carpio, Glenda R. "What Does Fiction Have to Do with It?" *PMLA* 128.2 (2013): 386–88. *MLA International Bibliography*. Accessed 20 Jan. 2014. http://eds.a.ebscohost.com.proxy.libraries.rutgers.edu/ehost/detail/detail?vid=3&sid=c0cfac02-c508-4201-80a4-ebd44dbc7dc5%40sessionmgr4001&hid=4205&bdata=JnNpdGU9ZWhvc3QtbGl2ZQ%3d%3d#db=mzh&AN=2013381447.

Carretta, Vincent, and Philip Gould, eds. *Genius in Bondage: Literature of the Early Black Atlantic*. Lexington: UP of Kentucky, 2001.

Cassidy, Richard. *Paul in Chains: Roman Imprisonment and the Letters of St. Paul*. New York, NY: Crossroad, 2001.

Cherokee Advocate. 23 October 1845. *Interlibrary Loan Request*. Rutgers University Libraries.

Childress, Brad. "Louisville Workhouse." *The Encyclopedia of Louisville*. Ed. John E. Kleber. Lexington: UP of Kentucky, 2000. 971–72.

Childs, Dennis. "'You Ain't Seen Nothin' Yet': *Beloved*, the American Chain Gang, and the Middle Passage Remix." *American Quarterly* 61.2 (2009): 271–97. *JSTOR*. Accessed 9 June 2013. http://www.jstor.org.proxy.libraries.rutgers.edu/stable/pdfplus/10.2307/27734990.pdf

Chiles, Katy. "Within and Without Raced Nations: Intratextuality, Martin Delany, and Blake; or, The Huts of America." *American Literature* 80.2 (2008): 323–52. *MLA International Bibliography*. Accessed 11 Oct. 2011. http://eds.a.ebscohost.com.proxy.libraries.rutgers.edu/ehost/pdfviewer/pdfviewer?sid=cocfaco2-c508-4201-80a4-ebd44dbc7dc5%40sessionmgr4001&vid=11&hid=4205.

Christianson, Scott. *With Liberty for Some: 500 Years of Imprisonment in America*. Boston, MA: Northeastern UP, 1998.

Cobb, Lyman. *The Evil Tendencies of Corporal Punishment as a Means of Moral Discipline in Family and Schools, Examined and Discussed*. New York: Mark H. Newman, 1847. Internet Archive, U of Toronto. Accessed 20 Aug. 2009. https://archive.org/details/eviltendenciesofoocobbuoft.

Cock, Simon. *The Narrative of Robert Adams, a sailor*. . . . London: John Murray, 1816. Rpt. in Adams, ed. 1–145.

Cock, Simon, and Robert Ellms. "The Narrative of Robert Adams. . . . " *Robinson Crusoe's Own Book*. . . . Ed. Robert Ellms. Boston, MA: Joshua V. Pierce, 1843. 403–31. *Google Books*. 8 Sept. 2010. http://books.google.com/books/about/Robinson_Crusoe_s_Own_Book_Or_The_Voice.html?id=R1_QAAAAMAAJ.

Colley, Linda. *Captives*. New York, NY: Pantheon, 2002.

Colley, Zoey A. *Ain't Scared of Your Jail: Arrest, Imprisonment, and the Civil Rights Movement*. Gainesville: UP of Florida, 2013.

Collins, Patricia Hill. *Black Feminist Thought: Knowledge, Consciousness, and the Politics of Empowerment*. Rev. ed. New York, NY: Routledge, 2000.

Conley, Robert J. *The Cherokee Nation: A History*. Albuquerque: U of New Mexico P, 2005.

Cooper, Afua. "The Fluid Frontier: Blacks and the Detroit River Region: A Focus on Henry Bibb." *Canadian Review of American Studies*. 30.2 (2000): 129–49.

Cornish, Samuel, and John B. Russworm. "To Our Patrons." *Freedom's Journal* 16 Mar. 1827. *African American Newspapers: The 19th Century*. Accessed 1 May 2012. http://www.accessible.com.proxy.libraries.rutgers.edu/accessible/docButton?AAWhat=builtPage&AAWhere=FREEDOMSJOURNAL.FR18270316o1.00001&AABeanName=toc3&AANextPage=/printBrowseBuiltPage.jsp.

Cowan, William Tynes. *The Slave in the Swamp: Disrupting the Plantation Narrative*. New York, NY: Routledge, 2005.

Curtin, Philip D. *The Image of Africa: British Ideas and Action, 1780–1850*. Madison: U of Wisconsin P, 1964.

Darby, Robert. *A Surgical Temptation: The Demonization of the Foreskin and the Rise of Circumcision in Britain*. Chicago, IL: U of Chicago P, 2005.

Davidson, Michael, Tobin Siebers, and Rosemary G. Feal. Introduction. *PMLA* 120.2 (2005): 498–501.

Davis, Angela. *Are Prisons Obsolete?* New York, NY: Seven Stories P, 2003.

———. "Race, Gender, and Prison History: From the Convict Lease System to the Supermax Prison." *Prison Masculinites*. Ed. Don Sabo, Terry A. Kupers, and Willie London. Philadelphia, PA: Temple UP, 2001. 35–45.

Davis, Charles T., and Henry Louis Gates Jr., eds. *The Slave's Narrative*. New York, NY: Oxford UP, 1985.

Davis, Cynthia J. "Speaking the Body's Pain: Harriet Wilson's *Our Nig*." 27.3 (1993): 391–404. *MLA International Bibliography*. Accessed 5 June 2010. http://eds.a.ebscohost.com.proxy.libraries.rutgers.edu/ehost/detail/detail?sid=6562b228-f975-414a-848e-ddac408e3bd5%40sessionmgr4002&vid=8&hid=4205&bdata=JnNpdGU9ZWhvc3QtbGl2ZQ%3d%3d#db=mzh&AN=0000300063.

Delany, Martin R. *Blake; or, The Huts of America: A Tale of the Mississippi Valley, the Southern United States and Cuba*. 1859–62. Ed. Floyd J. Miller. Boston: Beacon Press, 1970. *Uncle Tom's Cabin and American Culture*. Accessed 10 Feb. 2013. http://utc.iath.virginia.edu/africam/blakehp.html.

———. *The Condition, Elevation, Emigration, and Destiny of the Colored people of the United States*. 1852. *Project Gutenberg*. Accessed 22 Oct. 2012. http://www.gutenberg.org/files/17154/17154-h/17154-h.htm.

Desrochers, Robert, Jr. "'Surprizing Deliverance'?: Slavery and Freedom, Language and Identity in the Narrative of Briton Hammon, A Negro Man." Ed. Carretta and Gould 153–74.

Dickens, Charles. *American Notes for General Circulation*. Ed. Patricia Ingham. New York, NY: Penguin, 2000.

Dix, Dorothea L. *A Review of the Present Condition of the State Penitentiary of Kentucky*. . . . Frankfort: A. G. Hodges, 1846. Rpt. in *On Behalf of the Insane Poor: Selected Reports*. New York, NY: Arno P, 1971. 1–40.

Dodge, L. Mara. *"Whores and Thieves of the Worst Kind": A Study of Women, Crime, and Prisons, 1835–2000*. Dekalb: Northern Illinois UP, 2002.

Doran, Michael. "Negro Slaves of the Five Civilized Tribes." *Annals of the Association of American Geographers* 68.3 (1978): 335–50. *EBSCOhost*. Accessed 6 Apr. 2011. http://eds.a.ebscohost.com.proxy.libraries.rutgers.edu/ehost/pdfviewer/pdfviewer?sid=163ef144-4c12-46d1-9977-a20d42adb538%40sessionmgr4005&vid=6&hid=4205.

———. "Population Statistics of Nineteenth Century Indian Territory." *Chronicles of Oklahoma*. 53.4 (1975–76): 492–515.

Douglass, Frederick. *My Bondage and My Freedom*. 1855. Ed. Philip S. Foner. Mineola, NY: Dover, 1969.

———. *Narrative of the Life of Frederick Douglass, an American Slave, Written by Himself*. 1845. Ed. William L. Andrews and William S. McFeely. New York, NY: Norton, 1997.

Drinnon, Richard. *Facing West: The Metaphysics of Indian-Hating and Empire-Building*. Minneapolis: U of Minnesota P, 1980.

Dudden, Faye. *Serving Women: Household Service in Nineteenth-Century America*. Middletown, CT: Wesleyan UP, 1983.

Dusinberre, William. *Them Dark Days: Slavery in the American Rice Swamps*. New York, NY: Oxford UP, 1996.

Dyson, Michael Eric. *Holler If You Hear Me: Searching for Tupac Shakur*. New York, NY: Basic Civitas, 2001.

Elaw, Zilpha. *Memoirs of the Life, Religious Experience, Ministerial Travels and Labors of Mrs. Zilpha Elaw*. Ed. Andrews *Sisters of the Spirit*. 49–160.

Ellis, R. J., and Henry Louis Gates, Jr. "'Grievances at the Treatment She Received': Harriet E. Wilson's Spiritualist Career in Boston, 1868–1900." *ALH* 24.2 (2012): 234–64. *MLA International Bibliography*. Accessed 4 Sept. 2013. http://eds.a.ebscohost.com.proxy.libraries.rutgers.edu/ehost/detail/detail?vid=10&sid=6562b228-f975-414a-848e-ddac408e3bd5%40sessionmgr4002&hid=4205&bdata=JnNpdGU9ZWhvc3QtbGl2ZQ%3d%3d#db=mzh&AN=2012381479.

Ellison, Ralph. *Invisible Man*. New York, NY: Vintage, 1995.

Ernest, John. *Chaotic Justice: Rethinking African American Literary History*. Chapel Hill: U of North Carolina P, 2009.

———. "Economies of Identity: Harriet Wilson's *Our Nig*." *PMLA* 109.3 (1994): 424–38. *EBSCOhost*. Accessed 21 Oct. 2000. http://eds.b.ebscohost.com.proxy.libraries.rutgers.edu/ehost/detail/detail?vid=3&sid=45882d6e-531a-40ea-a5ef-7546b5aa53df%40sessionmgr113&hid=126&bdata=JnNpdGU9ZWhvc3QtbGl2ZQ%3d%3d#db=aph&AN=9412072249.

Escott, Paul D. "The Art and Science of Reading WPA Slave Narratives." Ed. Davis and Gates. 40–48.

Fabian, Ann. *The Unvarnished Truth: Personal Narratives in Nineteenth Century America*. Berkley: U of California P, 2000.

Fairhead, James, Tim Geysbeek, Svend E. Hosloe, and Melissa Leach, eds. *African-American Exploration in West Africa: Four Nineteenth-Century Diaries*. Bloomington: Indiana UP, 2003.

Fehrenbacher, Don E. *The Dred Scott Case: Its Significance in American Law and Politics*. New York, NY: Oxford UP, 1978.

Ferguson, Roderick A. "The Lateral Moves of African American Studies in a Period of Migration." Ed. Hong and Ferguson. 113–30.

Foote, Julia. *A Brand Plucked from the Fire: An Autobiographical Sketch by Mrs. Julia Foote*. Ed. Andrews *Sisters of the Spirit*. 161–234.

Foreman, P. Gabrielle. Introduction. *Our Nig; or, Sketches from the Life of a Free Black*. 1859. By Harriet E. Wilson. xxv–lv.

Foster, Frances Smith. "Briton Hammon's Narrative: Some Insights into Beginnings." *CLA Journal* 21 (1977): 179–86.

———. "Resisting *Incidents*." Ed. Garfield and Zafar. 57–75.

———. *Witnessing Slavery: The Development of the Antebellum Slave Narrative*. Westport, CT: Greenwood P, 1979.

Foucault, Michel. *Discipline and Punish: The Birth of the Prison*. Trans. Alan Sheridan. New York, NY: Vintage, 1977.

Franklin, H. Bruce. *Prison Literature in America: The Victim as Criminal and Artist*. New York, NY: Oxford UP, 1989.

Frawley, Maria. *Invalidism and Identity in Nineteenth-Century Britain*. Chicago, IL: U of Chicago P, 2004.

Frost, Natasha, Judith Greene, and Kevin Pranis. *Hard Hit: The Growth in the Impris-*

onment of Women, 1977–2004. National Criminal Justice Reference Service, NCJRS, 2007. Accessed 9 Sept. 2010. https://www.ncjrs.gov/App/publications/abstract.aspx?ID=238811.

Frustenberg, François. "Beyond Freedom and Slavery: Autonomy, Virtue, and Resistance in Early American Political Discourse." *Journal of American History* 89.4 (2003): 1295–1330. *ProQuest*. Accessed 13 May 2009. http://search.proquest.com.proxy.libraries.rutgers.edu/docview/224893913/fulltextPDF?accountid=13626.

Fuente, Alejandro de la. *Havana and the Atlantic in the Sixteenth Century*. Chapel Hill: U of North Carolina P, 2008.

———. "Slaves and the Creation of Legal Rights in Cuba: Coartacion and Papel." *Hispanic American Historical Review* 87.4 (2007): 659–92. *EBSCOhost*. Accessed 1 Nov. 2012. http://eds.b.ebscohost.com.proxy.libraries.rutgers.edu/ehost/pdfviewer/pdfviewer?vid=7&sid=45882d6e-531a-40ea-a5ef-7546b5aa53df%40sessionmgr113&hid=126.

Gagnon, Jeffrey. "'They Us'd Me Pretty Well': Briton Hammon and Cross-Cultural Alliances in the Maritime Borderlands of the Florida Coast." *Journeys of the Slave Narrative in the Early Americas*. Ed. Nicole N. Aljoe and Ian Finseth. Charolettesville: U of Virginia P, 2014. 74–100.

Gallay, Alan. *The Indian Slave Trade: The Rise of the English Empire in the American South, 1670–1717*. New Haven, CT: Yale UP, 2002.

Gardner, Brian. *The Quest for Timbuctoo*. New York, NY: Harcourt, Brace, and World, 1968.

Gardner, Eric. "Of Bottles and Books: Reconsidering the Readers of Harriet Wilson's *Our Nig*." Ed. Boggis, Raimon, and White. 3–26.

———. *Unexpected Places: Relocating Nineteenth-Century African American Literature*. Jackson: U of Mississippi P, 2009.

Garfield, Deborah M. "Earwitness: Female Abolitionism, Sexuality, and *Incidents in the Life of a Slave Girl*." Ed. Garfield and Zafar. 100–130.

Garfield, Deborah M., and Rafia Zafar, eds. *Harriet Jacobs and Incidents in the Life of a Slave Girl: New Critical Essays*. New York, NY: Cambridge UP, 1996.

Garrison, William Lloyd. Preface. *Narrative of the Life of Frederick Douglass, an American Slave, Written by Himself*. By Frederick Douglass. Ed. William L. Andrews and William S. McFeely. New York, NY: Norton, 1997. 3–10.

Gates, Henry Louis, Jr. *Figures in Black: Words, Signs, and the "Racial" Self*. New York, NY: Oxford UP, 1987.

Gates, Henry Louis, Jr., and Richard J. Ellis. Introduction. *Our Nig; or, Sketches from the Life of a Free Black*. By Harriet Wilson. New York, NY: Vintage, 2011. xiii-lxviii.

Gellner, Ernest, and Charles Micaud. *Arabs and Berbers: From Tribe to Nation in North Africa*. Lexington, KY: Lexington Books, 1972.

Goldman, Anita. "Harriet Jacobs, Henry Thoreau, and the Character of Disobedience." Ed. Garfield and Zafar. 233–50.

Goldsby, Jacqueline. "'I Disguised My Hand': Writing Versions of the Truth in Harriet Jacobs's *Incidents in the Life of a Slave Girl* and John Jacobs's 'A True Tale of Slavery.'" Ed. Garfield and Zafar. 11–43.

Gollaher, David L. "From Ritual to Science: The Medical Transformation of Circumcision in America." *Journal of Social History* 28.1 (1994): 5–32.

Gould, Philip. "'Remarkable Liberty': Language and Identity in Eighteenth-Century Black Autobiography." Ed. Carretta and Gould. 116–29.

———. "The Rise, Development and Circulation of the Slave Narrative." *The Cambridge Companion to the African American Slave Narrative*. New York: Cambridge UP, 2007. 11–28.

Green, Lisa. "The Disorderly Girl in Harriet Wilson's *Our Nig*." Ed. Boggis, Raimon, and White. 139–54.

Green, Tara. *From the Plantation to the Prison: African-American Confinement Literature*. Macon, GA: Mercer UP, 2008.

Green-Barteet, Miranda A. "'The Loophole of Retreat': The Interstitial Spaces in Harriet Jacobs's *Incidents in the Life of a Slave Girl*." *South Central Review* 30.2 (2013): 53–72. *Project Muse* Accessed 18 Jan. 2014. http://muse.jhu.edu.proxy.libraries.rutgers.edu/journals/south_central_review/v030/30.2.green-barteet.pdf.

Greenberg, Kenneth S. *Honor and Slavery*. Princeton, NJ: Princeton UP, 1996.

Gross, Kali N. *Colored Amazons: Crime, Violence, and Black Women in the City of Brotherly Love, 1880–1910*. Durham, NC: Duke UP, 2006.

Gundaker, Grey. *Signs of Diaspora, Diaspora of Signs: Literacies, Creolization, and Vernacular in African American Practice*. New York, NY: Oxford UP, 1998.

Gunning, Sandra. "Nancy Prince and the Politics of Mobility, Home, and Diasporic (Mis) identification." *American Quarterly* 53.1 (2001): 32–69. *JSTOR*. Accessed 18 Sept. 2009. http://www.jstor.org.proxy.libraries.rutgers.edu/stable/30041872?seq=1#page_scan_tab_contents.

Hall, Stuart. "What Is This 'Black' in Black Popular Culture?" *Black Popular Culture*. Ed. Gina Dent. Seattle, WA: Bay Press, 1992. 21–36.

Halliburton, Rudi, Jr. *Red over Black: Black Slavery among the Cherokee Indians*. Westport, CT: Greenwood P, 1977.

Hammon, Briton. "Narrative of the Uncommon Sufferings and Surprizing Deliverance of Briton Hammon, A Negro Man." *Unchained Voices: An Anthology of Black Authors in the English-Speaking World of the Eighteenth Century*. Ed. Vincent Carretta. Lexington: UP of Kentucky, 1996. 20–25.

Harrold, Stanley. "John Brown's Forerunners: Slave Rescue Attempts and the Abolitionists, 1841–1851." *Radical History Review*. 55 (1993): 89–110.

Hartman, Saidiyah V. *Scenes of Subjection: Terror, Slavery, and Self-Making in Nineteenth-Century America*. New York, NY: Oxford UP, 1997.

Haslam, Jason. *Fitting Sentences: Identity in Nineteenth- and Twentieth-Century Prison Narratives*. Toronto: U of Toronto P, 2005.

Hawthorne, Nathaniel. *The Scarlet Letter*. New York, NY: Penguin, 2003.

Hedin, Raymond. "The American Slave Narrative: The Justification of the Picaro." *American Literature* 53.4 (1982): 630–45.

Heffernan, Micahel. "'A Dream as Frail as Those of Ancient Time': The In-credible Geographies of Timbuctoo." *Environment and Planning D: Society and Space* 19 (2001):

203–25. *EBSCOhost*. Accessed 5 Sept. 2011. http://www.envplan.com.proxy.libraries.rutgers.edu/epd/fulltext/d19/d231t.pdf.

Heglar, Charles. Introduction. *The Life and Adventures of Henry Bibb, an American Slave*. Madison: U of Wisconsin P, 2001. v-xxxv.

Herndl, Diane Price. *Invalid Women: Figuring Feminine Illness in American Fiction and Culture, 1840–1940*. Chapel Hill: U of North Carolina P, 1993.

———. "The Invisible (Invalid) Woman: African-American Women, Illness, and Nineteenth-Century Narrative." *Women's Studies* 24 (1995): 553–72.

Herndon, Ruth Wallis. "'Proper' Magistrates and Masters: Binding Out Poor Children in Southern New England, 1720–1820." Ed. Herndon and Murray. 39–51.

Herndon, Ruth Wallis, and John E. Murray, ed. *Children Bound to Labor: The Pauper Apprentice System in Early America*. Ithaca, NY: Cornell UP, 2009.

———. "'A Proper and Instructive Education': Raising Children in Pauper Apprenticeship." Ed. Herndon and Murray. 3–18.

Higginbotham, Evelyn. *Righteous Discontent: The Women's Movement in the Black Baptist Church, 1880–1920*. Cambridge, MA: Harvard UP, 1993.

Hill, Patricia Liggins, Bernard W. Bell, Trudier Harris, William J. Harris, R. Baxter Miller, and Sondra A. O'Neale, eds. *Call and Response: The Riverside Anthology of the African American Literary Tradition*. Wilmington, MA: Houghton Mifflin, 1998.

Hindle, Steve, and Ruth Wallis Herndon. "Recreating Proper Families in England and North America: Pauper Apprenticeship in Transatlantic Context." Ed. Herndon and Murray. 19–36.

Hirsch, Adam J. *The Rise of the Penitentiary: Prisons and Punishment in Early America*. New Haven, CT: Yale UP, 1992.

Hoffman, Katherine E., and Susan Gilson Miller, eds. *Berbers and Others: Beyond Tribe and Nation in the Maghrib*. Bloomington: Indiana UP, 2010.

Hogue, W. Lawrence. *The African American Male, Writing, and Difference: A Polycentric Approach to African American Literature, Criticism, and History*. Albany: State U of New York P, 2003.

Hong, Grace Kyungwon, and Roderick A. Ferguson, ed. *Strange Affinities: The Gender and Sexual Politics of Comparative Racialization*. Durham, NC: Duke UP, 2011.

Horton, James Oliver, and Lois E. Horton. *Black Bostonians: Family Life and Community Struggle in the Antebellum North*. New York, NY: Holmes and Meier, 1979.

Ilahiane, Hsain. *Historical Dictionary of the Berbers*. New York, NY: Scarecrow Press, 2006.

Jackson, Cassandra. *Barriers between Us: Interracial Sex in Nineteenth-Century American Literature*. Bloomington: Indiana UP, 2004.

———. "Beyond the Page: Rape and the Failure of Genre." Ed. Boggis, Raimon, and White. 155–65.

Jackson, George. *Soledad Brother: The Prison Letters of George Jackson*. Foreword by Jonathan Jackson Jr. Chicago, IL: Lawrence Hill Books, 1994.

Jacobs, Harriet. *Incidents in the Life of a Slave Girl, Written by Herself*. 1861. Enlarged ed. Ed. Jean Fagan Yellin. Cambridge, MA: Harvard UP, 2000.

Jacobs, John S. "A True Tale of Slavery." *Incidents in the Life of a Slave Girl, Written by Herself*. 1861. Ed. Jean Fagan Yellin. Cambridge, MA: Harvard UP, 2000. 207–28.

James, George. "Rapper Faces Prison Term for Sex Abuse." *New York Times* 8 Feb. 1995. Google Search. Accessed 25 Apr. 2010. http://www.nytimes.com/1995/02/08/nyregion/rapper-faces-prison-term-for-sex-abuse.html.

James, Jennifer, and Cynthia Wu. "Race, Ethnicity, Disability, and Literature: Intersections and Interventions." *MELUS* 31.3 (2006): 3–13.

Johnson, Paula C. *Inner Lives: Voices of African American Women in Prison*. New York: New York UP, 2003.

Johnson, Walter. *Soul by Soul: Life inside the Antebellum Slave Market*. Cambridge, MA: Harvard UP, 1999.

Johnston, Norman Bruce, with Kenneth Finkel and Jeffrey A. Cohen. *Eastern State Penitentiary: Crucible of Good Intentions*. Philadelphia, PA: Philadelphia Museum of Art, 1994.

Joy, Natalie. "Cherokee Slaveholders and Radical Abolitionists: An Unlikely Alliance in the Antebellum Era." *Common-Place* 10.4 (2010). *Common-Place*. American Antiquarian Society and the University of Connecticut, 2010. Accessed 1 Oct. 2011. http://www.common-place.org/vol-10/no-04/joy/.

Kang, Nancy. "'As If I Had Entered a Paradise': Fugitive Slave Narratives and Cross-Border Literary History." *African American Review* 39.3 (2005): 431–57.

Kazanjian, David. *The Colonizing Trick: National Culture and Imperial Citizenship in Early America*. Minneapolis: U of Minnesota P, 2003.

Kete, Mary Louise. "Slavery's Shadows: Narrative Chiaroscuro and *Our Nig*." Ed. Boggis, Raimon, and White. 109–22.

King, Debra Walker. *African Americans and the Culture of Pain*. Charlottesville: U of Virginia P, 2008.

King, Lovalerie. "Counter Discourses on the Racialization of Theft and Ethics in Douglass's *Narrative* and Jacobs's *Incidents*." *MELUS* 28.4 (2003): 55–82. *MLA International Bibliography*. Accessed. 12 Feb. 2010. http://eds.a.ebscohost.com.proxy.libraries.rutgers.edu/ehost/pdfviewer/pdfviewer?vid=15&sid=cocfac02-c508-4201-80a4-ebd44dbc7dc5%40sessionmgr4001&hid=4205.

Kryza, Frank. *The Race for Timbuktu: The Search for Africa's City of Gold*. New York, NY: Harper Collins, 2006.

Lacan, Jacques. "The Mirror Stage as Formative of the Function of the *I* as Revealed in Psychoanalytic Experience." *Ecrits: A Selection*. Trans. Alan Sheridan. London, UK: Routledge, 1977. 1–6.

Lambert, David. "'Taken Captive by the Mystery of the Great River': Towards an Historical Geography of British Geography and Atlantic Slavery." *Journal of Historical Geography* 35 (2009): 44–65. *EBSCOhost*. Accessed 5 Sept. 2012. http://www.sciencedirect.com.proxy.libraries.rutgers.edu/science/article/pii/S0305748808000595.

Lane, Lunsford. "The Narrative of Lunsford Lane. . . " *North Carolina Slave Narratives: The Lives of Moses Roper, Lunsford Lane, Moses Grandy, and Thomas H. Jones*. Ed. William L. Andrews, et al.. Chapel Hill: U North Carolina P, 2003.

Lawrence-McIntyre, Charshee Charolette. *Criminalizing a Race: Free Blacks during Slavery*. New York, NY: Kayode, 1992.

Lee, Jarena. *The Life and Religious Experience of Jarena Lee*. Ed. Andrews *Sisters of the Spirit*. 25–48.

Lee, Julia Sun-Joo. *The American Slave Narrative and the Victorian Novel*. New York, NY: Oxford UP, 2010.

Leveen, Lois. "Dwelling in the House of Oppression: The Spatial, Racial, and Textual Dynamics of Harriet Wilson's *Our Nig*." *African American Review* 35.4 (2001): 561–580. *MLA International Bibliography*. Accessed10 Mar. 2009. http://eds.b.ebscohost.com.proxy.libraries.rutgers.edu/ehost/pdfviewer/pdfviewer?vid=3&sid=efb2824a-3c3c-4b0d-a1fe-15c639833ae9%40sessionmgr110&hid=126.

Lewis, Bernard. *Race and Slavery in the Middle East: An Historical Enquiry*. New York, NY: Oxford UP, 1996.

Li, Stephanie. *Something Akin to Freedom: The Choice of Bondage in Narratives by African American Women*. Albany: State U of New York P, 2010.

Linebaugh, Peter, and Marcus Rediker. *The Many-Headed Hydra: Sailors, Slaves, Commoners and the Hidden History of the Revolutionary Atlantic*. New York: Beacon, 2000.

Linton, Simi. *Claiming Disability: Knowledge and Identity*. New York: New York UP, 1998.

———. "What Is Disability Studies?" *PMLA* 120.2 (2005): 518–22.

Litwack, Leon. *North of Slavery: The Negro in the Free States, 1790–1860*. Chicago, IL: U of Chicago P, 1961.

Livingstone, David. *The Geographical Tradition: Episodes in the History of a Contested Enterprise*. New York, NY: Oxford, 1992.

Lovejoy, Paul E. *Transformations in Slavery: A History of Slavery in Africa*. Cambridge, UK: Cambridge UP, 1983.

Lovett, Laura. "African and Cherokee by Choice: Race and Resistance under Legalized Segregation." Brooks, ed. 192–222.

"Lucius C. Matlack." *Wheaton History A to Z*. Wheaton College, n.d. Accessed 12 June 2010. http://www.wheaton.edu/A-to-Z.

M, D. J. "Africans at Home." *The Southern Quarterly Review*. Vol. 10. Charleston: C. Mortimer, 1854. 70–96. *Google Books*. Accessed 12 Mar. 2012. https://books.google.com/books?id=5GJRAAAAYAAJ&pg=PA245&lpg=PA245&dq=Africans+at+Home+southern+quarterly&source=bl&ots=a0EBrE703T&sig=IWgAjSlBtqMApiafFmtUI9x03p0&hl=en&sa=X&ei=—3HVMbOC4i1sQTU6IKwAQ&ved=0CDwQ6AEwBQ#v=onepage&q=Africans%20at%20Home%20southern%20quarterly&f=false.

Macpherson, Crawford Brough. *The Political Theory of Possessive Individualism, Hobbes to Locke*. Oxford, UK: Clarendon P, 1969.

Mancall, Peter C. *Deadly Medicine: Indians and Alcohol in Early America*. Ithaca, NY: Cornell UP, 1995.

Mann, Eric. *Comrade George: An Investigation into the Life, Political Thought, and Assassination of George Jackson*. New York, NY: Harper, 1972.

Marrant, John. *A Narrative of the Lord's Wonderful Dealings with John Marrant*. . . . Ed. Adam Potkay and Sandra Burr. New York, NY: St. Martin's P, 1995. 75–105.

Mather, Cotton. *The Glory of Goodness. . . .* Baepler, ed. 61–70.

May, Cedrick. "John Marrant and the Narrative Construction of an Early Black Methodist Evangelical." *African American Review* 38.4 (2004): 553–70.

McClintock, Anne. *Imperial Leather: Race, Gender, and Sexuality in the Colonial Contest.* New York, NY: Routledge, 1995.

McClinton, Rowena. Introduction. *The Moravian Springplace Mission to the Cherokees.* Vol. 1: 1805–1813. Lincoln: U of Nebraska P, 2007. 1–40.

———, ed. *The Moravian Springplace Mission to the Cherokees.* Vol. 1: 1805–1813. Lincoln: U of Nebraska P, 2007.

McDowell, Deborah. "In the First Place: Making Frederick Douglass and the Afro-American Narrative Tradition." *Critical Essays on Frederick Douglass.* Ed. William L. Andrews. Boston, MA: G. K. Hall, 1991. 195–208.

McEntee, Grace. "The Ethos of Motherhood and Harriet Jacobs's Vision of Racial Equality in *Incidents in the Life of a Slave Girl.*" *The Literary Mother: Essays on Representations of Maternity and Child Care.* Ed. Susan C. Staub. Jefferson, NC: McFarland, 2007. 200–223.

McHenry, Elizabeth. *Forgotten Readers: Recovering the Lost History of African American Literary Societies.* Durham, NC: Duke UP, 2002.

McLoughlin, William G. *Cherokee Renascence in the New Republic.* Princeton, NJ: Princeton UP, 1986.

McMurty, Gerald R. "The Influence of Riley's Narrative upon Abraham Lincoln." *Indiana Magazine of History* 30 (1934): 133–38. *JSTOR.* Accessed 8 June 2011. http://www.jstor.org/discover/10.2307/27786655?sid=21105717953243&uid=4&uid=2&uid=3739256.

McNeill, John Robert. *Atlantic Empires of France and Spain: Louisburg and Havana, 1700–1763.* Chapel Hill: U of North Carolina P, 1985.

Meranze, Michael. *Laboratories of Virtue: Punishment, Revolution, and Authority in Philadelphia, 1760–1835.* Chapel Hill: U of North Carolina P, 1996.

Miles, Tiya. *Ties That Bind: The Story of an Afro-Cherokee Family in Slavery and Freedom.* Berkeley: U of California P, 2005.

Minges, Patrick, ed. *Black Indian Slave Narratives.* Winston-Salem, NC: John F. Blair, 2004.

Moore, R. Laurence. "The Spiritualist Medium: A Study of the Female Professional in Victorian America." *AQ* 27.2 (1975): 200–221.

Naylor, Celia E. *African Cherokees in Indian Territory: From Chattel to Citizens.* Chapel Hill: U of North Carolina P, 2008.

———. "'Born and Raised among These people, I Don't Want to Know Any Other': Slaves' Acculturation in Nineteenth-Century Indian Territory." Brooks, ed. 161–91.

Owens, Louis. "As If an Indian Were Really an Indian: Native American Voices and Postcolonial Theory." *Native American Representations: First Encounters, Distorted Images, and Literary Appropriations.* Ed. Gretchen M. Bataille. Lincoln: U of Nebraska P, 2001. 11–24.

Painter, Nell Irvin. "Soul Murder and Slavery: Toward a Fully Loaded Cost Accounting of Slavery." *Southern History across the Color Line*. By Nell Irvin Painter. Chapel Hill: U of North Carolina P, 2002. 15–39.

Parramore, Thomas C. "Harriet Jacobs, James Norcom, and the Defense of Hierarchy." *Carolina Comments* 38.3 (1990): 82–87.

Patterson, Orlando. *Slavery and Social Death: A Comparative Study*. Cambridge, MA: Harvard UP, 1982.

Pease, Jane J., and William H. Pease. *The Fugitive Slave Law and Anthony Burns: A Problem in Law Enforcement*. New York, NY: Lippincott, 1975.

Peterson, Carla L. *Doers of the Word: African American Women Speakers and Writers in the North, 1830–1880*. New York, NY: Oxford UP, 1995.

Perdue, Theda. "Cherokee Planters: The Development of Plantation Slavery before Removal." *The Cherokee Indian Nation: A Troubled History*. Ed. Duane H. King. Knoxville: U of Tennessee P, 1979. 110–28.

———. *Slavery and the Evolution of Cherokee Society, 1540–1866*. Knoxville: U of Tennessee P, 1979.

Pfaff, John F. "The Empirics of Prison Growth: A Critical Review and Path Forward." *Journal of Criminal Law and Criminology* 98.2 (2008): 547–619. *EBSCOhost*. Accessed 2 June 2010. http://eds.a.ebscohost.com.proxy.libraries.rutgers.edu/ehost/pdfviewer/pdfviewer?vid=14&sid=110bd9a4-b755-4152-b2c5-995ecf289168%40sessionmgr4003&hid=4205.Piep, Karsten H. "'Nothing New Under the Sun'": Postsentimental Conflict in Harriet E. Wilson's *Our Nig*." *Colloquy* 11 (2006): 178–94. *EBSCOhost*. Accessed 12 Apr. 2012. http://artsonline.monash.edu.au/colloquy/download/colloquy_issue_11_may_2006/piep.pdf.

Pierson, Michael D. "'Slavery Cannot Be Covered with Broadcloth or a Bandana': The Evolution of White Abolitionist Attacks on the 'Patriarchal Institution.'" *Journal of the Early Republic* 25.3 (2005): 383–414. *JSTOR*. Accessed 22 Apr. 2009. http://www.jstor.org.proxy.libraries.rutgers.edu/stable/pdfplus/30043336.pdf?acceptTC=true.

Plasa, Carl. "'Tangled Skeins': Henry Timrod's 'The Cotton Boll' and the Slave Narratives." *The Southern Literary Journal* 65.1 (2012): 1–20. *EBSCOhost*. Accessed 5 Jan. 2013. http://eds.a.ebscohost.com.proxy.libraries.rutgers.edu/ehost/pdfviewer/pdfviewer?vid=10&sid=110bd9a4-b755-4152-b2c5-995ecf289168%40sessionmgr4003&hid=4205.

"Politicized Curriculum in Texas." *New York Times*. 26 May 2010. *ProQuest*. Accessed 5 Aug. 2012. http://search.proquest.com.proxy.libraries.rutgers.edu/docview/1461204803?accountid=13626.

Potter, Eliza. *A Hairdresser's Experience in High Life*. Ed. Xiomara Santamarina. Chapel Hill: U of North Carolina P, 2009.

Pratt, Mary Louise. *Imperial Eyes: Travel Writing and Transculturation*. 2nd ed. New York, NY: Routledge, 2008.

Prince, Nancy. *A Narrative of the Life and Travels of Mrs. Nancy Prince. Written by Herself*. 3rd ed. Boston, MA: published by the author, 1856.

Quashie, Kevin. *The Sovereignty of Quiet: Beyond Resistance in Black Culture*. New Brunswick, NJ: Rutgers UP, 2012.

Raimon, Eve Allegra. "Miss Marsh's Uncommon School Reform." Boggis, Raimon, and White, eds. 167–81.

Randle, Gloria. "Between the Rock and the Hard Place: Mediating Spaces in Harriet Jacobs's *Incidents in the Life of a Slave Girl*." *African American Review* 33.1 (1999): 43–56. *MLA International Bibliography*. Accessed 2 June 2010. http://eds.a.ebscohost.com.proxy.libraries.rutgers.edu/ehost/pdfviewer/pdfviewer?vid=12&sid=78e8f37f-4caa-4045-be24-fb62d73df02d%40sessionmgr4003&hid=4205.

Rediker, Marcus. *Between the Devil and the Deep Blue Sea: Merchant Seamen, Pirates, and the Anglo-American Maritime World, 1700–1750*. Cambridge, UK: Cambridge UP, 1987.

Richardson, Riché. "*Push*, *Precious*, and New Narratives of Slavery in Harlem." *Black Camera* 4.1 (2012): 161–80. *Project Muse*. Accessed 5 June 2013. http://muse.jhu.edu.proxy.libraries.rutgers.edu/journals/black_camera/v004/4.1.richardson.html.

Ripley, Peter. "The Autobiographical Writings of Frederick Douglass." *Narrative of the Life of Frederick Douglass, an American Slave, Written by Himself*. Ed. William L. Andrews and William S. McFeely. New York, NY: Norton, 1997. 135–46.

Robbins, Archibald. *A Journal Comprising an Account of the Brig Commerce, of Hartford, Conn. . . .* Hartford, CT: Silas Andrus and Son, 1847. *Google Books*. Accessed 7 May 2010. http://books.google.com/books/about/A_Journal_Comprising_an_Account_of_the_L.html?id=o8wTAAAAYAAJ.

Rodriguez, Dylan. "Against the Discipline of 'Prison Writing': Toward a Theoretical Conception of Contemporary Radical Praxis." *Genre: Forms of Discourse and Culture* 35 (2002): 407–28.

Rorabaugh, W. J. *The Alcoholic Republic: An American Tradition*. New York, NY: Oxford UP, 1979.

Rothman, David J. *The Discovery of the Asylum: Social Order and Disorder in the New Republic*. Rev. ed. New York, NY: Adline de Gruyter, 2002.

Runyon, Randolph Paul, researched in collaboration with William Albert Davis. *Delia Webster and the Underground Railroad*. Lexington: UP of Kentucky, 1996.

Rush, Benjamin. "An Inquiry into the Effects of Public Punishments upon Criminals, and upon Society." *Essays, Literary, Moral, and Philosophical*. 2nd ed. By Rush. Philadelphia, PA: Thomas and William Bradford, 1806. 136–63. *Google Books*. Accessed 10 Mar. 2011. https://books.google.com/books?id=xtUKAAAAIAAJ&pg=PA136&lpg=PA136&dq=An+Inquiry+into+the+Effects+of+Public+Punishments&source=bl&ots=aK2uN3n3aN&sig=gVZWGJtAisWWe9NvW3geEO1sO68&hl=en&sa=X&ei=Ig7IVPGpMqaxsATMzoHoCA&ved=0CCYQ6AEwAQ#v=onepage&q=An%20Inquiry%20into%20the%20Effects%20of%20Public%20Punishments&f=false.

Saad, Elias N. *Social History of Timbuktu: The Role of Muslim Scholars and Notables, 1400–1900*. Cambridge, UK: Cambridge UP, 1983.

Sampsell-Willmann, Kate. *Lewis Hine as Social Critic*. Jackson: UP of Mississippi, 2009.

Sánchez-Eppler, Karen. *Dependent States: The Child's Part in Nineteenth-Century American Culture*. Chicago, IL: U of Chicago P, 2005.

———. *Touching Liberty: Abolition, Feminism, and the Politics of the Body*. Berkeley: U of California P, 1993.

Santamarina, Xiomara. *Belabored Professions: Narratives of African American Working Womanhood*. Chapel Hill: U of North Carolina P, 2005.

Sartwell, Crispin. *Act Like You Know: African American Autobiography and White Identity*. Chicago, IL: U of Chicago P, 1998.

Saunders, Daniel. *A Journal of the Travels and Sufferings of Daniel Saunders*. . . . Leominster, MA: Charles Prentiss, 1797. *ECCO*. Accessed 8 Mar. 2011. http://find.galegroup.com.proxy.libraries.rutgers.edu/ecco/retrieve.do?sgHitCountType=None&sort=Author&tabID=T001&prodId=ECCO&resultListType=RESULT_LIST&searchId=R1&searchType=BasicSearchForm&currentPosition=1&qrySerId=Locale%28en%2C%2C%29%3AFQE%3D%280X%2CNone%2C58%29A+Journal+of+the+Travels+and+Sufferings+of+Daniel+Saunders%3AAnd%3ALQE%3D%28BA%2CNone%2C124%292NEF+Or+0LRH+Or+2NEK+Or+0LRL+Or+2NEI+Or+0LRI+Or+2NEJ+Or+0LRK+Or+2NEG+Or+0LRF+Or+2NEH+Or+0LRJ+Or+2NEM+Or+0LRN+Or+2NEL+Or+0LRM%24&retrieveFormat=MULTIPAGE_DOCUMENT&userGroupName=new67449&inPS=true&contentSet=ECCOArticles&&docId=CW3308392242&retrieveFormat=MULTIPAGE_DOCUMENT&docLevel=FASCIMILE&workId=CW3308392242&relevancePageBatch=CW108392242&showLOI=&contentSet=&callistoContentSet=ECLL&docPage=article&hilite=y.

Scarry, Elaine. *The Body in Pain: The Making and Unmaking of the World*. New York, NY: Oxford UP, 1985.

Scott, Joan W. "Experience." *Women, Autobiography, Theory: A Reader*. Ed. Sidonie Smith and Julia Watson. Madison: U of Wisconsin P, 1998. 57–71.

Sekora, John. "Black Message/White Envelope: Genre, Authenticity, and Authority in the Antebellum Slave Narrative." *Callaloo* 32 (1987): 482–515.

———. "Red, White, and Black: Indian Captivities, Colonial Printers, and the Early African-American Narrative." *A Mixed Race: Ethnicity in Early America*. Ed. Frank Shuffleton. New York, NY: Oxford UP, 1993. 92–104.

Seymour, George L. "Extracts from *The Journal of the Journey of George L. Seymour to the Interior of Liberia, 1858*." Fairhead et al., eds. 124–55.

Sewall, Samuel. *The Selling of Joseph: A Memorial*. Ed. Sidney Kaplan. Amherst: U of Massachusetts P, 1969.

Shakur, Tupac. "Dear Mama." *All Eyes on Me*. Interscope, 1995. CD.

Shanley, Kathryn. "The Indians America Loves to Love and Read: American Indian Identity and Cultural Appropriation." *Native American Representations: First Encounters, Distorted Images, and Literary Appropriations*. Ed. Gretchen M. Bataille. Lincoln: U of Nebraska P, 2001. 26–51.

Siebers, Tobin. *Disability Theory*. Ann Arbor: U of Michigan P, 2008.

Singley, Carol. *Adopting America: Childhood, Kinship, and National Identity in Literature*. New York, NY: Oxford UP, 2011.

Slotkin, Richard. *Regeneration through Violence: The Mythology of the American Frontier, 1600–1860*. Middletown, CT: Wesleyan UP, 1973.

Smith, Caleb. *The Prison and the American Imagination*. New Haven, CT: Yale UP, 2009.

Smith, Valerie. *Self-Discovery and Authority in Afro-American Narrative*. Cambridge, MA: Harvard UP, 1987.

Sollors, Werner. *Neither Black nor White yet Both: Thematic Explorations of Interracial Literature*. New York, NY: Oxford UP, 1997.

Sparks, Jared. "The Narrative of Robert Adams: A Review Essay." *North American Review* 5 (1817): 204–24. Rpt. in Adams, ed. 162–82.

Speck, Frank G., and Leonard Broom, in collaboration with Will West Long. *Cherokee Dance and Drama*. Norman: U of Oklahoma P, 1983.

Spillers, Hortense. "Mama's Baby, Papa's Maybe: An American Grammar Book." *The Black Feminist Reader*. Ed. Joy James and T. Denean Sharpley-Whiting. Oxford, UK: Blackwell, 2000. 57–87.

Starling, Marion Wilson. *The Slave Narrative: Its Place in American History*. Boston, MA: G. K. Hall, 1981.

Stewart, Maria. "Lecture Delivered at the Franklin Hall." 1832. *Maria W. Stewart: America's First Black Woman Political Writer, Essays and Speeches*. Ed. Marilyn Richardson. Bloomington: U of Indiana P, 1987. 45–49. *Black Thought and Culture*. Accessed 1 May 2012. http://solomon.bltc.alexanderstreet.com.proxy.libraries.rutgers.edu/cgi-bin/asp/philo/contextualize.pl?p.10214.bltc.256.264.274.277.281.290.

Stodola-Derounian, Kathryn Zabelle, and James Levernier. *The Indian Captivity Narrative: 1550–1900*. New York, NY: Twayne Publishers, 1993.

Storrow, Samuel A. "Interiour of Africa." *North American Review* 5 (1817): 11–26. Rpt. in Adams, ed. 147–61.

Stowe, Harriet Beecher. *Uncle Tom's Cabin. A Norton Critical Edition: Authoritative Text, Backgrounds, and Contexts, Criticism*. Ed. Elizabeth Ammons. New York, NY: Norton, 1994.

Sumner, Charles. *White Slavery in the Barbary States*. Boston, MA: John P. Jewett and Co., 1853. *Google Books*. 5 Feb. 2011. http://books.google.com/books?id=mwsUAAAAIAAJ&printsec=frontcover&source=gbs_ge_summary_r&cad=0#v=onepage&q&f=false.

Sundquist, Eric J. *To Wake the Nations: Race in the Making of American Literature*. Cambridge, MA: Harvard UP, 1993.

Sweeney, Megan. *Reading Is My Window: Books and the Art of Reading in Women's Prisons*. Chapel Hill: U of North Carolina P, 2010.

Taney, Roger B. *Dred Scott v. John A. Sanford*. 60 US 393–529. Supreme Court of the United States. 1857. *Supreme Court Collection*. Legal Information Inst., Cornell U Law School, n.d. Accessed 15 Sept. 2011. http://www.law.cornell.edu/supremecourt/text/60/393.

Tate, Claudia. *Psychoanalysis and Black Novels: Desire and the Protocols of Race*. New York, NY: Oxford UP, 1998.

Taylor, Douglas. "From Slavery to Prison: Benjamin Rush, Harriet Jacobs, and the Ideology of Reformative Incarceration." *Genre* 35.3/4 (2002): 429–48.

Thomas, Hugh. *Cuba; or, The Pursuit of Freedom*. New York, NY: Da Capo P, 1998.

Thompson, George. *Prison Life and Reflections*. Hartford, CT: Alanson Work, 1855.

Thompson, Robert Farris. "Dance and Culture. An Aesthetic of the Cool: West African Dance." *African Forum* 2.2 (1966): 85–103.

Thomson, Rosemarie Garland. *Extraordinary Bodies: Figuring Physical Disability in American Culture and Literature*. New York, NY: Columbia UP, 1997.

Thoreau, Henry David. "Resistance to Civil Government." *The Higher Law: Thoreau on Civil Disobedience and Reform*. Ed. Wendell Glick. Princeton, NJ: Princeton UP, 2004. 63–90.

Titus, Mary. "'The Poisonous System': Body Ills, Social Ills, and *Incidents in the Life of a Slave Girl*." Garfield and Zafar, ed. 199–215.

Tomkins, Silvan S. "The Psychology of Commitment: The Constructive Role of Violence and Suffering for the Individual and for His Society." *Affect, Cognition, and Personality: Empirical Studies*. Ed. Silvan S. Tomkins and Carroll E. Izard. New York, NY: Springer, 1965. 148–71.

Turner, Mary, ed. *From Chattel to Wage Slaves: The Dynamics of Labour Bargaining in the Americas*. Bloomington: Indiana UP, 1995.

Twain, Mark. *The Adventures of Tom Sawyer*. Ed. John Seelye. New York, NY: Penguin, 2006.

Varella, Claudia. "The Price of Coartacion in the Hispanic Caribbean: How Much Freedom Does the Master Owe to the Slave?" *International Journal of Cuban Studies* 4.2 (2012): 200–210. *EBSCOhost*. Accessed 2 Feb. 2013. http://eds.a.ebscohost.com.proxy.libraries.rutgers.edu/ehost/pdfviewer/pdfviewer?vid=3&sid=6af34df3-2bac-4a64-b5b6-5b26762a0a0f%40sessionmgr4005&hid=4205.

Vollaro, Daniel. "Sixty Indians and Twenty Canoes: Briton Hammon's Unreliable Witness to History. *Native South* 2 (2009): 133–47. *Project Muse*. Accessed 9 Sept. 2011. http://muse.jhu.edu.proxy.libraries.rutgers.edu/journals/native_south/v002/2.vollaro.pdf.

Wacquant, Loïc. "From Slavery to Mass Incarceration: Rethinking the 'Race' Question in the U.S." *New Left Review* 13 (2002): 41–60.

Wade, Richard C. *Slavery in the Cities: The South, 1820–1860*. New York, NY: Oxford UP, 1964.

Wallace, Maurice O. *Constructing the Black Masculine: Identity and Ideality in African American Men's Literature and Culture, 1775–1995*. Durham, NC: Duke UP, 2002.

Walker, Alice. *The Color Purple*. New York, NY: Harcourt, 1992.

Ward, Brian. *Just My Soul Responding: Rhythm and Blues, Black Consciousness, and Race Relations*. Berkley: U of California P, 1998.

"Warrant for the Arrest of Bill." Issued by James Bayman, Justice of the Peace. May 1826. Chowan County Court Records. North Carolina State Archives.

"Warrant for the Arrest of Edward and Anthony." Issued by Alex Dixon, Justice of the Peace. 19 Apr. 1857. Chowan County Court Records. North Carolina State Archives.

Warren, Kenneth. *What Was African American Literature?* Cambridge, MA: Harvard UP, 2011.

Watson, Alan D. "County Buildings and Other Public Structures in Colonial North Carolina." *North Carolina Historical Review* 82.4 (2005): 427–63.

Welter, Barbara. "The Cult of True Womanhood: 1820–1860." *American Quarterly* 18.2

(1966): 151–74. *JSTOR*. Accessed 5 May 2011. http://www.jstor.org.proxy.libraries.rutgers.edu/stable/pdfplus/10.2307/2711179.pdf.

Weyler, Karen. "Race, Redemption, and Captivity in the Narratives of Briton Hammon and John Marrant." Carretta and Gould, ed. 39–53.

Wheatley, Phillis. "On Being Brought from Africa to America." *The Norton Anthology of African American Literature*. 2nd ed. Ed. Henry Louis Gates Jr. and Nellie Y. McKay. New York, NY: Norton, 2004. 219–20.

White, Barbara A. *Growing Up Female: Adolescent Girlhood in American Fiction*. Westport, CT: Greenwood P, 1985.

———. "'Our Nig' and the She-Devil: New Information about Harriet Wilson and the 'Bellmont' Family." *American Literature* 65.1 (1993): 19–52.

Whitman, T. Stephen. "Orphans in City and Countryside in Nineteenth-Century Maryland." Herndon and Murray, ed. 52–70.

Williams, Roland, Jr. "Briton Hammon." *The Oxford Companion to African American Literature*. Ed. William Andrews, et al. New York, NY: Oxford UP, 1997. 337.

Wilson, Harriet E. *Our Nig; or, Sketches from the Life of a Free Black*. 1859. Ed. P. Gabrielle Foreman and Reginald H. Pitts. New York, NY: Penguin, 2009.

Yanuck, Julius. "The Garner Fugitive Slave Case." *Mississippi Valley Historical Review* 40.1 (1953): 47–66.

Yellin, Jean Fagan. *Harriet Jacobs: A Life*. New York, NY: Civitas, 2004.

Youcha, Geraldine. *Minding the Children: Child Care in America from Colonial Times to the Present*. New York, NY: Scribner, 1995.

Zafar, Rafia. "Capturing the Captivity: African Americans among the Puritans." *MELUS*. 17.2 (1991): 19–35.

———. *We Wear the Mask: African Americans Write American Literature, 1760–1870*. New York, NY: Columbia UP, 1997.

Index